Alive and Well

The Emergence of the
Active Nonagenarian

Alive and Well

The Emergence of the Active Nonagenarian

William F. Powers

Rutledge Books, Inc.   Bethel, CT

Rutledge Books, Inc.
8 F.J. Clarke Circle, Bethel, CT 06801

Manufactured in the United States of America

Library of Congress Cataloging in Publication Data
Powers, William F.
    Alive and well : the emergence of the
active nonagenarian / William F. Powers
    p. cm.
    ISBN 1-887750-14-2
    1. Longevity.   2. Happiness in old age.
3. Aged--Health and hygiene. I. Title
305.26--dc20   95-72544

For my mother, DELIA MITCHELL POWERS,
who at age 87 was too young to be included in this book

****

To die at the age of a hundred
will be dying young.
Isaiah 65:20

Contents

The Active Nonagenarians

Acknowledgments

Although writing is a solitary activity, I had the sense that many individuals were sitting beside me as *Alive and Well* was being composed and that others were cheering me on from the bleachers. Those right there with me were, of course, the active nonagenarians themselves, the dozens of wonderful people who invited me into their homes and so generously shared with me tea or coffee and the stories of their lives. In a sense, they are the authors of this book, and I their spokesman. Especially as I transcribed the audio tapes of interviews and looked at the photographs which I had taken, they were present.

Also, contributions of the scores of other men and women with whom I corresponded or spoke on the phone have enriched the book even if they are not named individually. They helped convince me that the phenomenon which I was recording—the emergence of the active nonagenarian—is indeed a widespread social reality and not some rare occurrence.

Among those who cheered from the sidelines, several deserve special recognition. Patty Moosbrugger of the Curtis Brown literary agency helped in the daunting task of preparing the manuscript for publication and, more importantly, believed in what I was doing. Myta Floyd, the author of several books herself, encouraged me to continue writing and drew from her own experience to offer valuable suggestions. A photographer, Suzanne Jacobson, was enthusiastic about the project and for a time we planned to collaborate. I am especially grateful to her for facilitating the trip that I made to Florida to interview several nonagenarians. In the early stages of my work, Betty Dunlap of the Suffolk County Department of Aging was very helpful as was my friend John Ryan, Ph.D., who read a draft of the manuscript and gave me valuable feedback.

My colleagues in the Psychology/Sociology department of Suffolk Community College on Long Island, New York, have been supportive of my work, especially Albin J. Cofone, Lawrence A. Propper, and

Acknowledgements

William L. Hoover. Professional encouragement as well as friendship are precious gifts and they have bestowed them liberally.

Most of all, a deep debt of gratitude is due to my wife, Ann, who as a faculty member in the Child Study Department of St. Joseph's College, knows how to guide students as they struggle to express themselves clearly and concisely. I have been her "student" now for twenty-five years and know that *Alive and Well* is a better book because of her patient and skilled assistance.

Introduction

In his 1933 novel *Lost Horizons*, James Hilton takes the reader to a hidden world high atop a Tibetan mountain. The journey to Shangri-La is long and arduous. Few people reach it, but once there a marvelous transformation occurs. Not only do men and women live to an advanced age—perhaps two hundred years—but they become more fully developed human beings. They grow in wisdom as well as age because they have the leisure to focus on essentials. With their mental and physical faculties intact, the residents of the utopia uncover depths of human potential seldom reached in the hurried "short" life of ordinary mortals.

Long considered little more than a gentle tale in the tradition of the search for the Fountain of Youth, Hilton's dream world may come true after all. In 1992, a physiologist at the University of Texas said that his research on controlling the aging process of rodents leads him to believe that it is possible to extend the human life span considerably, giving us an extra hundred years. Another scientist, working with roundworms at the University of Colorado, is similarly convinced that a doubling of the present life span is conceivable.

As if such forecasts were not awesome enough, Dr. Michal Jazwiski, studying yeast at the University of Louisiana Medical Center, says that should the genes that control aging be discovered, it may be possible for people alive today still to be alive four hundred years from now.

Alive and Well is a suggestion that the climb up the mountain toward Shangri-La has already begun. Active nonagenarians are men and women who not only are still alive in the rarefied air of the tenth decade of life but are happy, healthy, growing human beings. And their numbers are increasing rapidly. To live to ninety or beyond is neither an impossible dream nor something to be dreaded as a wasteland of losses. The people whose stories are related in this book are scouts on the frontier of the longevity miracle which is transforming human life.

Put another way, the active nonagenarians you will meet here are the early experiments in the laboratory of our expanding life expectancy. They are the preliminary data, the early models, the trial run of what is coming. Although the subjects of this study are in many respects very ordinary people, they stand on a higher rung of the ladder of life than the rest of us. Some can tell us what they see with greater clarity than others, but each represents a facet of the diversity and richness that can characterize life after the ninetieth birthday.

While public attention focuses on those elderly people who are in nursing homes and hospitals, the active nonagenarians quietly go about the business of daily life. Aside from a mention in a local newspaper, they gain scant attention because they do not pose a problem to society. What they do, however, is to present to all of us a prospect which until recently was too remote to be given serious consideration, namely, the possibility of living to ninety and beyond with enough physical and mental vigor to look to the future with enthusiasm. More than one nonagenarian said to me, "I'm anxious to see what it's like to be one hundred."

Alive and Well documents the emergence of the active nonagenarian not so much with statistics as with living examples of life in the nineties. The heart of the book is the profiles of more than forty people, including four nonagenarian married couples, who invited me into their homes and shared with me the story of their lives.

Americans are familiar with nonagenarian celebrities like George Burns and Bob Hope. The people in this book are what might be called "run of the mill nonagenarians," men and women with whom anyone might identify. One woman put it succinctly when she said, "I'm just an ordinary ninety-five year old woman." She didn't know why anyone would be interested in her. But, of course, we are interested in her. The reason is quite selfish. If she can do it, why not I?

Along with the striking increase in the number of active nonagenarians is the equally rapidly rising number of children of such people—and grandchildren and great grandchildren for that matter. Family members take pride in the competence of their venerable relative.

They brag, "Mom is amazing. She's 92 and taking a college course—in Human Sexuality, no less!" Or "Pop is unbelievable. He's still driving at 93, and he has a girlfriend!" At the same time there is concern. Life has been extended but no one is immortal. Crises occur, like the woman who breaks a hip or the man who needs a hernia operation. To such solicitous children, the nonagenarians in *Alive and Well* offer a number of suggestions and coping strategies. Sometimes it is a very simple modification or intervention that enables the older person to remain independent and the "child" to feel that Mom or Dad is safe.

Chapter One establishes the fact of the aging of the population, and in particular, the emergence of the active nonagenarian. It sets the stage for meeting the people whom I interviewed and provides a framework for listening to them. Some readers might prefer to skip this chapter for a time, coming back to it after reading some of the interviews.

Chapter Two moves closer to the wonderful reality being reported, presenting dozens of brief vignettes of nonagenarians other than the ones whom I interviewed. These broad brush-strokes are organized around a number of themes and styles which should be helpful for not getting lost in the striking uniqueness of the individuals interviewed. Readers should find here a perspective for approaching the interviews more profitably, for dealing with what certainly will be the questions in everyone's mind: "How did they do it? What is their secret? Is there anything I can do to experience their good fortune?"

The heart of the book is the first person accounts of the nonagenarians themselves. Hopefully, enough material was selected from the lengthy interviews to bring these individuals to life, to uncover something of the special blend of experiences, thoughts, and feelings that have brought them to this moment. Each life, of course, is complex and a few pages never can capture the full richness of any person, least of all someone who has lived for over ninety years. Nevertheless, after reading the profiles, it is hoped that readers will feel as though they have encountered a group of interesting human beings and been enriched and inspired thereby—as though they have walked through a portrait gallery, paused for a minute at each picture, and then moved on carrying away a precious memory.

A title or label is affixed to each nonagenarian, such as "Concert Violinist," "Auditing College Courses," "Practicing Attorney," or "Real Estate Agent." The label identifies a significant aspect of that person's life, of course, but is meant mainly to highlight the wide range of possibilities available to active nonagenarians. Readers might read first those profiles which have labels corresponding to their own interests or those of their loved ones.

Each interview has an introduction which is meant to give some general information about an aspect of the experience of being active in the nineties, such as housing options, participation in the work world, and the relationship to family members. Taken together, the introductions provide a sort of primer on social gerontology.

Finally, **the Epilogue attempts to draw some conclusions** from a year of interviewing truly fascinating people. It is an effort to step away from particular flesh and blood men and women and see if there might be any common themes, any recurring messages to help us unlock the secret of a vibrant old age. Obviously, no one can control all the genetic, physical, environmental, and lifestyle factors which are blended together to fashion a human life. Nevertheless, there is much to be learned from those who have beaten the odds, who have blown out the candles on their ninetieth birthday cake and looked up with a warm smile on a circle of proud and loving relatives and friends.

But of course, in the long run, whether we live for seventy or eighty years is not as important as living well whatever be our allotted number of days. The wisdom of these nonagenarians is not primarily a matter of calendar years but of meaningful years.

CHAPTER ONE

THE AGE OF THE ACTIVE NONAGENARIAN

One Friday in July, Olga Loeb put in a day's work at the Bronx-Lebanon Hospital Center in New York where, as a volunteer, she had managed the gift shop for more than thirty years. She became ill over the weekend and died on Sunday. Mrs. Loeb was 97 years old. She had a reputation for knowing exactly what was in the shop's inventory and for handling the accounts skillfully.

A few days later Frank Blazek parachuted from a plane over the airport in East Moriches, Long Island. By so doing, he earned a place for himself in the *Guinness Book of World Records*. Blazek was 91. After the jump he said, "I was enjoying the scenery on the way down. It was fun falling."

At the nation's capitol in Washington, D.C., Strom Thurmond goes about his work as a senator from South Carolina as he has done since 1952. Thurmond is 94 years old and was first elected to public office in 1928, eighteen years before President Bill Clinton was born.

In February 1993, Lillian Gish, the last of the great silent film stars, died at the age of 99. When she was 92 years old, she starred in the film, *The Whales of August*, as alert and photogenic as when in 1915 she had dazzled audiences with her beauty in D.W. Griffith's, *The Birth of a Nation*.

George Burns, who died early in 1996 at the age of 100, was certainly America's favorite nonagenarian. Well into his late nineties he delighted millions with his humor.

In 1982, Beatrice L. Cole wrote an article for *Parade* magazine titled, "The Joys of Being Eighty." In 1991, at the age of 90, she wrote a sequel titled "I Greet Each Day As A Gift." Her picture shows a smiling woman with a poodle on her lap. In the article she says, "At 90 I can truthfully say that the last 10 years have been the most satisfying.... I greet each day as a gift that I unwrap with anticipation and live each day as if it were the last."

Manny Levy of Nassau County, New York, plays nine holes of golf every weekday. Mr. Levy is 98.

Irene Corbally, at 94, continues her lifelong career as a writer, serving as contributing editor of *Gourmet* magazine.

Chester Tosini, 96, works out with weights two or three days a week at the North Shore Gym in Manhasset, New York, and that's after the half-mile walk from his home.

As a girl, Orlena Stevenson picked cotton in Arkansas and remembers being so hungry, "I chewed my tongue." She gave birth to thirteen children. At age 40 she moved to St. Louis, Missouri, where she worked as a domestic until well into her 60's. At age 91 in 1992, she was a pillar of the Prince of Peace Baptist Church and as she planned to vote in the November election, remembered times when she couldn't vote because she was a woman and because she was black.

At the age of 98, Nellie Dick was guest speaker at a Queens College class on "The History of Anarchism." Mrs. Dick, a Russian-born Jew, was a lifelong anarchist, who in the 1920's had established and taught in "anarchist schools" in England and the United States. She said that the schools "emphasized children's freedom to develop their own potential at their own pace."

At 91, the actress Helen Hayes was still busy presenting and receiving awards at public events. When asked where she got her energy she said, "I don't know. I do go to Mass and maybe that helps and I do rest all day long."

David Rockefeller calls Hermann J. Abs, "the most important banker of our time." Abs, at the age of 90, was still attending board meetings and putting in a full day's work at the Deutsche Bank headquarters in Frankfurt, Germany. Associates said that his memory remained prodigious.

The Emerging Longevity Miracle

These are but a few of the scores of nonagenarians who have been featured in newspapers and magazines in the past few years.

They are the tip of the iceberg of a phenomenon which is transforming the world of the elderly and is destined to change forever human longevity expectations. We have entered the age of the active nonagenarian.

In the Foreword to *Going Strong*, a 1991 book about people 75 and older who were still "going strong," Norman Cousins wrote:

> What is perhaps most striking about [this] book is that, only a generation ago, it would have been about people over sixty-five who were still in the prime of life and who were active, purposeful, healthy. Today, the fact of a full and rewarding existence after sixty-five is so commonplace that it would seem almost strange that it should command special attention. In the early years of the twenty-first century, there will probably be books about the enjoyment of living after eighty-five.

Cousins himself died shortly after writing those words. He did not live to be an octogenarian himself, let alone a nonagenarian. Nor did he realize that long before the twenty-first century, it would already be time to celebrate not only eighty-five-year-olds, but ninety-year-olds who were "going strong."

The nonagenarians in this book are not a representative sample, but rather a selection of superstars. Much has been written about Alzheimer's disease and nursing homes and soaring health care costs and loneliness and pain. Certainly such things are real and of great concern for society. However, it is important to celebrate success stories, to hold up to view models of healthy, happy older people. In the years ahead ever increasing numbers of people will enter the now rarefied world of the active nonagenarian. Today it is noteworthy that people are still driving cars, working, and playing tennis at 90. Twenty years from now such occurrences will be so common that they will be taken for granted.

The Age of the Active Nonagenarian

What is an "Active Nonagenarian"?

Although surviving to celebrate one's ninetieth birthday is an achievement worth the attention it typically receives, being "active" at that age is yet more remarkable. The word "active" defies precise definition and encompasses a wide range of behaviors. In simplest terms, it means that the man or woman lives relatively independently and has no serious debilities, either physical or cognitive.

To be physically active means not confined to bed, able to go up and down stairs, and capable of leaving the house in order to attend to one's affairs. There is no immediate life-threatening condition such as advanced cancer or coronary heart disease. There may be handicaps such as blindness, deafness, or confinement to a wheel chair, but such conditions must not limit the person any more than they might a younger person with the same disability. Certainly, many blind people and those who use wheelchairs for mobility are productive members of society, although in need of some assistance. However, as a matter of fact, few of the nonagenarians interviewed for this book had any such disabilities. Some hearing loss was common but usually corrected with hearing aids.

Cognitive or mental competence is more difficult to measure. Although Harvard University Professor Gerald Fischbach insists that memory loss is not an inevitable part of aging, numerous studies show that memory loss, slower reaction time, and greater difficulty in solving problems are predictable accompaniments of advancing years. One study commissioned by the Charles A. Dana Foundation, which has committed $25 million to study the brain and its ailments, found that nearly half the 600 adults surveyed had some memory loss problem, and that two-thirds said their parents had memory ailments that interfered with their daily lives. Losses are an unavoidable dimension of the human condition, and what is most dreaded is the loss of the capacity for rationality. "Take away anything, but leave me my mind" is a common refrain.

An active nonagenarian, then, is one who exhibits no dementia or confusion, is able to remember the past, manage the present, and plan for the future. Such a person can hold a sensible conversation, is aware of current events, and shows no obvious signs of clinical depression or other psychoses.

In interviewing nonagenarians I was alert for inappropriate responses to questions, mental wandering, forgetfulness, or repetition. What was striking was how logical and consistent people were. Most had a lively sense of humor, interest in a wide range of issues, and enthusiasm for life. They were well-adjusted individuals who had made age-appropriate modifications in their routines, enabling them to remain substantially self-sufficient.

A common modification was the extension of their social network to include a helper of some sort, typically someone who did the heavy housekeeping, performed outdoor chores such as shoveling snow and mowing the grass, perhaps prepared meals, and served as chauffeur. Frequently, this person was a younger spouse, daughter, or other relative who worked in a sort of partnership relationship with the nonagenarian, receiving as well as providing service. For example, the younger person might do the grocery shopping while the nonagenarian cooked the dinner, watered the plants, and cared for the family pet.

What Happens to the Human Mind?

Statistics generated by research into human mental functioning can be misleading. Averages obscure individual variations. Many people perform substantially above the average. For example, although on average, IQ begins to decline significantly in the period from age 60 to 67, many individuals function at near optimum levels much longer. Likewise, although declines appear in short-term memory as people age, the decline is gradual and for many individuals does not pose a serious problem. In general, the nonagenarians interviewed showed striking retention of cognitive capacity, ability that would be envied by many people half their age.

However, there were memory lapses. One man wanted to show me something in his bedroom. By the time he arrived there, he couldn't recall what he was looking for. On another occasion, a woman offered to give me a tour of her retirement community. As we walked around, several times she repeated something she had recently said. Short-term memory can be like writing a message in the sand. A wave comes and washes it away.

Memory is a fickle friend, pulling forth from the recesses of the mind an assortment of recollections, jumbling that which is central to the life of a person with the puzzling details which inhabit the recesses of that mysterious storehouse of knowledge, feelings, beliefs, and hopes. Talk to me today and I will tell you things which tomorrow I might not mention. Is it that my memory is failing, or is it that, like a deck of cards, on each day a different hand is drawn?

To Know a Stranger

One of the unavoidable risks of spending an hour or two with a stranger, and never seeing him again, is that the story told will be inaccurate, the impressions gained flawed, and the picture taken out of focus. When interviewing people who have lived more than ninety years, it is particularly daunting, frustrating, and perhaps even cruel to ask them to synthesize their lives into such a short period of time. But how much time does it take to "really" get to know someone? If an hour is inadequate, what then would be enough—five hours, ten? Isn't it our experience that even after years of living with others, we may not really know them as well as we thought?

One way to double check the account given by a nonagenarian would be to interview someone who knows the subject well or to send such a person a copy of the interview tape for a reaction. This is what was done in the case of Dr. Ruth Bennett who was interviewed a few days before her 96th birthday. After listening to the tape, her son Claude phoned and filled what would seem to be important gaps in his mother's account of her life.

Dr. Bennett had said that she spent seven years as a medical missionary in India, but that when she returned to the United States and married a farmer, she practiced medicine only when friends and neighbors called upon her for help. Her account sounded like the traditional expectation of the time, namely, that a married woman, especially a mother, remain at home.

The son, now in his fifties, said that, to the contrary, his mother had a very busy career after her marriage. First of all, while pregnant with him she served for several months as a physician in the women's prison where she had worked shortly after completing medical school. Her motive was to help the fragile finances of the family. Next, after Claude was born, she returned to India, bringing the infant child with her and worked at the Friends Mission for three years, her husband remaining on their Colorado farm. When she did return to the farm, Dr. Bennett regularly relieved three or four country doctors when they vacationed. Claude remembers being left with an aunt so often that he considers that he had two mothers.

As if this were not enough proof of a lifetime commitment to her career, during World War II his mother was contacted by the War Department and enlisted to work as an ophthalmologist on a victory ship. Finally, at age 65, after the mother-in-law for whom she cared had died (at the age of 96!), Dr. Bennett returned to California where she had been licensed while serving with the military and worked in a hospital for retarded children until mandatory retirement at age 70. As will be seen, none of this full and far flung medical career was mentioned in the interview.

It is possible that similar gaps exist in the stories of other nonagenarians. In several cases conversations with relatives or friends did help to verify facts. But to have sought to check and amplify every subject's account would have been prohibitively time consuming. What are presented are not detailed biographies, but the broad strokes of life as painted by willing subjects in an all too brief period of time. The stories have a ring of authenticity to them. Taken together, they present a panoramic view of the varied worlds of the very old.

Use It or Lose It

Is it possible to predict who will retain above average mental functioning into the eighties and nineties? More important, is it possible to enhance one's chances of remaining mentally alert? These are questions which challenge researchers working on the frontiers of the human aging experience. While intriguing hints as to answers can be detected in the life stories of these nonagenarians, it will take much more controlled investigation to arrive at definitive conclusions. By way of anticipation, it seems that one characteristic found almost universally in the men and women interviewed was a profoundly positive attitude toward life. Might it be that mental health is enhanced by "happy thoughts"? Is there some chemical or "energy" that is released when humans consistently see light rather than dark, hope rather than despair?

Also, although it may seem redundant to say that active nonagenarians are active, there is abundant research evidence that "exercising" the mind (and the body for that matter!) helps to maintain intellectual ability. Adults who read books, take classes, and have regular interaction with friends show less IQ decline than more isolated and inactive adults. Also, it has been found that better educated adults not only outperform their less well educated peers, but maintain their intellectual power longer in old age. The fact that many of the men and women interviewed are well educated may represent an unintended bias in the sample. On the other hand, it may suggest that better educated people are precisely those who are more likely to enter the ranks of active nonagenarians.

Genes vs. Lifestyle

Longevity runs in families. To live to be a nonagenarian, pick your parents and grandparents carefully, because if they lived to advanced age, chances are good that, barring accidents and infectious diseases, you will also. All the people interviewed were asked about the ages of family members and, predictably, many had nonagenarian relatives. Several had brothers and sisters in their nineties. Ann Jordan introduced herself as the "baby" of her family with two older sisters who also are active nonagenarians, one of them married to a nonagenarian. The power of the genetic contribution to longevity is supported by studies of twins, which show that identical twins die within 37 months of each other compared with 78 months for fraternal twins.

However, as significant as genetics and heredity may be, they are not the major causes for the rise of the active nonagenarian; environmental factors are. At present, there is no way to control genetic inheritance, but it is possible to modify behavior and to take advantage of the advances made in medical knowledge. For example, it is estimated that smoking two or more packs of cigarettes a day reduces life expectancy by twelve years. We would expect that nonagenarians don't smoke, and they don't. Tonio Selwart said that he was a heavy smoker until thirty years ago. The fact that he was then in his sixties might offer encouragement to those who have smoked for many years and wonder if it is too late to stop.

Proper diet also contributes to longevity. Moderation in eating and limiting the intake of fat and sugar decrease the prospect of cardiovascular disease, the major cause of death in old age. Life expectancy in Japan is among the highest in the world, and the traditional Japanese diet is low in cholesterol. However, as American fast food chains proliferate in Japan, rates of diseases associated with high cholesterol intake are soaring. On the other hand, many Americans seem to have learned their lesson and are shifting away from high cholesterol foods such as eggs and beef. Of course, nonagenarians lived most of their lives before the current "health food" consciousness emerged, yet invariably they report moderation in food intake. None are true vegetarians, but all limit meat consumption. Although no detailed dietary history was attempted, it would seem that wise nutrition habits were the norm.

Adequate nutrition is a serious issue with older Americans. Even when poverty is not a factor, many older people fail to eat balanced meals. Those living alone are especially vulnerable, often lacking the motivation or energy to prepare healthy meals. Congregate feeding centers for those able to get out and Meals-on-Wheels for shut-ins are valuable services for frail or disabled elders. The active nonagenarians reveal patterns which facilitate and encourage appropriate eating habits. Those who live in retirement communities are required to take one meal a day in the communal dining room. Others have hired someone to come in and prepare a meal for them. For example, Dr. Harriet Strachstein, a clinical psychologist, has an employee who serves as combination receptionist-cook. Others are fortunate enough to live with a spouse or other family member. Sister John Baptist lives in a religious community, and Magnus Lundstrom has dinner with the family in whose home he rents a room.

Other lifestyle features such as moderation in the use of alcohol, getting adequate sleep, exercising regularly, interacting with friends, and having periodic medical check ups also enhance the prospects for a happy old age. Most important of all, and what is clearly revealed in the stories of the nonagenarians, is engagement with life. Each day has its plan and projects. There is a schedule, a reason to get up, to get dressed, to groom oneself, to be alert.

Why Do Healthy People Die?

Some years ago a book titled *Nobody Ever Died of Old Age* made the point that old age is not a disease, that people die from heart disease or cancer or a cerebrovascular disorder but not from old age itself. However, what is emerging in the United States and other developed countries is that more and more people are dying not so much from a specific disease as from old age. Their biological systems reach the outer limit of viability and simply stop. Death certificates may require something more specific than "old age," but often that's what it comes down to. It is not unusual now to read obituaries that state that the deceased died "from natural causes."

An intriguing term, "natural causes." It implies that death is built into nature and not a mistake or tragedy. Just how to explain "natural" death is still debated by experts. Some hold that cells are genetically programmed to divide a set number of times, perhaps fifty. It is as if the body were a slowly unwinding clock.

Another theory proposes that over time larger biological systems, in particular the immune system, lose their capacity to sustain and protect the body when it encounters normal environmental assaults, such as a virus. The cause of death of Mrs. Loeb, mentioned at the beginning of this chapter, was "an asthma attack." Quite possibly, when younger, Mrs. Loeb's body would have been capable of defending her from the "attack."

Assuming an outer limit to life, what is the limit? In February 1996, Jeanne Calment, who lives in Arles, France, celebrated her 121st birthday. According to the *Guinness Book of World Records*, she is the oldest person in the world. At the celebration attended by government officials and other dignitaries, Mrs. Calment, noted for her sense of humor, said, "I see badly, I hear badly, I can't feel anything, but everything's fine." So it would seem that at the present time, human *life span* is about 120 years. There is no one for whom documented evidence exists who has lived longer. But even if life span is not increasing, *life expectancy,* that is, the actual experience of people in a population, certainly is. So today in the United States life expectancy for women is 78 and for men 71. In this century alone life expectancy has increased by over twenty years. More and more Americans are moving closer and closer to that outer limit, presently 120 years. In fact, one expert forecasts that just as life expectancy increased by twenty years in this century, it will increase by a similar amount in the next. Should that occur, to live to be a nonagenarian will be the *average* human's experience.

Another forecast calls for a more compressed period of *morbidity,* that is, the age at which significant disability occurs. People will maintain good health for a longer and longer period and then, like Mrs. Loeb, die rather quickly.

What is Old?

In light of the extraordinary developments in life expectancy and health, classifying people as old becomes increasingly problematic. In strictly chronological terms, the active nonagenarians were "middle aged" when they were 65. Some of them refuse to label themselves as old at 90! On the other hand, restaurants offer Senior Citizen menus and discounts for people 60 and over. Membership eligibility for the American Association of Retired Persons (AARP), whose 32,000,000 members constitute the world's largest organization promoting the interests of the elderly, begins at age 50.

Even retirement no longer serves as a rite of passage into the world of the old. Millions of people retire early, many in their mid-fifties, and cannot be considered old. Social Security allows workers to begin collecting retirement benefits, although reduced, at age 62. In fact, the average retirement age has decreased in recent decades and now stands at 62. On the other hand, a contrary trend has developed with many people continuing to work well beyond 70. To facilitate this option, mandatory retirement has been eliminated for most job categories. Several of the active nonagenarians continue to work full time. Mrs. Cassidy would be lost without her demanding but energizing job in real estate sales. Edward Corcoran saw me in his law office where he works every day. Russell Wilson doesn't want to spend too much time away from his paid position as a library page.

However, it must be noted that many of those interviewed were forced to retire decades ago. Eugene Curry, a dynamic man at age 92, had to relinquish his position as director of a retirement home more than twenty years ago when he reached age 70. Mrs. Donovan had the same experience as a registered nurse.

There is a paradox in American society today. People readily accept the label "senior citizen" in order to qualify for theatre discounts and lower air fares but refuse to see themselves as old in the classic sense of the revered but retired ancient ones. A new set of age norms has emerged. To be a senior member of society does not signify disability, dependence, or inactivity. Quite the contrary. Advertising directed at older people creates an image of vigor, adventure, and creativity. Even those who retire from paid employment frequently commence volunteer "careers" which may last for decades, as was true of Mrs. Loeb and her "work" as manager of a hospital gift shop. It is not unusual to hear people say that retirement is the most fulfilling stage of life because they are doing what they freely choose to do.

Furthermore, typically by their mid-fifties, middle class Americans have completed the responsibilities of child rearing, paid off the mortgage on their house, and provided themselves with an income which enables them to maintain their accustomed life style. Despite the valid concerns about soaring health costs and low interest rates on savings, the men and women entering old age today are the most affluent, healthy, and politically powerful generation of older people in the history of the world.

Affluence in Their Nineties

Although several of the interviewees said that their income was "just enough to get by," it was obvious from their homes, furnishings, and lifestyle that most of the subjects of this study were comfortably middle class. Also, it will be noticed that all the people included are white. Efforts were made to locate poorer and minority group active nonagenarians but with little success. Certainly there are such people, and the picture of life in the nineties would be more complete were they to be represented. However, the demographics of American life show that the active nonagenarian profile is to be found predominantly among affluent whites. On average, better educated people live longer than less well educated people, whites longer than blacks, and white collar workers longer than blue. A Census Bureau study of people over 100 found that most centenarians were native born, in spite of the fact that they were born at the time of high immigration to the United States.

Race reveals an especially striking contrast. A white girl born in the United States in 1987 had a life expectancy of 78.8, while a black girl could expect to live until age 73.8. A white male's life expectancy was 72.1 and a black male's 65.4. Particularly troubling is the fact that this gap has been increasing. In 1984 the average difference was 5.6 years, while in 1987 it had risen to 6.2. Life expectancy is shorter yet for Mexican-Americans and shortest of all for Native Americans.

Pictures of extremely old black men and women could give the impression that blacks actually live longer than whites. And strangely enough, among the very old this turns out to be true. Nonwhite eighty-five-year-olds have longer life expectancy than whites. This crossover phenomenon is explained in terms of the unusual hardiness required for blacks to reach such an advanced age. The lower overall life expectancy of minority group members is attributed to the greater likelihood that they are poor, have worked in high risk occupations, and have received less adequate health care.

More Men Than Women?

Although on average American women outlive men by seven years and comprise about 75% of the population over 85, half the active nonagenarians included in this book are men. Two factors may provide an explanation. First, men may have been more willing to volunteer than women. Cultural norms deter women from inviting an unknown man into their homes. Also, they may not believe that they are "important" enough to be included in a book. Several women expressed such disclaimers as, "I don't know why you would want to talk to me; I have never done anything special." The second reason is a phenomenon similar to nonwhite 85-year-olds having longer life expectancy than whites. There is some evidence that those males who live to 85 remain more healthy for a longer period of time than do women who live to 85. Thus, a distinction can be made between life expectancy in general and *active life expectancy*, the time that an individual can expect to live free of serious disability.

While death rates are readily available, there is scant evidence on rates of morbidity and disability, that is, the age at which a person ceases to be active or independent. Nursing homes are filled with people who have physical and/or mental disabilities as well as people obviously in terminal decline. On the other hand, some individuals have no period of morbidity at all. One day they are fine and the next day they die. This of course is what everyone wants. In mantra-like fashion older people say, "I want to remain healthy to the end and die in my sleep."

Gerontologists use various instruments to measure the level of independence of older people. Two of them were included in the interviews with the active nonagenarians as an informal screening mechanism. One is called the Activities of Daily Living (ADL). The ADL measures walking, bathing, getting outside, getting into and out of a bed or chair, dressing, using the toilet, and eating. The other instrument is the Home Management Activities (HMA) which includes heavy housework, shopping, light housework, preparing meals, managing money, and using the telephone.

Since the number of nonagenarians interviewed is small and not selected randomly, comparing the level of independence of men and women would not be meaningful. However, a study of a more representative sample of people 85 and older found that 58.8% of the females and 39.9% of the males reported difficulty with one or more ADL. A similar difference emerged on the HMA, with 60.5% of the females and 43.2% of the males reporting some difficulty. Although such findings support the thesis that males over 85 are hardier than their female counterparts, it must be cautioned that the data may reflect the greater reluctance on the part of men to admit difficulties.

How Many Active Nonagenarians?

It was only in the late 1980's that major research funding from the National Institute on Aging focused attention on persons aged 85 and older. This subgroup—variously called "the oldest old," "the frail elderly," and "the extreme aged"—became the center of attention because it was growing rapidly and had relatively high rates of illness and disability. Because of the implications for health care and social services, most funded research has centered on the problems encountered by the elderly, often focusing on nursing home residents and other individuals already identified as in need of help. For the most part, those who maintain robust health and independence have been ignored.

Until the 1960's, the elderly suffered from a distressingly high rate of poverty and were given scant national attention. All that changed with the "War on Poverty" and other reforms of the 60's and 70's. Helped by their growing political power, the elderly enhanced their status in the United States to the point where today more than half of the federal domestic budget is devoted to assistance for older Americans, with "entitlement" programs such as Social Security and Medicare the most costly. To a large extent the stereotype of the elderly has changed from meek, decrepit, and lonely individuals to an assertive, well-organized, and affluent class competing for benefits with their economically hard-pressed children and grandchildren.

The concern of the government and younger generation is well founded. The ranks of the elderly, and in particular the oldest old, are growing rapidly. The 1990 census counted 3,000,000 Americans 85 or older, of whom nearly 1,000,000 were nonagenarians and more than 50,000 centenarians. Since 1980, the population 65 and over has more than doubled; the number of people 85 and older has increased almost fivefold and the number of centenarians more than ten times. This was happening while the population of the nation as a whole increased by 10%. The country is getting older and the old are getting older.

The National Center for Health Statistics reports that an 85-year-old white man has a life expectancy of 5.0 years and an 85-year-old white woman 6.3 years. (Comparable projections for blacks are even higher.) If life expectancy continues its upward movement, by the year 2030 when the baby boomers begin to reach 85, the number of centenarians will be approaching one million. The demands placed on health care services will be enormous. But also, by then, the active nonagenarian will be a familiar part of the American scene.

How many of today's men and women over ninety can be classified as active nonagenarians? It is impossible to give anything other than a rough estimate. Much depends on how rigorously the term is defined. If all those who are not institutionalized are counted, then the figure is more than half a million. However, many nonagenarians living at home suffer serious physical and mental infirmities, which severely restrict their autonomy. Many others, especially those in their late nineties, remain alert but have limited mobility. My opinion is that upwards of 100,000 people are as active as the men and women interviewed for this book and that the number will double before the year 2000.

Where to Live

Although the majority of elderly people, including active nonagenarians, live in their own homes, an ever-expanding range of alternatives has emerged. With patience and knowledgeable assistance, it should be possible for nearly all older people, especially those with financial assets, to locate housing that is appropriate to their needs and lifestyle.

For decades there have been "retirement communities," which essentially are age-segregated neighborhoods providing services such as security and a recreation center. Older couples, in particular, buy a house or condo in a development restricted to people over 50 or 55. One purpose of this restriction is to preclude the addition of school age children to the local population together with its tax implications. These "leisure" communities range from mobile home parks to high rise condominiums to large luxury houses. Basically, residents of retirement communities have many of the advantages of home ownership together with opportunities for companionship with people who share their stage of life. The absence of younger people in the neighborhood may or may not be experienced as an advantage.

Recently, as more and more people not only reach retirement age but move into their eighties and nineties, additional housing options have been developed. The National Association of Senior Living Industries, a 1,000-member organization of builders who specialize in housing for the elderly, divides the various alternatives into three broad categories: congregate-living communities, assisted-living facilities, and continuing-care retirement communities.

Congregate-living housing is characterized by substantial independence. Although meals are provided and some personal-care services such as assistance with bathing, dressing, and grooming, no nursing care is available. Residents with serious medical or nursing needs are transferred to a hospital or nursing home. Dominican Village in Amityville, Long Island, is representative of such a facility. A community of nuns, saddled with an underutilized fifty-five-acre convent campus, have developed a 266-unit rental project with two main living formats. Those in need of minimal services live in one-bedroom apartments and receive one meal a day, free transportation for outings, and are welcome to participate in numerous activities, including sharing in religious services with the nuns. For more frail residents there is "assisted living," which includes three meals a day as well as help with personal care and housekeeping. The monthly rent for this more comprehensive plan is $1,500. All residents must be ambulatory or be able to use a wheelchair unassisted. Free use of a laundry is included, and a security system connects each apartment to the front desk.

In assisted-living facilities residents live independently, usually in studio or one-bedroom units, but are provided with twenty-four hour supervision and a variety of services, including minimum health care assistance.

Finally, continuing-care communities are the most comprehensive, providing a continuum of care from independent living to skilled nursing facilities. One type of continuing-care community is the "life-care community" in which residents pay an up front endowment fee as well as monthly maintenance fees for which they are entitled to full lifetime health care, even if financial resources should be depleted. Three of the active nonagenarians in this book— Dorothy Redfield, Alice Wheeler, and Ruth Bennett—live in life-care communities. It might be of interest to read these three interviews in conjunction with one another in order to get a variety of viewpoints on three different residences, noting in particular that although such complexes contain a nursing home component, most of the residents live independently, have considerable privacy, own cars, and come and go as they please. Most of all, they have peace of mind. They know that all contingencies have been provided for. The negative image which many people have of nursing homes should not be applied to these pleasant and dignified facilities.

Freedom or Conformity?

Research suggests that while people are working and raising a family they conform to social expectations, that is, they shape their lives to fit the requirements of their positions. Once retired and no longer responsible for guiding the young, the uniqueness of the individual is set free. As one nonagenarian said, "No more bullshit!" If this is true, then as men and women age they should become increasingly themselves, unshackled from convention, less and less concerned with the opinions of others. Theoretically, therefore, nonagenarians should be the most liberated people on earth. But are they?

There is a characteristic openness and trust in responding to questions and expressing views. On the other hand, no matter how old one may be, the social dimension of life remains powerful and the tendency to measure oneself against others continues. Those living in housing for the elderly are motivated to "put on a front," to present themselves as competent and appropriate in their behavior. There is little appeal to being considered "odd." On the contrary, there remains the need to be perceived in a positive light by peers, of not crossing the line and joining the "confused" or "old ones." So, like it or not, most continue to walk the thin line of conformity.

Those living in the general community have a similar need to "behave themselves." They realize that their children are alert for signs of failure, that the slightest slip is likely to be cause for alarm and a discussion about their capacity to remain independent. Therefore, the nonagenarians, perhaps more than younger people, are required to be on their guard lest their cherished freedom be taken from them and they be obliged to join those in need of custodial care.

So a tension exists beneath the surface. On the one hand there is that urge toward singularity and free expression. On the other is the desire to be appraised as competent. To be an active nonagenarian is to juggle with skill the balls of personal individuality and social conformity.

Is There Ageism?

In March 1993, *The New York Times* reported the end of eighteen years of court supervision over former residents of the notorious and now closed Willowbrook State School, which once housed more than 5,000 mentally retarded people in what was little more than a filthy warehouse. A picture accompanying the article showed Federal Judge John R. Bartels who had presided over the complex case for many years. Although it is not unusual to mention the age of participants in such proceedings, it is interesting to note what might be a subtle hint of ageism in this front page item. It was mentioned *twice* that Judge Bartels was 95 years old and *twice* that he had to hold legal papers close to his eyes in order to read them.

Despite many reported cases of age discrimination in employment practices, negative stereotypes of elderly drivers, and jokes about the sexual behavior of older people, few nonagenarians made any mention of encountering ageism on their long journey through old age. It may be that by temperament they don't notice or don't attract obstacles or critical remarks based on their age. By their vitality they may in fact be contributing to the erosion of the residual ageism in American society. Even if attention is drawn to Judge Bartels' failing eyesight, it is difficult not to be favorably impressed by the ability of a 95-year-old man to occupy such a responsible position.

The Aging Daughter

In a moment of candor, this is how the daughter of one of the nonagenarians spoke about her mother:

> I'm in my mid-sixties myself, but Mom continues to treat
> me like a child. She has always been tyrannical. She bosses
> her brothers and sisters, her children and her grandchildren.
> Oh yes, when you meet her she is a lovely little old lady,
> but believe me, if the Devil himself were as charming,
> we'd all be in the Garden of Eden. She likes to be the boss
> and when the children feel that they are of an age to
> be in charge of their own lives, it's very difficult.

Despite her age, the older woman continues to wield power and to generate the sort of anger mixed with guilt that is common in mother-daughter relationships. The emergence of the active nonagenarian is creating the phenomenon of the daughter in her 60's or even 70's who, as someone's child, is subjected to criticism of her clothing, friends, home decorating, and cooking. A woman who is a Senior Citizen herself still being scolded by her mother!

Yet there is another side to the complex relationship mentioned above. Besides being the child, the daughter in some respects is also the parent, wondering every day if her mother is all right. As active and alert as the mother may be, she is after all 95 and living alone. The daughter calls her mother daily, does the heavy grocery shopping, and visits weekly. When she is away, she makes arrangements for another relative to look in on Mom. The daughter feels restricted, hesitant to take a vacation, relocate, or—God forbid—get sick or disabled herself. By a strange twist of nature, some nonagenarians have buried their own children—sons and daughters who have died of old age.

But relationships are complex and stories are many-sided. Thus, besides at times being frustrated and angry with her mother, the daughter referred to above has deep love for her mother, admires her, and credits her with a valuable role in the family. She says:

> We are close-knit and get together about once a month
> for one occasion or another. And I'm talking about
> thirty-five people. Mom, as the oldest, holds us together.
> And she has a fantastic memory. I go out of the house
> in the morning and can't remember where I parked my
> car the night before, but Mom can remember everyone's
> birthday and anniversary. She's amazing!

What Is It Like to be Ninety?

With the steady extension of life expectancy, it is perhaps appropriate to think in terms of several generations within the aging population. The young-olds are those roughly between 60 and 70 who still have one foot in middle age and may be denying that they are old. The middle-olds are those between 70 and 85. Almost all are retired, notice increasing infirmities in themselves or their peers, and are taking seriously the reality that human life is finite. Finally, there are the old-olds, those over 85 who, no matter how healthy, experience the inevitable physical and mental changes which are daily reminders that the gift of life inevitably must be relinquished.

It is likely that the young-olds cannot really identify with the old-olds. At 60 someone is culturally as well as chronologically as far removed from an 85-year-old as he is from a 35-year-old. One of the elderly people interviewed by Glenn Busch for his book, *You Are My Darling Zita*, communicates from personal experience the impossibility of understanding what it's like to be old:

> Old age is something that you think is never going to come upon you. It's like a disease; it creeps up on you. It creeps and creeps and then all of a sudden it comes upon you with a rush.

It is as impossible to fully understand what it's like to be 90 as it is for a man to understand what it's like to be a woman or a white person to understand what it's like to be black. The best we can do is listen to the stories and try to approach, if not enter, their world.

Life is a process, a gradual unfolding. Today's nonagenarian was once a child looking out at the world through the bars of a crib. He or she had the dreams, joys, and heartaches of adolescence, entered the adult world with its promise and its disappointments, worked, loved , and gradually grew old. Each life is like a plant which grows slowly over time. As we look at the blossom which is the active nonagenarian, we can only wonder about all those years and experiences which shaped the beautiful flower.

A social worker in a county office for the aging said that when a very old person dies without his or her story being recorded, it is as if a whole library were lost. Only parts of stories are recorded in this book. It is up to younger relatives to preserve the memories of a loved one before it is too late. Oral history is facilitated today by audio and video recorders. Just as for generations photo albums have been treasured repositories of the memories of a family, so also now should be the tapes on which Grandma's voice and image are preserved as she tells her story. It is said that most human beings are completely forgotten within three generations. With today's technology it is possible to keep people alive indefinitely, at least electronically. And as individuals are thus preserved, so also is the history of a family.

CHAPTER TWO

PATHWAYS TO THE TENTH DECADE

E ach human being's journey along the road of life is unique. Nevertheless, the cultural and historical period in which men and women live has an impact on the opportunities available to them and the choices they make. For example, because of the policies in place at the time, many nonagenarians were obliged to retire at age 65 or 70. Today, with the elimination of mandatory retirement for most occupations, workers have greater flexibility with regard to retirement from work

Even more significant is the revolution which has taken place in the lives of women in American life. Today's female nonagenarians were raised in an age which offered women much more circumscribed options than are available to women today. In the light of this fact, it is striking how many female active nonagenarians were "liberated women" long before the term was coined and before "women's rights" became a paramount societal value.

In *Revolution from Within*, Gloria Steinem wrote that as she went around the country promoting the women's movement, she continuously encountered talented women who suffered from self-doubt and insecurity. As true as this undoubtedly is, the women interviewed for this book, although products of their times, seem to have surmounted cultural obstacles to inner growth and social achievement. There were few complaints about gender-based handicaps Their voices communicate self-confidence and strength.

Besides the tendency of culture and gender to squeeze individuals into predetermined molds, so also social class, ethnicity, religion, and family have an impact on one's life trajectory. In listening to the nonagenarians it is not difficult to hear echoes of such shaping forces. Nevertheless, what is most impressive is the uniqueness of each individual.

"Types" of Nonagenarians

Having made this point, it can still be asked whether or not the nonagenarians can be clustered into a few basic patterns or types. The initial plan of the book was to group the subjects into several broad categories so as to present a few core models that would simplify what might otherwise be a bewildering parade of apparently completely individual men and women. Sociologists have a penchant for what are known as "ideal types," idealized or even stereotypical formulations which are designed to uncover and highlight major dimensions of some social reality. For example, the terms "upper class," "middle class," and "lower class" are an effort to take millions of discrete individuals and cluster them under these three headings. Many people don't fit comfortably into any one of these classifications, of course, but the practice of looking at society in terms of "classes" has its utility. It helps to see the forest and not just the trees, to discern ways in which some people are similar to one another and different from others.

How then might active nonagenarians be "classified?" One way to look at them could be as *Family-Integrators, Social Networkers,* or *Solitaries.*

Family-Integrators would be those men and women who are either married or living with other kin and finding their principal satisfaction in their relationships within the small world of the family.

Social Networkers would be those with significant non-kin relationships, such as at work, in voluntary associations, or in church groups.

Solitaries would be those people who not only live alone, but find their principal satisfaction with gardening, listening to music, or other solitary pursuits.

As the interviewing progressed it was decided that although such a model might have some value, the more important value of stressing the uniqueness of each subject would be compromised. Hence, the subjects are presented in alphabetical order. Nevertheless, with some degree of arbitrariness, the interviewees if not assigned to one or another of the categories suggested, might be imagined as on a scale from most socially active to most solitary.

A practical value of imagining the subjects in this fashion is to assist the reader in answering what certainly will be an implicit if not an explicit question: *Which of these people is living their advanced old age closest to how I envision my own?* However, since no one of the nonagenarians presented is likely to offer an exact blueprint for anyone else's old age, it might be useful to select several with whom one might identify, perhaps making notes or keeping a journal in which the process of shaping one's own unique future is begun. The challenge is to fashion a self which is the authentic embodiment of one's own vision and values and which takes into account physical, intellectual, and economic realities. The people in this book cannot take others by the hand and lead them into their company. But they can offer suggestions, witness, and hope.

Are Memories the Truth?

Interviewing nonagenarians, while fascinating and energizing, was also frustrating. How can the richness of a long life be encapsulated in a few pages? What is "the truth" about these people? Do they know themselves well enough to share what is most central? Did what I "heard" and decided to include do them justice?

In her book of memoirs, *Remembering the Bone House,* Nancy Mairs wrestles with a similar problem. She speaks of the past as "a ramshackle structure" and contents herself with saying that she did not deliberately invent any of the "facts" she relates. Mairs' aim is not so much to have absolute accuracy as to give the past "a new life." Certainly, the nonagenarians also were giving "a new life" to their past, rearranging and reshaping the picture of themselves. Listening to those stories, I could not avoid filtering them through the story of my own life. All biography is approximation.

Decisions had to be made at every stage of the process. Not only were the nonagenarians drawing forth but a few items from the rich storehouse of memory, but I was selecting and highlighting. What results, then, are not biographies but all-too-brief sketches of human complexity. When subjects sit for an artist, they may be more or less satisfied with what ends up on the canvas. Even photographers use shadows and camera angles to bring out the "truth" of the subject as they see it. I'm certain that all my subjects will recognize themselves, although some might take issue with the tone or perspective which has emerged. Hopefully, the profiles are faithful to the larger truth, which is the quest for an understanding of the various roads which a privileged few have taken into the world of the active nonagenarian.

A Brief Glimpse of Many

Most of the 150 nonagenarians brought to my attention were generated by an "Author's Query" which appeared in the October 11, 1992 *New York Times Book Review*. Although the majority could not be interviewed personally, the letters from them and from their friends and relatives reveal the geographic and lifestyle diversity of American nonagenarians. Before proceeding to the profiles based on interviews, excerpts from such correspondence can illustrate not only the diversity but also the enthusiasm which people have for sharing their good fortune:

"Contact my father-in-law. He still drives, walks a mile daily, cooks, gardens and writes beautiful letters." (East Hebron, New Hampshire)

"When I visited my great aunt last summer, I noticed that her driveway had recently been sealed. I mentioned it and learned—to my astonishment—that she had done it herself. She then told me that the flat-roofed porch of her house had been leaking, so she got out a ladder and climbed up with a bucket of tar. That fixed the problem!" (Indianapolis, Indiana)

"You might wish to approach my father. He's 92, healthy and quite active (church, concerts, causes, wood-splitting). Whether you can get cooperation is up to you! He's courteous, but busy and tired." (Montpelier, Vermont)

"My aunt lives on her own, will read your palm, analyze your handwriting and probe your life with an intensity rarely found today. We think she's truly a phenomenon. She looks decades younger than her 95 years." (New York, New York)

"My father is 96 and cooks on all burners—better than I!" (Marblehead, Massachusetts)

"My step-aunt is 96. When I last visited her she was out in the garden working. Also, she usually has a quilting project going." (Milford, Iowa)

"I am 95 years old and had a complete physical last spring. My doctor says I'm in very good health." (Winter Harbor, Maine)

Why Not Centenarians?

Nida Neel, one of the subjects of this book, did not consider it noteworthy that she was 97. As if to underscore her position, she followed up my visit to her Connecticut home by sending me a newspaper clipping that gave the names and ages of fifty-four centenarians living in western Connecticut. The article noted that May was Centenarians Month. Mrs. Neel's point, of course, was that no one celebrates Nonagenarians Month.

Indeed, there is something awesome about a centenarian. However, although their numbers are growing, people who live for a century are still a rarity and few of them are "active" in the sense that the nonagenarians in this book are active. Centenarians have not been included because it seems more realistic to emphasize what is a plausible expectation rather than a far out dream. On the other hand, for those like Mrs. Neel who are well into their nineties to become, shall we say, an "active centenarian" is a very likely prospect. Two of the people whose profiles are presented, both men, were ninety-nine and confidently anticipating their one-hundredth birthday.

Early in this research, I interviewed a ninety-nine-year-old woman, who although intellectually alert and living alone in her own apartment, had limited vision and difficulty walking. After writing up the interview, I phoned the woman's only child, a daughter, to get some additional information. The daughter had heard about the interview after the fact and for whatever reason did not want her mother identified in the book. Respecting the daughter's wish, the interview is not included. However, what the ninety-nine-year-old woman said is instructive because not untypical of how nonagenarians feel about living to 100.

She related that her father had twin aunts, both of whom had lived in three centuries. They were born at the end of the 18th century and died within a few months of each other at about the age of 107 early in the 20th century. She then said, "I was born in the 1890's and it's possible that I also might live in three centuries. I'm 99 now and feel OK." Unfortunately, she died three months later, a few months short of her one-hundreth birthday.

Government agencies have paid more attention to centenarians than to nonagenarians. In the 1960's, the Social Security Administration began issuing a series of volumes consisting of very brief interviews with centenarian repicients of Social Security. In 1982, Osborn Segerberg supplemented the questions asked by Social Security field representatives with more in-depth questions. In particular, Segerberg compared U.S. government guidelines for preserving health with the practices of the long-lived. Then, in 1987, the Bureau of the Census published a brief book titled *America's Centenarians* based on data from the 1980 census.

Two more recent books also offer a view of life over 100. Belle Boone Beard includes information on more than 500 people in *Centenarians* (1991). Finally, the most accessible primer on centenarians is Jim Heynen's *One Hundred over 100* (1990), a collection of color photos of 100 people with an accompanying one-page narrative about each.

Several of the people who wrote to me referred to the prospect of living to be 100 or were well positioned to do so:

"On my 92nd birthday I started my memoirs which I have titled 'A Life in Three Centuries.' In it I wrote: 'If I manage to hang on for ten years more, the title will not be a complete misnomer.' Also at that time it will be interesting to round up others in the same age group and form a Three Centuries Club, since all of us will have lived in three centuries." (San Francisco, California)

"I've a candidate for your study of active nonagenarians, but you must hurry. In January she will be 100. When I saw her a couple of weeks ago at her younger sister's 95th birthday celebration, she was planning a trip to Texas with a young woman. They were going in a pickup truck." (Woodburn, Kentucky)

"I had a sister who lived to be 103; another one is 96. I'm only 92. Albert Schweitzer said, 'There are two means of refuge from the miseries of life—music and cats.' I happen to like both!"

"My mother would interest you. She will celebrate her 100th birthday in six months. In spite of two broken hips, a broken shoulder (from falls) and a gall bladder operation in the past five years, she is in reasonably good health. She lives alone in an apartment where she cares for herself and a canary, as well as numerous house plants." (Jenkinstown, Pennsylvania)

"I am 99 years old and practice law daily in this office. I attend continuing legal education seminars regularly. I was a judge and retain the title." (Minneapolis, Minnesota)

"You will want to talk to a friend of mine, age 99, who still takes business trips. In fact, I have taken this long to contact you because I was waiting for her to return from her latest trip to South Dakota where she has been establishing a chair in nutrition at the Brookings Institute. She herself has worked in nutrition all her life and is the author of several books on this subject." (Chicago, Illinois)

"My father-in-law is 98 years old, lives alone and by-and-large takes care of himself, although he has loving children and grandchildren living nearby who look in on him regularly. The back yard of his modest home is devoted to vegetable gardens and fruit trees which he tends and harvests for his own consumption and that of family and friends." (Tucson, Arizona)

"Soon I will be 98 and am healthy and able. I volunteer at the medical library in the hospital in my area. I don't use a cane or walker to get around; thank God." (Far Rockaway, New York)

"I lived alone until I was 90 when I moved to a high rise building for senior citizens. I embroider, crochet, sing and play the organ. I love to play bingo with my friends. I'm 98." (Pittsburgh, Pennsylvania)

"I'm 97 and each day bring a rose from my garden to my wife who is in a nursing home. I'm going to try to make 100 and then the hell with it!" (Southold, New York)

More Men Than Women

It has been noted that the majority of nonagenarians brought to my attention were men. While most of the extremely old people in nursing homes are women, a high proportion of the nonagenarians living in the general community are men. Several reasons explain this, including the fact that men are more likely than women to have adequate financial resources as well as a living, younger spouse.

"My father-in-law gardens, hunts, putters with his vast collection of tools, and with my 85-year-old mother-in-law commutes weekly between their house in town and their ranch, where they still raise stock for family consumption." (Stanford, California)

"My father is 95 and lives alone since my mother died last year at 91. His walking is not too good as he has some trouble with his legs. But he has learned to cook and reads *The New York Times* and *Wall Street Journal* daily. Good shape mentally." (Palm Desert, California)

"A former colleague of mine at Westminster College is 94, very active, very alert and in very good health. Recently he has spent several periods of time 'housesitting' for one of his sons who lives in the wilds of Montana. He spends summers at a family cabin in Northern Michigan and has appeared in various plays at the summer theatre and still works on sets." (Fulton, Missouri)

"I am 90 and healthy and still writing for publication. Will send you some samples of my recent work." (Eureka, Montana)

"I am 94 and am in very good health with considerable vigor and still in business as a general contractor." (Mill Valley, California)

"I am a lawyer and was in active practice until two years ago, when I retired at the age of 90. I had to give up golf a year ago, but can still swim, drive my own car, walk on my own power—sometimes with a cane which I was advised to use, especially when I have to walk on terra that is not very firma." (St.Louis, Missouri)

"This 'grand old man' of Chicago real estate is reigning national tennis champion in his age group: 85 and over. There is no 90 and over category, so he faces younger and younger men. He still heads the company at 91." (Chicago, Illinois)

Women Who Take Initiative

Women now in their nineties may have been taught not to be assertive, but that did not restrain many of them from going to college long before it was fashionable, entering demanding careers, and developing strong, independent personalities. Nor did the female role stereotype of passivity deter many from volunteering for the study of active nonagenarians. Several actually wrote twice, wanting to be sure that I realized that they were really interested in participating. Responses from women included the following:

"I am 93 years old, quite busy and like it. I belong to the Golden Senior Club and attend all their dinner dances. I love to dance." (Pittsfield, Massachusetts)

"This is what I typed into the Macintosh computer recently: 'I was born in Russia October 4, 1898 and came to this country when I was seven. I have lived from seeing the first light bulb to watching a man walk on the moon.'" (Santa Cruz, California)

"My young friend, the local librarian, found your notice in the newspaper. She was intrigued and since I am one of her few nonagenarian friends she urged me to write to you. My eyesight is not good at all and I am not as quick on my feet as I was fifty years ago, but my brain is still in fair working order." (Schertz, Texas)

"I read your notice in the *Book Review* section. What do you want to know? I'm 92, active, healthy—and busy!" (Bronx, New York)

"I was born December 1900 and worked in an office until the age of 81. I am a subscriber to the New York Philharmonic matinee concerts, attend art exhibits and maintain an extensive correspondence in English, German and French." (Forest Hills, New York)

"I'm over 90, but in this retirement community of 16,000, people age 90-plus in good health are not unusual. This is a great place to study the aged. They play tennis, swim, dance, volunteer, and golf, golf, golf." (Green Valley, Arizona)

Ninety-Plus Club

Although, as indicated, one optimistic man is considering the formation of a Three Centuries Club, there already exists at least one Ninety-Plus Club. A woman in her late 70's who lives in a life-care home for the elderly in Altadena, California has established it. The woman is a student at Cal State in Los Angeles and has received a certificate in gerontology. She wrote that a number of people who were admitted to the home two decades ago when they were 70 are still functioning well. As a project for school, she initiated the club and says that it delights the nonagenarians, although "at first I encountered some resistance. Several people did not want to acknowledge their age."

It is not clear what the activities of the Ninety-Plus Club might be, but its formation suggests that the practice of having one club for "Senior Citizens" of all ages might need reconsideration in light of the ever expanding life expectancy. "Seniors" of sixty or seventy are a different generation from those who are eighty or ninety and may have different interests. It will be interesting to see if indeed programs designed for "Junior Seniors" and "Senior Seniors" might emerge in the near future.

Nonagenarians at Work

The basic purpose of senior clubs is to provide leisure programs for retirees. Relatively few active nonagenarians belong to such clubs. They have other interests to fill their time or, mirabile dictu, they are not retired and so do not identify at all with people who play bingo in a church hall, eat lunch in a Golden Age center, and go on bus trips to state parks. Try to imagine any of the following people engaged in standard Senior Citizen activities:

"This gentleman, at 92, is senior Judge, sitting on the Court of

Appeals for the Eleventh Circuit in Atlanta. He still sits on cases, keeps up with his work, and still pins lawyers with hard questions." (Atlanta, Georgia)

"There is in this New England village a lovely old lady who is in her 90's and a practicing chiropractor. She is legally blind but feels her patients and gets around with a companion who writes and reads for her. Otherwise she is quite mobile." (Meredith, New Hampshire)

"My former father-in-law who will soon be 91 is currently teaching his last course at the William Mitchell Law School. He 'retired' from the University of Minnesota Law School at age 65 and went directly to William Mitchell. He has had an illustrious career." (Minneapolis, Minnesota)

"Sister Mary Alma taught biology at Notre Dame College from 1938 until 1987 when she retired from teaching. She then became Special Assistant to the President and works in the office responsible for college fundraising. She was 90 recently and keeps moving both physically and mentally. She currently teaches a class on the brain at the College's Renaissance Institute, which is a program for women and men 55 years or better." (Baltimore, Maryland)

"I have a friend who is 92. She gives lectures and workshops on death and dying and has written a book titled *Life's Finishing School*. It's about time someone wrote about healthy old people!" (Townsend, Washington)

"I was born January 24, 1900, have been practicing law since 1925 and still am." (Dallas, Texas)

"My uncle is 91 and raises award-winning camellias. He continues to operate a small farm about 100 miles from his home to which he makes weekly trips and puts in a full day of work. He is active in vocational agricultural activities and drives all over the state to attend various functions." (Jackson, Mississippi)

"At our college here is a 95-year-old nun who continues to instruct harp students. By means of a videotape, she even critiques a harpist in Montana." (Marylhurst, Oregon)

"A man, 91, binds books for me with help from a granddaughter and grandson who drop in regularly. He told me he has a friend in his eighties who claims my friend is just as sharp as he ever was.' To which my friend replies, 'That's a lot of hooey. I forget a lot worse than I used to.'" (Lincoln, Nebraska)

"She received her college degree in 1967 at the age of 65. When an invitation for her 25th class reunion arrived in 1992 she called the Alumni Office to let them know that she was too busy to attend. She teaches daily piano lessons, writes for the local newspaper, volunteers for the American Red Cross, is a lay reader in her church, and is gearing up for the annual Audubon bird count." (Livingston, Montana)

Physical Exercise

Letters nominating candidates for this study focused on two particularly striking aspects of the active nonagenarians: their intellectual acuity and their capacity for physical activity. As the interviews will show, it is important not to exaggerate the extent to which nonagenarians are physically active. While some have an impressive fitness regimen, others never exercise. Similarly, although all the subjects reveal no cognitive impairment, not all are "in a study group that reads and discusses James Joyce's *Ulysses*" as one man wrote about his 90-year old mother. It is important to realize that while the range of interests and activities is extensive, what is possible for some is not required of all. More energetic respondents included the following:

"Two nonagenarians who are members of our bicycle club completed a 100-mile bike ride in Texas in the middle of August." (Wichita Falls, Texas)

"I am 93. I jogged until six years ago. Now I walk two or three miles daily unless there is ice. Then I use an exercise bicycle. I am a fortunate person to have made good recoveries from several operations and to have gone back to jogging and yard work in a month or at most six weeks." (Cedar Falls, Iowa)

"I'm 93 and keep active. I work in my garden, saw wood and chop it and work around the grounds, about two acres. I live here with my wife of 55 years and drive the 75 miles to Boston. Please excuse my penmanship. I have two pinched nerves in my neck and lack full control of my left hand." (Martha's Vineyard, Massachusetts)

"I have a 95-year-old mother who is in perfect health and living in her own apartment in a retirement area. She has made hundreds of stuffed dolls for a women's exchange in our town and is still doing so. She goes to exercise class three times a week and walks every morning, weather permitting." (Chagrin Falls, Ohio)

"My husband, who is 89, and I live in Leisure World. I spoke to several other residents in our gym about your work and they gave me permission to send you their names and addresses. I'm sending only three names. These folks just happened to be there when I asked about those over 90 who frequent the gym. This is a retirement community of about 22,000 and there are many more active nonagenarians." (Laguna Hills, California)

"I'd like to bring two people to your attention. Ruth took up running at age 70, ran 10 marathons and recently switched to fast walking. She is 91, lives in Brookline but winters in Florida. The other is a retired dentist, age 92, who plays 18 holes of golf three times a week, carrying his own bag. By the way, this gentleman has fascinating stories about being a black professional sixty years ago." (Stamford, Connecticut)

Intellectual Interests

Even more striking than their physical fitness was the mental strength of the nonagenarians. Scientific measurements show that cognitive functioning declines with advanced age and several of the subjects interviewed said that they noticed some decrements. Nevertheless, in the dozens of interviews I conducted there was no one whom I felt had any noticeable difficulty with memory, communication, or abstract thinking. If anything, I came to expect and usually experienced very stimulating conversations with people who continuously surprised me with the depth of their reasoning and the breadth of their interests.

Many of those who wrote to me revealed a similar high level of intellectual ability, including one who wrote from Israel:

"I am 93, a physician and have a deep interest in public health, Jewish law and classical music. I am ready to participate in your project as long as the Almighty agrees and will give me strength to continue as usual." (Jerusalem, Israel)

"The major theme of my life has been the sponsorship of a financial philosophy which I call 'Existential Capitalism.' I am sending you some literature about my ideas. At 93, I continue my struggle to promote them." (New York, New York)

"My mother is 94 and lives alone in an old farmhouse. She beat me at Scrabble last month, fair and square, two games out of two, and I'm a reasonably good Scrabble player. I hope you will acknowledge her, even if you don't need her—she hates to be ignored!" (Buffalo, New York)

"Our next door neighbor is 97. She is a wise, kind, extraordinary woman who feels she's 'lived too long' because all of her friends have already passed on. It would be wonderful to involve her in a project that puts some attention on a life so well lived." (Freemont, California)

"I guess I am just the right example of the kind of 90-year-old guy you are looking for. I retired as a modern language professor in 1968 and became a radio reporter for the Belgian State radio. Now I am busy promoting the work of my late wife, a well known ceramist and sculptor." (West Nyack, New York)

"I'm heading into 93 and since 1972 have been active in alternative medicine. I'm expecting proofs to arrive any day for my book *Preventive Homeopathic Medicine*." (Edgewater Park, New Jersey)

"At 75 I retired as a business executive and became affiliated with the Retired Senior Volunteer Program. Until three years ago I taught 'pitcraft' at the Morris County Adult Day Center. Pitcraft involves using fruit pits, rinds and other natural materials to create miniature works of art. I'm now 94 and still give lectures by request." (Morristown, New Jersey)

"I'm glad you are writing a book on this particular class of human beings. It used to be that books on children were the rage, now it seems to be books on that rapidly growing segment of humanity referred to as 'Senior Citizens.' I am 93 and travel, write and lecture on vegetarianism and what I call the 'cosmic law.' Come to see me and I'll tell you all about it." (Bronx, New York)

Not All Were Cooperative

In dealing with so many nonagenarians, I anticipated complications, such as people refusing to cooperate, getting sick, or forgetting about our appointment. As it turned out, the problems were minimal. Only once was an appointment canceled. A woman in Hyannis, Massachusetts, indicated interest in meeting me. In her letter she shared her reactions to a book she had just read, *The Courage to Grow Old* by Phillip Berman. I phoned her, talked with her for a time, made an appointment, and got directions to her house. As was my practice throughout, I called to confirm our meeting the night before. Since she had seemed so enthusiastic about seeing me, I was surprised when she said that her family had advised her not to see me, that "it would be too much of a strain" on her.

In a trip to Florida, I hoped to meet a 91-year-old man whose friend had written. He had just returned from Siberia "because he wanted to see Lake Baikal. He is thinking of going to Costa Rica for the deep sea fishing. He lives alone, writes outstanding letters, knows everyone, and drives himself pretty much all over the country." As I did to all the people who had been referred to me, I sent a form letter explaining the study and indicating that I might be in contact. When I phoned this Cocoa Beach resident and identified myself, he said that he had not heard from me and didn't know anything about me. Saying that he was very busy and not interested, he hung up. Certainly, "nuisance" phone calls are a problem and there are many cases of unscrupulous people preying on the elderly. In light of such unfortunate social reality, it is perhaps surprising that there were not more such negative reactions. The all but universal trust, courtesy, and cooperation which I experienced was not only gratifying but perhaps revealed a common trait of active nonagenarians.

In an effort to add at least one black nonagenarian to the roster of subjects, I telephoned a woman about whom I had read in a local weekly newspaper. This was the only truly blind contact that I made. The woman, 92, and believed to be the oldest resident of her Long Island town, is the matriarch of a community descended from Indians who intermarried with slaves. The small community survived for generations largely through employment opportunities on nearby estates. When I called her, the woman listened patiently but refused to participate saying, "I'm old and not feeling well and have had enough publicity."

To Live in the Present Moment

Sister John Baptist Hull, one of the nonagenarians who will be met in the pages that follow said, "I have a long and interesting past and a miniscule future." Although this is true of all nonagenarians, such knowledge never led to depression or fear, not in Sister Hull and not in any of the other men and women interviewed. There seems to be a sense of immortality in nonagenarians as well as in young people. In fact, research shows that very young and very old adults have less fear of death than do middle-aged adults. It seems that the awareness of mortality which surfaces in the forties and fifties is assimilated into the life structure of the elderly. They see age peers become infirm and die but do not let it disturb them in any substantial way. However, death is only deferred, not defeated. The black woman with whom I spoke on the phone identified the three interrelated characteristics of those who have crossed the boundary line from being active nonagenarians to being people preparing for the final summons:

"I am old and not feeling well."

Many of the nonagenarians interviewed said in effect that they did not *feel* old. They were healthy and identified feeling old with feeling sick. There was another nonagenarian who refused to see me. He is a prominent music composer living in New York City. When I called him he told me to read the autobiography which he had written thirteen years ago when he was eighty and then to call him again. In effect, he told me, "Don't waste my time asking me about things you can learn from my book." I read the 600-page book, wrote a summary of it, sent it to the man, and then called again. After putting me off several times, he finally refused to see me. On one level he told me that he would write his own story. On another, he indicated that recently he had fallen and injured himself and that he had not recovered fully. The brash tone of our earlier conversations was replaced with what I felt was a note of sadness and dread. Perhaps it was over. Perhaps he had written his last page of music and he who thought himself immortal had to face life's ultimate demand. My intuition was that between the first and last time that I spoke to this man, he became old.

"I've had enough publicity."

Much attention is paid to the active nonagenarians. Many have had their stories featured in local papers, received certificates and proclamations, and had elaborate birthday parties. For most, reaching age ninety was the most newsworthy event of their lives. They emerged from anonymity to at least local celebrity status. For a time, they basked in the long delayed attention and readily gave interviews while modestly fending off compliments. My attention to them was an aspect of this experience. But a moment comes when fame and fortune count for nothing. A professor of history at the University of Wisconsin, Madison, wrote to recommend a colleague of his who at 95 "is a remarkable man, one who reads and converses for five of us." Decades before, the nonagenarian had won the Pulitzer Prize in History. When I contacted the nonagenarian he sent back a brief note: "This is to give you good wishes in your project but to let you know that I do not want to be any part of it. No more questionnaires, oral interviews, or whatever."

"No more"

The stories which follow are for the most part joyful and upbeat. An active nonagenarian is someone who is not only happy to be alive but busy with the tasks of life, still contributing, still independent, still in charge. Rejoice with the good fortune of these people; hope to experience it yourself. But let there be no forgetting that there is one more stage of life to go. The sands continue to flow through the narrow opening of the hourglass. Only a few grains remain. The active person of February may be the bedridden person of July. The parades of spring become the funeral processions of fall. But citing Sister John Baptist once more, "The trip through life was wonderful!"

SENIOR OLYMPIAN AT 96:
RUTH BENNETT, M.D.

*F*riends House, a retirement community located in Sandy Spring, Maryland, is sponsored by the Religious Society of Friends (Quakers). Various housing options are available, but most residents, including Mrs. Bennett, occupy private efficiency apartments in a motel-like complex, the wings of which are connected to lounges, laundry rooms, a library, and other facilities. Dinner is included with the monthly charge, and although other meals can be purchased, most residents prepare breakfast and lunch in their small but fully equipped kitchens. Each apartment is furnished by the resident as he or she wishes. Mini-bus service provides transportation to the bank, post office, and grocery stores.

In the center of the campus-like setting is a large nursing home which offers intermediate and full nursing care. Mrs. Bennett pointed out a man whose wife had suffered a stroke and had to be transferred to the nursing home while he remained in their apartment.

When I was a young woman I spent two years in prison for debt and then was exiled to India. That's what I tell people. More specifically, after receiving my medical degree I interned in Boston and then, in order to earn money to pay back my student loans, I worked as a physician in the Women's House of Detention in Framingham, Massachusetts. After that I went to India and worked as a medical missionary for seven years.

I was born 96 years ago in Tobias, Nebraska. My father was a country doctor in the horse and buggy days. He had thought to retire, but when World War II came all the younger doctors were needed in the service, so he remained in practice until his death in 1944 at the age of 90.

I am what is called a birthright Friend or Quaker. Besides being a physician, my father was a Quaker minister and had the power to officiate at marriages. In fact, he married me and my husband.

A major tragedy struck my family when I was six years old. My mother died of acute bronchitis and just four months later my older brother died also. My father was in great anguish, losing his wife and eldest child whom he thought might study medicine and join him in his practice. A few years later, when I was twelve years old, my father remarried. My stepmother was very good to me.

After the ninth grade in the local public school, I transferred to a private academy associated with Nebraska Central College, one of several small Methodist colleges which dotted the Great Plains. I went right through college there. Then for one year I taught first grade at a Quaker school. It was a disaster. I had such discipline problems. After that I taught for a couple of years at the college I had attended.

However, I knew that what I really wanted was to become a doctor. At the University of Nebraska College of Medicine in Omaha, there were four girls in the first year class. Two of them didn't make it through what we called the "Star Chamber," an oral exam at the end of that year. The third one went to Minnesota, and so I was the only girl in the class in second year of medical school. The fellows were my pals. Also, I loved athletics and got involved in swimming, playground games, camping, and hiking. Exercise had been important to me since my days on the farm. Although my father was a doctor, we had our own cows and I had to milk them and perform other chores.

At age nineteen I had gotten engaged but didn't marry until I was 39. I wanted to finish college, to study medicine, to do a lot of things. It's a wonder my fiancé waited, but he did. My husband had a farm in Colorado not far from the Nebraska border. When we married, I became the farmer's wife and remained such until my husband died in 1975. I was called upon a great many times but never set up my own practice.

I didn't miss being a full-time physician. I had had many challenging and exciting professional experiences in those ten or eleven years after I graduated from medical school. My dream all through school had been to be a missionary with the Society of Friends. At first I was supposed to go to Africa, but they didn't need another doctor at the mission. Then I was to go to China, but it happened that because of the politics at the time, the missionaries were coming home. Finally, the Mission Board asked if I would go to India. I went.

A woman doctor was very welcome there because of the way that they shielded women from men. If an Indian woman had to see a male doctor, she would be in bed all covered up, face and all. Only a hand would be sticking out. Just by feeling the pulse at the wrist, the doctor was supposed to diagnose her condition. I got along very well. Some of the women even asked me to see their husbands.

I never came home during the seven years that I was in India. The journey by ship took a month each way. Also, it was the 30's and money was scarce.

When I did return to the United States I had to "itinerate," that is, talk to the people who had sent me—go around to meetings and explain life on the mission.

Finally, I decided that it was time to get married. My mother-in-law told her son, who had waited for me for twenty years, that I would probably never have children because I was so old. His response was that he didn't care because there were too many people in the world anyway. As it turned out I had a son, our only child, ten months after the marriage. My son lives with his wife and children just a short distance from here.

It was on a visit to my son that I had learned about Friends House, and so when my husband died of a stroke, I applied for an apartment. However, I was on the waiting list for several years. Some people don't like to move from their homes, but I was delighted. I knew that Friends House was where I wanted to be. Change had been part of my life. I welcomed it. I've been in this apartment for thirteen years now and have never regretted it.

It has been a new life for me, to some extent picking up where I left off when I returned from India and settled down to be a wife and mother. My travels have taken me to all the continents and helped me to experience such a range of stimulating people and situations. Last year when I read in a travel booklet about a trip to western Greenland, I decided that I would like to go and so asked my daughter-in-law if she would come with me. She had not traveled very much and was happy to do it. When I had been to Norway a few years back, I had gone to the southern part of Greenland but was anxious to see the north, which I had heard was quite different. It is the land mass nearest to the North Pole. The year before that I had journeyed to Antarctica and so I have gotten close to both poles.

The collage on that wall was made by my granddaughter. It recalls my trip up the Amazon River in South America. We flew from Florida to a city which is half way up the Amazon. There we boarded a ship that went up toward the source. I know people worry about malaria and other tropical diseases, but I seem to be pretty much immune. I take the medicine with me but end up giving it to someone else. I don't have any more trips planned, but one never knows when something good might come along.

Each year I participate in the Maryland Senior Olympics. There is a leisurely walk and also a competitive walk around the track. I always wanted the competition. That silver medal was because I walked faster than a woman who was much younger than I, in her 80's.

There's an exercise program here. A young woman has us sitting in chairs and doing our exercises. I prefer to get down on my back and get my feet up. Every morning I exercise here in my room. You should see me with my feet going up and down, up and down.

My health is good. Aside from childhood diseases and on one occasion a duodenal ulcer, I have never had any problems. My vision used to be so keen that I could read a license plate number a mile away. Now I need glasses but see just fine. I have a hearing aid but don't have it in now. I use it only when I'm in a setting where background noise makes it hard to hear people talking. I have some arthritis in my hands but not to bother me and I can walk all over the place. The only medication I take is one baby aspirin a day. I think the doctor just wanted to prescribe something, but I don't believe it does anything.

I feel fine, but have my name in for the intermediate care nursing home in case I should be unable to care for myself in my apartment. One never knows. I think I'm prepared for whatever happens. My son has power of attorney over my funds and I have a living will. I'm getting to the age when I might not be responsible, especially if there should be something the matter with my brain.

I have no special diet. I don't drink coffee, because that's a drug. But I love ice cream, Ben and Jerry's Rainforest Crunch. I keep it on hand all the time. Would you like some?

Life here is a wonderful mix of privacy, freedom, companionship, and security. I come and go as I please, just the same as if I were in my own home. Yet by having dinner each day in the dining room, I have people with whom to talk and there are no end of scheduled programs. They have housekeepers to take care of the halls and common areas. For an additional fee they will clean an apartment. If something should happen, it is very easy to call for assistance. So far I have never needed help.

Religion remains important to me. There is a Friends meeting in the lounge every Wednesday morning. I read the Scriptures, usually getting through the whole Bible about once a year.

I would like to live until I'm 104. I saw a bit of the 1800's and nearly all the 1900's. Should I live to 104 I would see some of the next century as well.

I think I have lived so long, because I have always done just as I please.

CONTENT TO LIVE ALONE AT 92:
HELEN PAGE BURNS

*W*hen asked to define maturity, Sigmund Freud replied that maturity was determined by one's capacity for love and for work. For most people, including active nonagenarians, love is experienced in the context of marriage, in the give and take, joys and sacrifices of shared spousal life and parenting. As far as work is concerned, most adults invest a substantial part of their lives in economically productive activity, not only to provide for material needs but for a sense of self worth. The script is clear: get married, have children, work.

Helen Burns is a striking exception to the norm and can serve as an example of an alternative route to the nineties.

Miss Burns never married; never had children; never worked. It is true that she devoted her early adult years to caring for her ailing mother and then her widowed father. Such dedication, not unusual for daughters, certainly reflected love and entailed work. However, even when her father died in the late 1930's, she did not alter significantly her solitary way of life. For more than fifty years she has lived alone and had minimal social involvement.

Helen Page Burns

As will be seen, most nonagenarians attribute their longevity to keeping busy. Miss Burns can serve as a model of someone who eschews activity and yet has attained a long and satisfying life.

I was born in Philadelphia and was what was called "a delicate child." I used to get sick spells and couldn't keep anything down. One winter, when I was about seven, I was too sick to go to school and so lost a year. All my life I have had a low energy level. For a while during World War II, I worked mornings as a nurse's aide in a hospital but was so fatigued that I had to spend the afternoons in bed. I couldn't continue. I have never held a full time job.

My father took over from his father a business which baked cookies and biscuits. We lived comfortably. I had one sister, six years younger than I. She died seven years ago of cancer. My mother died in her forties and my father in his sixties. However, my grandparents on both sides lived to advanced ages, so if longevity runs in families, I guess it skipped a generation and is coming out again in me.

I went to Wellesley College and at one time thought that I might write, but it didn't amount to anything. Actually, I never considered a career. My mother suffered severely from rheumatoid arthritis and had a practical nurse for years. When I finished college, I remained at home caring for her and managing the house. When she died, I stayed on and cared for my father until he died a few years later. In the meanwhile, my sister had married, so I was alone in the house.

Where we lived was pleasant enough, but I didn't know many people. I wanted to find a place that had more of a community character. One of my friends from college lived in Hingham, Massachusetts. So I spent a winter with her, liked it, and decided to relocate. That was in 1939. I bought an old Cape Cod style house, installed plumbing and electricity, and have lived here ever since. I've never regretted it.

When my aunt died in 1938 she left a house in New Hampshire to me. I spend summers there; it gives some variety to my year.

I would have liked to have married but never met the right person.

Because of my low level of energy I never expected to live beyond seventy. I can't stay on my feet very long. However, I have not had many other health problems. I did have a bad case of shingles in 1978 and my shoulder and arm still are painful, but it's superficial. I have some arthritis but it doesn't impede my mobility much.

For several years I have experienced dizzy spells. Once, when I was walking across Boston Common, I just blacked out. I don't remember a thing. When I woke up I was in the hospital. Last year I had surgery to replace a heart value and hoped that the operation would end the dizzy spells, but it didn't accomplish a darn thing. So, a few months ago I stopped driving. I was afraid that I might have a spell while behind the wheel.

Throughout life, I found that I was all right if I didn't do too much at a time. Of course now I'm not doing too much of anything. I have always had help. A few years after moving to Hingham, I hired a house-keeper. She not only took care of the house but became a good friend. She was with me for twenty-seven years until she got too old to work. Since then I have had several other people come in to help me.

When I need transportation now, I call upon a local man who has a car. He's God's gift to elderly ladies. It's frustrating not being able to get around on my own. I also have friends who will give me a ride.

Religion never has played much of a role in my life. My parents were non-practicing Presbyterians. My father gave up religion as soon as he could get away from his parents. My mother thought I should go to Sunday school, but really religion was not important in our home. I do remember very interesting religion courses at Wellesley. One was on the Old Testament prophets, the other on the Gospels. I used to go to chapel services at college; the preaching was very good. However, I was never a church member until I moved to Hingham, where I joined the Unitarian Church across the street. For twenty-five years I served as the Clerk of the parish.

I've always had dogs and have two at the present time. They are good company and they tell me when it's time to go for a walk.

I do a lot of gardening and have no trouble finding things to keep me busy. I never watch television during the day.

Years ago I helped a distant cousin get his Masters at Boston University. He became a teacher, married, bought a house in

Hingham, and had two children. He was like a son. But he had a bad heart and died. His widow still lives nearby and I see her occasionally. Twice a year I visit a niece who lives in western Massachusetts. Now that I can't drive, she comes and picks me up. Apart from these things I have no contact with relatives.

Friends drop by my house for tea, and of course, I know people from church, but basically I live by myself.

Am I happy? Yes, by and large. "Contented" might be a better word. My life today is not much different than it has been for decades. I have simple routines; live quietly; don't worry. When you ask me why I think I have lived so long or what thoughts I have about life, I just don't know what to say. I live by myself, take care of my affairs, and just hope that I can continue on a while longer.

CREATOR OF A RENOWNED GARDEN AT 90:
LeROY A. CAMPBELL, Ph.D.

*O*ne of the first things that Mr. Campbell did was show me a paper on which he had written information which he had prepared for use in his obituary. His demeanor suggested not that he was apprehensive about or anticipating death, but rather that he wished to have his affairs in order. The obituary, which seemed no more stressful to him than having a will, includes the following information:

He was born in Amherst, Maine, and graduated from Bangor High School with the highest scholarship award. He earned a B.A. degree from Harvard, a Bachelor of Divinity degree from Andover Newton Theological School, and a Ph.D. from Yale Graduate School. He was a Professor of Ancient History in Hiram College in Ohio for several years and then Headmaster of Worcester Academy. He retired from the faculty of Classical Languages and Literature at Brooklyn College at age 65. He and his wife, Catherine, began building their retirement home in South Harwich, Massachusetts, in 1950.

In recent years it has become widely known for its flower gardens. Catherine died in the 63rd year of their marriage. He is survived by his son, Bruce who, with his wife, Joy, has been living with him for three years.

Like most nonagenarians, Mr. Campbell showed me trophies and certificates and pictures dating back to his high school days. Referring to such mementos, one woman said, "They keep me company." The people interviewed frequently had photographs of six generations: their own grandparents and parents; themselves with their spouse and siblings, their children, grandchildren, and great grandchildren. Although usually they are the oldest living members of the family, locating themselves more or less in the middle of a family history gives them a perspective which younger people may not appreciate.

One of my treasures is this original letter written by John Greenleaf Whittier. It was given to me by the granddaughter of the woman to whom it is addressed. She had a whole bundle of his letters and asked if I would like to have one. She just pulled that one from the bundle. Notice especially the sentences near the end:

> Have you been able to enjoy some of these
> delicious September days? They have always
> been a surprise to me, veritable days of the
> Lord. On such days if I am able to be out, I
> almost feel youth come back to me although
> the truth is I am forced generally to confess to
> myself that I am one of the oldest inhabitants
> most of the time. In this connection, I enclose
> a letter I have just had from O.W. Holmes
> which I will thank thee to return to me.
> Emerson, Longfellow and Holmes have
> always been dear and generous friends of
> mine and as our shadows lengthen in the
> setting sun, they fall still closer together.

When Whittier wrote that in 1879 he was much younger than I am now, but of course people didn't live as long in those days.

Although I spent many years as a college professor, the only book

I had published was *Mithraic Iconography and Ideology* (1968). Mithra was a Persian god and the religion associated with him was popular with soldiers. It didn't admit women. For a time it competed with Christianity but died out in the fourth century. Any religion that doesn't accept women is going to be in trouble sooner or later! I spent about thirty years on that book, on and off. It's good to read if you want to go to sleep.

I was raised a Protestant and served as the Pastor of a church in Camden, Maine, for six years after completing college. But I really wanted to teach. I was in the wrong pew, figuratively speaking. So I went to Yale graduate school. I haven't been affiliated with any church for a long, long time. It wasn't a crisis of faith but an evolution. I just got tired of hearing old-fashioned doctrine being pounded in, things which I just didn't believe. (Excuse me for saying so.) Catherine and I went to a Universalist Church in New York for a time years ago, but I got bored. My garden is my church. If I didn't have it to work in, I don't know if there would be any reason to hang on. What would I do? Sit here, read, look out the window?

A man who retired from a nursery has been helping me with the garden for three or four years. The two of us enjoy working together. Generally, I put in two to four hours each morning. There are several dozen small gardens, each with different species. Most are labeled. People were always asking me the names of the various plants.

I want people to visit the gardens and have a guest book out there for them to sign. Last year about 1,400 people signed and others come but don't bother to write their names. Here's one recent entry: "Four generations of our family were so thrilled to be here on Mother's Day. Thank you so much for sharing." It's all word of mouth. We're not on a main road or anything, but people all over Cape Cod know about it and bring family and friends. My daughter-in-law was somewhat concerned about having strangers around the house. I told her that people who enjoy gardens don't steal. But I'm prejudiced.

Fortunately, we had this place for vacation while I was teaching at Brooklyn College. I'd be climbing the walls if I had to spend all summer in an apartment. When I retired, my wife and I moved here full time. That's when I really started to develop the garden, cutting down trees and gradually extending it. I used to grow vegetables behind the house, but my daughter-in-law has taken that over.

My health is good. In fact, it's only since I had pneumonia two years ago that I have a family physician. I should have gone to him sooner and gotten antibiotics because I nearly coughed my lungs out. If I got pneumonia again I'd take the medicine promptly. Around the same time I had cataract operations. I'm OK now, but I have to admit that I tire easily and can't work as long in the garden as I used to. You know, until the pneumonia, I had not been in a hospital in more than sixty years. I don't take any medication, but for thirty or forty years I've been taking vitamins and minerals daily. People pooh-pooh it, but I think they help.

It was when I had pneumonia that I stopped driving. My son was here by then and urged me to do it. He said they would take me any place I wanted to go.

My wife was a talented woman, very artistic. Unfortunately, she contracted Alzheimer's disease. For two years I cared for her here, did the cooking, tended the gardens. I was down to skin and bones. Finally, my son said that I had to do something. So, for the last four-teen months of her life she was in a nursing home. Tragic. It breaks you up. She ceased to be the same person. Also, it was very expensive. The nursing home cost nearly $50,000 a year. But that's not the worst part of it. She was going up and down the corridor of the nursing home asking for me and wanting to go home. But when she was here, she wanted to go home also. Toward the end, she thought that I was her father. She lapsed back to her childhood. It was a blessing when she died. Life had ceased to mean anything to her.

I say to people they should hope to die of a heart attack. That's a clean way to go; I mean, if it's fatal. It's not dragging on for years like with Alzheimer's. I don't worry about death. I guess I hope that when it comes, I just drop dead!

Science is what I really enjoy reading. Between you, me, and the lamppost, I often wonder if I should have gone into physics instead of the classics. As a freshman at Harvard I got an "A" in physics and an

"A" in Greek. The professor of physics wanted to know if I'd become his assistant. Well, I weighed it but went in the direction of the classics instead. Actually, I never was that good in languages. Some Greek, Latin, Spanish, German, etc, but not fluent in any. I feel more competent in science. I subscribe to *Science Weekly*, *Science News*, *Natural History*, and *Archaeology* magazines. I have all my magazines here and spend some time each day reading.

I'm not rich by any means but have a good income, the equivalent of about 6% on a million dollars. What do I need that much for? When my wife died, I gave $25,000 in her memory to the local library. And I gave $50,000 to the church in Maine where I had served as pastor. Now that I don't need much money, I'm giving it away! My son is retired and doesn't need it. I enjoy giving the money to good causes the same as I enjoy having people come to see the gardens.

REAL ESTATE AGENT AT 91:
ANNA CASSIDY

*A*lthough most workers retire, some have no interest in leaving the work force, even in their nineties. They work not so much for financial reasons as for a sense of personal satisfaction. They love to work; can't imagine themselves not gainfully employed. Anna Cassidy is one of those people who have never left the world of work.

There are others who do retire but become, as one nonagenarian put it, "unretired," at least on a part time basis. Work gives them a reason to get up, dressed, and out of the house. It enhances self-esteem, provides a social life, and supplements a retirement income eroded by inflation. One man quipped, "I flunked retirement."

Certain types of work lend themselves more readily than others to continued involvement. Professionals, such as doctors, lawyers, and psychologists have considerable control over their work life and can modify their schedules without relinquishing the prestige and satisfaction they experience in occupying high status positions. Representatives of the three *professions mentioned are included among the active nonagenarians.*

Another occupational category which lends itself to continued employment is creative work, such as that engaged in by musicians, artists, and writers. Again, such individuals are included among the people featured in this book.

Finally, there are people who work on commissions. Mrs. Cassidy, a real estate agent, is such a person. As long as she generates business, the realtor for whom she works is happy to have her. At the same time, she has some control over her hours and can accept clients at a pace with which she is comfortable. Energized by her continued productivity, she considers the fact that she is 91 irrelevant.

I left school after two years of high school because I wanted to go to work and I've wanted to work ever since. I still work, sometimes seven days a week, selling real estate. My children tell me I should slow down, but I love it.

I was born 91 years ago in East Hartford, Connecticut, the youngest of three sisters. One of them died at about 83. The other was also rather old when she died of cancer. Both my parents lived into their 80's. My father fell down the cellar stairs and my mother had cancer.

My first job was with the Travelers Insurance Company where I remained for years. When I was twenty-five, I married a man who also worked for the Travelers. Since he was living in Brooklyn, we decided to buy a house there in the Sheepshead Bay section. It was a wonderful neighborhood. There was a great spirit. We all had young families.

I had four boys, all of whom attended Catholic schools and colleges. I just had a call from one of my sons. He retired as Senior Vice President from a major corporation and is now teaching at Catholic University in Washington. He told his colleagues that he was retiring at age 60 because he wanted to go back to his alma mater and teach.

Another son, a psychologist, lives in Annapolis and yet another in Chicago. But I'm very fortunate because the fourth son lives with his wife just a few blocks from here. My daughter-in-law is very good to me; she visits all the time and keeps after me to eat properly.

When my children were raised, I went to work in Brooklyn for a real estate broker. But when my husband got sick and I was diagnosed as having diabetes, we bought this smaller house on Long Island. But I continued working. The broker had an office out here and, in fact, eventually moved out here himself.

On my ninetieth birthday, the office gave me a plaque commending me for my hard work and integrity for forty-four years. It is now forty-five years. In real estate it's quite unusual for someone to stay in the same place so long. They are always comparing how much money they are making with people in other agencies and switching.

Imagine me out there showing houses to customers. If it was me, I'd probably be saying, "You old bag!" People kid me all the time.

Because I have diabetes I have to be careful about what I eat. Maybe that's what helped me to live this long. But I didn't take insulin until about a year ago. I was on pills before that.

Since my husband died twenty years ago I've lived here alone. Nobody ever asked me to marry him! But that has never been a problem. I'm very happy with what I'm doing.

Someone does clean the house for me, and the man next door takes care of the lawn, changes light bulbs, and does other little jobs. I don't do anything but go to work. I have the freedom to take off a day when I want to, but I keep busy. I don't take any walk-ins; just recommendations. I'm in the next generation now. People say: "My mother told me to look for you." I've sold houses to the children of any number of my customers from years ago.

Work is my only social life. I'm not involved with any local organizations. Maybe I'll join the Senior Citizens when I retire. I used to have a number of friends, but they are dead. There isn't even anyone in the office now with whom I could socialize. They are so much younger. The death of friends didn't make me depressed. I just kept on going.

I say to my grandchildren, "Do you like what you are doing? If you don't, get out of it. And don't think of money." This is the philosophy which has guided me. My son kids me that I am always telling his children that they should like what they are doing. He says that I may not realize it, but my advice is good psychology. And he's a psychologist!

When will I retire? When I get old! My daughter-in-law worries about me. Some days I am very tired. I come home from work and go right to bed without eating. If I tell her, she brings over a meal to me.

In my whole life, I never had a car accident and was driving until I had a cataract operation a couple of months ago. The doctor said it would take eight or nine weeks to heal. In the meanwhile, I have loaned my car to a grandson. I said to him, "Remember, I want it back as soon as I'm able to drive again." For now, someone at the office picks me up. Or I take a cab. When I tell the customers that I'm not driving yet, they say, "Don't worry. We'll come around to your house and do the driving."

On Sunday I go to church but am not very involved. My daughter-in-law goes to weekday Mass, but I have never done that. I've always been too busy working. My work is my life. But my family is important too. My children are very good to me. I have a dozen grandchildren and now five great grandchildren. I keep up with all of them.

The only changes I notice in myself are some arthritis in my fingers and my hip. But I just say to myself, "Get going!" The doctor tells me to keep on doing what I'm doing. If I ask, "Should I retire?" he says, "No way!" When this eye began to bother me, I suggested to the eye doctor that I might retire. He said, "Not you!" He was right. Even if I'm home one day, I'm lost. I should have developed more of a social life, but my recollection of volunteer work in the church in Brooklyn is that people were so petty. I didn't like that.

I don't know why I enjoy work. We have conflicts. But the give-and-take is part of life. Other salespeople worry about making money. Thank God, that has never been my concern. I show clients a house. If they buy it, they do. If they don't, they don't. I'm not a good salesperson, but I'm honest. A lawyer refers people to me because he knows I'm trustworthy.

Although I'm not that good with paperwork, like checks, I manage my own affairs. Except my daughter-in-law in Chicago now helps me with health insurance forms. Charges not covered by Medicare she sends to the Travelers. All these years I had not submitted claims, although I knew I was covered. Travelers was good to me when I worked for them. I knew it was a stupid way to think. Now, though, I send Pat the bills for prescription drugs and the 20% of doctors' bills which Medicare doesn't pay, and she completes the forms. I send the money back to her, because I never would have had it if she didn't take care of it.

I don't know anyone else who is ninety. A woman whose house I am selling is in her eighties. She's moving to a nursing home. Another woman keeps asking me to go places with her, but I say that I can't take time off from work. I'll go with her for breakfast before work or to dinner after work, but I don't take time off.

A WORKING ARTIST AT 90 WITH A SUPPORTIVE WIFE OF 92:
MAX ARTHUR & SARAH COHN

*M*ax Cohn, an artist since age sixteen, paints every day in the studio in the 14th floor New York apartment he shares with his wife, Sarah, who serves as promoter and agent for the prolific but shy painter. Cohn's work is included in major collections around the world, and he has had numerous exhibitions extending from a 1930 showing at the New York Civic Gallery to a recent exhibit at the University of Wisconsin Milwaukee Art History Gallery.

On the easel in his studio is a work-in-progress, a mosaic-like composition of purple shapes bound by black paths. A shaft of late morning sunlight strikes the canvas, like a spotlight celebrating the creative work done that morning by a dedicated artist.

Sarah: It's only in the last 10 or 15 years that my husband has received any significant recognition, and in some respects, we are busier now than we have ever been. Dealers are in touch with us and Max has been interviewed several times. Just recently, a video documentary was made that traces his career and is included in a collection of lives of contemporary American artists for use in art schools and museums. The half-hour program describes what is considered Max's most important contribution, the use of silk screening to produce art.

His other major contribution occurred in the 1930's when, with other artists, he attempted to develop a purely American art style. His Depression era paintings of coal towers, piers, power stations, and gravel pits have gained considerable attention.

Frankly, the weeks spent producing the video have given Max a sense that his life's work has been successful. It encourages him to continue painting. But art has been his life and I'm sure he would still be in there working even had he not been recognized.

I know that I speak for him. I'm proud of what he has done and he's shy about it. Although I was a social worker by training, some forty years ago I retired from my job and have worked with Max ever since.

These cubistic cityscapes are a middle period between his realistic early stage and the more abstract period which began in the 1950's. It is the early period which has been gaining attention, including the WPA paintings.

Max: The Public Works of Art Project was predecessor to the Works Project Administration and enabled many of us to survive. In the Easel Project of the WPA, I was paid $26 a week and expected to produce an oil painting every six weeks. The paintings became the property of the government. I don't know where most of mine are. We do know that one is in the National Museum of American Art. Our dentist went to Washington, DC, and saw it.

For years we held regular meetings here of the WPA artists. Most are now gone or too frail to travel, so we have discontinued the group. But there are exhibits of our work.

Sarah: I was born in Boston 92 years ago and am the only survivor of ten children. Several lived into their 80's, but for some mysterious reason I am still here. I'm in the middle of writing a family chronicle, so I'm up-to-date on everyone. My father came here more than one hundred years ago from Lithuania and brought over my mother and oldest brother two years later. In Europe, father was a talmudic scholar. He and the other men would go to the temple three times a day to pray, while the wives assumed all the responsibility for the homes.

When he came here, father started a matzo business and became the Matzo King of New England. That was before Manischewitz and the technocrats came in with their machines. Father did a hand-rolled matzo. All of us worked in the business. I sewed the cloth bags for the flour.

My brothers went to Harvard and I attended Radcliffe. I don't know how we did it, really. We were not rich. I had a scholarship and didn't live on campus. Each day I walked across the bridge from Boston to Cambridge. I earned both my B.A. and Master's in Social Work while working. It wasn't a very productive way of doing it, but it was necessary.

I moved to New York in the depths of the Depression but had no difficulty finding a job. There was a demand for social workers. Up to that time the private agencies had provided most of the social welfare services. But with the increased problems during the Depression, public agencies began to emerge and grow. The private agencies just couldn't handle it all. I worked for the National Refugee Service, a private agency. Mainly, we helped refugees from Germany to get settled here, both before and after the Holocaust.

Max: I was born in England. My father, who was a tailor, had gone there from Eastern Europe. When I was two, the family had enough money to continue the journey to America. We arrived in New York but went to Cleveland where my mother died leaving four little boys. We were put in an orphanage. For that time period, it was a good place. I was eight.

At 16, I was required to leave the home and be on my own. I came to Kingston, New York where I had an uncle. It was there that I went to high school. They discovered that I was artistic and put me to work doing posters for businesses. I became an artist, not because I had talent but because of an inner urge. I just knew that art had to be my life.

Sarah: We were both in our thirties when we married. We wandered around for several years before settling down. First, we went to Mexico and had an inexpensive six-month honeymoon. Of course, it provided Max with a new setting in which to paint. Earlier, like most American artists at the time, he had spent a year in France. Rather late in life we had one child, a daughter. She is a Ph.D. archaeologist at the University of Wisconsin.

For many years we lived on 17th Street here in Manhattan and owned the Graphic Arts Studio, a commercial silk screening business. Max continued painting and doing the creative work, while I handled business affairs. Our life has been one of partnership. We complement one another well.

Our apartment on 17th Street was an old walk-up. My brother used to tease us about living so poorly. But we didn't need anything more. We have never been concerned about money or possessions. I learned from Max that you don't have to have a regular job to survive. We took risks, I suppose, but never felt any great stress about it.

When this middle income cooperative, Penn South, was built about thirty years ago we sold the business and moved. With the studio in the apartment and the monthly charges low, we have been able to manage, and Max can devote himself full-time to his art.

We used to have closets full of paintings but just recently moved 750 of them to climate-controlled storage. An artist needs a lawyer who understands the value of art. IRS tends to evaluate paintings based on what has been sold. So, if you sold one painting for $5,000, they just multiply everything you have by $5,000. The IRS now has a committee that helps them establish the true value of remaining work.

For many years, I have been on medication for high blood pressure. Aside from that we have no health problems. Both of us have had cataracts removed from our eyes. We feel just fine. We eat normal, wholesome meals every day. Walking is our only exercise. We make it a point to get out every day. We do the shopping. Once a week we go to the library. And I suppose that housekeeping is exercise. We do it all ourselves. Max has always done the vacuuming. I've been a modern woman since I marched with the suffragettes in Boston while a teenager.

Max: The secret of our long life is keeping active. Sarah is always busy. I go to the studio each morning and paint for three hours.

Sarah: We are as active today as we have ever been. It's due to the increased attention given to Max's work and to the greater involvement with relatives, because of the family history project I'm working on.

What does it feel like to be 90? I know I'm 92. It's a fact. But I don't really feel like 92. We've been well and can still function. That's it.

WRITING LETTERS TO THE EDITOR AT 90:
PETER J. COMERFORD

*P*erhaps the ideal situation for an active nonagenarian is that experienced by Peter Comerford. His wife, Ethyl, is seventeen years his junior. Although this means that she herself, at 73, is getting old, she is healthy and completely devoted to her husband. Since he is hard of hearing, she defines herself as "his ears." She also types the letters which he authors and in myriad ways cares for him as if they were newlyweds.

Ethyl Comerford is a composite live-in housekeeper, health care aide, and loving friend. She combines solicitude for his well-being with steady encouragement for his quixotic literary ventures and his passion for contemporary issues of church and state.

Marriages, like individual lives, go through stages from the honeymoon, through child rearing, to retirement and finally, for one partner, widowhood. Ethyl Comerford knows that the odds are great that she will be widowed some day, perhaps soon. However, she does not dwell on the inevitability of change and death, living in gratitude the richness of the present moment.

Peter J. Comerford

Some years ago Peter Comerford built a wishing well in the garden of their modest Long Island home. In the cement he impressed in small stones the letters "I L Y V V M" for "I love you very, very much." Family members began to write those letters on greeting cards and as conclusions to correspondence. When the Comerfords' daughter graduated from college, they were surprised and delighted to see that she had written these letters on her mortarboard for the commencement exercises. If not directly a factor in his longevity, certainly the quality of life of Peter Comerford is enriched because he knows that he is loved "very, very much."

We get *The New York Times* delivered and I spend a good part of each morning reading it. I read the editorials and the columnists. Even when I don't agree with something, I read it anyway; it gives me something to think about. Pope John XXIII said that we need to be in dialogue with everyone in the world.

The "Letters to the Editor" have always been my favorite part of a newspaper. Readers should be able to respond to what they read. A newspaper is a two-way conversation. I've written many letters myself to *The Long Island Catholic*, our diocese's weekly paper. Quite a few have been published, but the current editor rejects more than did the previous man. Many church issues interest me, in particular Catholic schools which I believe are very important. No, that's not strong enough. The schools are essential. I hate to see the bishop closing schools.

In 1979, I wrote a letter to Pope John Paul II urging him to tell the American bishops to promote Catholic schools more vigorously. When the Pope visited the United States, he did praise the role the schools have played. Well, the superintendent of Catholic schools wrote to me and said that the Pope's remarks were the result of my letter.

My parents were poor Irish immigrants. My father worked in the New York City garment district as a messenger and delivery man. My mother cared for the seven children. I have a sister two years older than me and one two years younger. Here's a picture of the three of us at my 90th birthday party last year.

Our mother lived in her own home until she died at the age of 107. Her mind remained clear and her sense of humor intact until the end.

Shortly before she died, her live-in helper said, "Here, put your arms around my neck, and I'll lift you up." Mom said, "Aren't you afraid that I might choke you?"

I attended St. Patrick's parochial school but was a dropout. I had to go to work to help support the family. I wasn't that good in school anyway. But I did develop a love for reading, and as a young man, read the Russian novels and the works of Catholic writers such as Belloc and Chesterton. All my life I have been devoted to the Church and very young began to pray the rosary each day. Maybe I have lived so long because of the rosary. When I had any problems as a young man, I would go to my room and quietly pray to Our Lady.

An important part of my daily routine is prayer and Bible reading. I have this book which gives a reading for each day of the year and a reflection on the reading. I sit here on the sofa each morning, read the Scriptures, and say my prayers. It helps me to feel peaceful now just as it did when I was young.

At age 16, I went to work for ITT as a cable operator. The messages came in on a long tape in Morse code. I would translate the message into English for delivery to the recipient. I can still read Morse code, although messages are transmitted very differently today. Later, when the company began to promote services more aggressively, I moved into sales and became a sales manager, even had my name on the door. Finally got a little recognition!

For many, many years I lived a very uneventful life at home with my mother. Two of my sisters had children and lived with us and I helped to raise them. Besides going to work and church, my life centered on my family.

Then, unexpectedly, my life really began. I met and fell in love with Ethyl. I was 54 and she was 37. Neither of us had ever met someone we felt was right for us. Ethyl had been working as a secretary. This picture of us on our wedding day I consider a picture of the day I was born.

Two years later we had our son. He was ten pounds. The doctor said that recently he had delivered twins, both of whom together didn't weight as much as our Peter. Three years later, when Ethyl was 41, our daughter was born.

We lived in Flushing, Queens, but when I was 64, after 48 years with the company, I was forced to retire. We didn't know what we would do, since the children were young and Ethel wasn't working. The family helped us to buy this house in the country. We could live more economically here than in the city. We've been here ever since. Ethyl is looking at new carpet, so I guess we will be here a while longer.

The children went to Catholic schools right through college. Ethyl, who had graduated from St. Joseph's College many years before, got a job teaching in a Catholic elementary school and worked there for 18 years. She gets a pension now. Both children are married and doing well, although neither of them has children.

When I retired I became something of a househusband. Ethyl was working and I was here taking care of the children and involved in the community. I did some real estate sales work and was active in the Knights of Columbus and civic groups. Since I was good at public relations, I have produced several souvenir journals. One was for the 100th anniversary of our local Catholic school, another for the K of C, and in 1987 I did one for the bicentennial of the U.S. Constitution. I believe that we live in the greatest secular democratic republic that ever existed, where there is freedom of religion and freedom from religion.

Once a week I spend several hours at the church recording the contributions people make in their envelopes. I just tabulated the contributions for last year and sent all the parishioners a statement for income tax purposes. It's a little job. They just raised my pay to $90 a month.

My health is good, except for my hearing which began to weaken many years ago. And I just got dentures but the bite isn't right. A few years ago I had a prostate operation, but it wasn't cancerous. My doctor has given me some pills which I think are to thin my blood. I've never smoked but have a scotch every evening before dinner.

Before you go, let me show you this book, *Savage Inequalities*, by Jonathan Kozol. My daughter used it for a course she was taking. Education is so important. Our country is so wonderful. We must make every effort to give all the children a real chance for a good education.

PRACTICING ATTORNEY AT 99:
EDWARD CORCORAN

When Eugene Curry was interviewed with his wife, Margery, he mentioned that their granddaughter had married a man who also had a nonagenarian grandfather. Mr. Curry recommended this other man quite highly, since he was 99 years old and still practicing law. Even to the 92-year-old Eugene Curry, this seemed amazing! Mr. Curry took the initiative of writing to his "co-great-grandfather," Edward Corcoran, to see if he would be willing to be interviewed.

In a very clear, legible hand Mr. Corcoran wrote a lengthy reply in which he reflected on the experience of being old. The letter is a rare glimpse into the world of nonagenarians communicating with one another:

> *I question whether the suggested interview with Dr. Powers would be of much benefit to him as material for his book. My impression of you is that you are a very cheerful person and that your old age has been filled with enjoyable*

events that were reflected in your interview. I,
on the other hand, despite my many blessings,
have not found old age to be 'the golden age,'
as it is sometimes described. While your interview,
I am sure, provided material that would be helpful
in the composition of the book, mine probably
would not because of my negative response to my
lifestyle during the past few years. For four years,
I have been unable to drive a car and am dependent
on my sons and others for transportation, and my
mobility in walking has been increasingly restricted.
The result is that I go few places except to the office,
to the homes of my sons, and to the market for
food. The discontent that sometimes assails me due
to my disabilities is surely unjustified in view of
the kindness of my sons and daughters-in-law
and the pleasure that my fourteeen grandchildren
afford me with their activities, and of course, the
thrill of the birth of each great-grandchild. I now
have eleven with another expected in a few weeks.
You wish me happy memories. I surely have
them, including the pleasure of witnessing the
marriage of our grandchildren and of meeting you.

I realize that I sounded rather unhappy with my life in the letter to Gene Curry. In fact, I was reflecting at Mass this morning that I have to control such a negative way of thinking. It's Lent and I attend daily Mass. The quiet time in church gives me an opportunity to put things in perspective. I get a lot of comfort from my religion. I do realize that I am blessed; in a few months I will be a hundred years old and am still able to work every day and am free of serious diseases. However, I have been experiencing losses and am grieving them.

In particular, I miss not being able to drive. All my life I have been independent. I love music and used to go to concerts. Now I can't go unless I ask someone to take me. I can't visit friends unless I impose on people. The doctor said that my eyes were not good enough for driving, but I think my sons told him to say that. They were concerned that my reflexes had slowed. And they were right. It would be horrible to have an accident and hurt someone. I understand it, but it's very restrictive. You have to go through it to realize what it's like.

Around the office I can walk with no difficulty, but for the past six months I have not felt steady on my feet, and so when I go out, I use a cane. It takes me about half an hour, but I walk the half mile to the shopping center. And every day I walk to the bank. It gives me exercise. My house is four miles from town. Sometimes I walk the quarter mile to get the bus, which brings me right to the door of my office here in town.

It doesn't matter how old you are, you still want to manage by yourself. You don't want to accept limitations. Especially since my mind is so clear, the advancing weaknesses of the body are annoying. I used to go out a lot; now I work here all day, go home, cook my own meal, and that's it. I can't get out. I miss the freedom. Life now has a sameness to it that it didn't have before. I have to fight the discontent. Actually, I know it's wrong to feel this way, because my children have me over regularly and I have grandchildren nearby. They are all very good to me.

I was born in Fall River, Massachusetts. My father, who had a jewelry shop there, died at the age of 38 when I was four years old. My mother, who had been born here in Newport, Rhode Island, moved back here with me, and I have lived here ever since. She worked as a housemaid in one of the estates, and that's where I grew up. Mother died at the age of 64. Although my parents died rather young, grandparents on both sides lived very long lives. In fact, my maternal grandfather was 93 when he died. It apparently skipped a generation!

I went to Brown University and Harvard Law School. In those days, anyone who wanted to be admitted to the bar first had to work as a clerk for a lawyer for six months. So I served my apprenticeship here in Newport, and when admitted to the bar I was taken in as a partner, and although the firm name has changed over the years as men died, I have spent all these years in the same place. Well over seventy years now.

We practice general law. Now, I mainly do estate and real estate work. Also, taxes, although I'm trying to get rid of that. It's just that I've been doing them for people for years and it's hard to say no. I have two sons in the firm with me and also one grandson. So there are four Corcorans. They do most of the work now. I don't go to court or get involved in any of the more complicated things.

My wife and I had four sons and a daughter. My daughter is a sister of the Sacred Heart of Mary and a graduate of Yale University Nursing School. She runs a medical clinic in Zimbabwe. My oldest son works here with me. The next oldest has an auctioneering business, is unmarried, and lives with me. They call us the odd couple. I'm very orderly and he's very disorderly. A woman comes in once a week and does the cleaning and the laundry. The next boy is the other lawyer here with me, and the youngest son is a Maryknoll missionary working in Nepal. So two of the children got as far away from me as they could, and the other three I see nearly every day.

I've been a widower for twenty-five years—a long time, but I have my children near me and have had a busy professional life. Newport has grown from a town where one knew everyone to what it is today, a large, busy city where most people are strangers and too busy to get to know their neighbors.

My health is all right. But I find that when I read in the evenings, I get drowsy and fall asleep, something I never experienced before. Also, I have arthritis in my hands and hip. If I were younger, I suppose I would have a hip socket operation. I do have pain if I sit in one position very long. But I sleep well, have a good appetite, and generally get along fine. Although I come to the office every day and still have clients, I practice very moderately. I notice now that some clients go to my son for help instead of me. They must think I'm too old. That's a little frustrating, but it's natural.

I'm sad about getting old. It's the friends that one loses. I've lost five in the last six months. Others are in nursing homes. Through my practice, I've made many friends. Today lawyers are looking at the clock and charging people by the minute. Business matters are to be conducted as quickly as possible. With me, it wasn't and it isn't like that. I might spend a half hour with someone on legal matters and then another half hour on interests we have in common and world events. Practicing law for me has always been a very social occasion. That's how friendships are made, how lasting relationships are formed. Law wasn't just business; it was life.

The Journal of the American Bar Association has had articles about how dissatisfied many young lawyers are with the profession and how many of them have left the field. That's particularly true in the big cities in the law factories. They work terrible hours and develop no relationships with clients. They practice law at the expense of their families and get nothing of personal satisfaction from their work. It is very different here. Evenings are for family. I leave here at six o'clock and go home. I read and visit family. Perhaps that's why I have never gotten burned out and why I still love to come here each day. My clients are my friends.

Retire? There's another old fellow in town. He's not as old as me, perhaps 90 or 91. When people ask him, "Jim, when are you going to retire?" he answers, "I'll retire when Ed Corcoran does." I want to keep going. When I look around me and see all the good that some people are doing, I feel like I have not done enough. Perhaps I could have been more generous, could have helped more people. I was reading about what Mother Teresa does and the terrible conditions in India.

I get disturbed with the way the country is going. I'm bothered about what the future will be for my grandchildren and great-grandchildren. The deficit puts an enormous burden on them. The Reagan years gave young people false expectations. They thought that making money would be easy and that there was no need to save. What a shock for them.

In earlier days middle class people had front porches on their houses. They sat on those porches and watched the world go by. That's unheard of today. People don't have time.

I realize that this is an old man talking and that the world has changed. Younger people just laugh at me when I talk like this.

Here I am practicing and earning money and because I'm over 70, I collect full Social Security. I shouldn't be getting it. Clinton is right.

People who don't need it shouldn't get it. I give most of the Social Security money to my grandchildren and to charities.

In some ways I'm glad I lived when I did, but in other ways I wish that I was starting my life now. When I was young there was a wall of hatred dividing Catholics and Protestants. The problem was on both sides. Today, with ecumenism, there is greater understanding and cooperation. I like that. Also, marvelous advances have been made in medicine. I had influenza during the 1938 epidemic. People died like flies. And polio ravaged the population before the Salk vaccine. In many ways, this has been a wonderful century and the wonders continue.

A LOVING PARTNERSHIP AT 92:
R. EUGENE & MARGERY CURRY

*T*he Currys have been married for 64 years. Although Margery is deaf and confined to a wheelchair by a broken hip, she continues to write poems which reflect her warm and joyful attitude toward life. Her husband, Gene, a vigorous, healthy man, exudes feelings of tenderness and support for his wife.

One of Margery's poems, "1928-1991," commemorates their 63rd wedding anniversary and can serve as a window to their daily routines as well as to a durable relationship:

> These days of ours start
> off with a morning kiss
> And that wonderful smile.
> You never fail to greet each
> morning cheerfully.
> Then you bring me that reviving cup of coffee.
> Dear heart, you are my source of strength.
> .....
> You bring me little gifts each time you come inside,
> Little flowers or brilliant leaves.

Tirelessly you write what you want to say, repeating
Conversations of others so that I may know
What it is all about....

Shortly after my visit to the Curry home in rural Armonk, New York, Gene had forty-three of Margery's poems printed privately in a booklet titled Verses. Her work reveals a range of moods from the happy recollections of her long life, to the awareness that the end cannot be far away. The final poem is titled "Death" and captures what is a common characteristic of active nonagenarians: the ability to face death without fear or anxiety:

Welcome, Death.
I bid you come.
Do not delay.
Through you I find the way
To leave all pain behind.
You bring to me some peace of mind
Knowing that you are near.
Do not grieve, my friends so dear,
Rejoice with me while I am here.

Margery (responding to written questions): I was born in Edinburgh, Scotland, of American parents. My family has been very globally oriented, which makes life interesting. My father, a physician, had been born in Syria to a medical missionary family. When I was three we came to America, and I was raised in Philadelphia. I have led a very protected life with an active guardian angel and an attentive husband.

I attended Wellesley College where I played on the championship baseball team. My first job out of college was with the Curtis Publishing Company working on correspondence for $16 a week. Later I became secretary to the editor of the company paper.

Gene and I met while I was at Wellesley and he was pursuing an MBA at Harvard. He took me to the Senior prom. After I had worked for a few years, I gave up my job, and my mother and I undertook an extended trip to Europe. Gene saw us off on the Cunard steamship, kissed me farewell, and we promised to write faithfully.

Mother and I traveled for some months, finally settling in Paris. Then came a telegram from Gene: "Letter too slow. Will you marry me?" I was completely bowled over and cabled back, "Do not believe in long distance engagements. Wait until I return." I hurried home, hoping that Gene would wait for me to say, "Yes."

The year after we married we bought this 1845 farmhouse in Westchester County, New York. The house consisted of just two rooms, had no plumbing, no electricity. We had to pay $25 a pole to bring the electricity in from the main road.

It was more than a year before we had our first child. I believe that every couple should have at least a year without children, because they change things so much. Eventually we had four, two boys and two girls. One daughter is married to the American ambassador to South Korea. Thanks to them we have seen many parts of the world. To visit one of our sons, a computer analyst, we went to Africa. Everyone who has children living abroad should try to visit them and the grandchildren. Many young children of Americans working in other countries don't see their grandparents. When we went someplace, they would have Gene and me visit the children's school, put us up in front of the class, and say, "These are grandparents!"

My life was busy with the children while they were young. And I did a considerable amount of volunteer work—with the town library, the church, and the garden club. I made the pottery you see around the house. Recently, I have settled on poetry as my main activity.

Gene: I was born in Kansas. Shortly after the Civil War, my father and his family had moved there from Indiana in a covered wagon. By the age of ten, I was driving a four-horse team and by 13 was lifting 90-pound bags of cement to help build a silo. Farm life was our life until we went off to college.

One of my brothers, John Stewart Curry, was a renowned artist linked with Thomas Hart Benton and Grant Wood as one of the three most significant regional painters. His murals decorate the walls of the Kansas capitol building in Topeka. They represent themes from the early days of the Kansas territory. Other of his murals are in the Department of State and the Department of the Interior.

Money for college was a problem. Nevertheless, after Princeton I decided to get an M.B.A. from Harvard. I went to a real estate agent in Cambridge and told him I could sell real estate. Well, I earned enough to buy a car, pay my tuition, and when I got my degree I had $1,600 in the bank.

Now I was ready to get a job and to marry Margery. She has related some of the details of our long distance courtship. Well, it just so happens that I'm three months younger than Margery. When she agreed that we would marry, she said that she wasn't going to marry a younger man. She insisted that we wait until the Saturday after my birthday. Then we would be the same age, 28!

My entire professional life was devoted to working for the elderly. For thirty-seven years, I was with the Osborn Retirement Center in Rye, New York. As administrator there I saw enormous changes in programs for older people and in state regulations. Today, a home has to hire a couple of people just to fill out forms for the government.

Perhaps I played a modest role in the progress that has been made in programs for the elderly. For twenty years, I served as chairman of the Westchester County Committee for the Aging. I helped to establish a Senior Information and Referral Service, which today is part of the County Office for the Aging.

I took an active role in the 1961 and 1971 White House Conferences for the Aging. I could go on, but it's all here in the Proclamation dated May 5, 1992 in which I was named "Senior Citizen of the Year" by the New York State legislature.

Although I retired more than twenty years ago, I have remained busy. For one thing, for years I was chairman of the board of the Mianus Gorge Preserve, the first land project of the Nature Conservancy, which subsequently has taken millions of acres to help preserve virgin forests.

During the Depression I went down to New York University and asked them what courses I could take to help me be more up-to-date. They said they didn't know what was going on in the economy and that they needed an instructor of economics. So I began teaching two nights a week. I carried that on for forty-three years, except for the three years I served in the Navy during World War II as a lieutenant-commander at a base in the Pacific. I loved teaching and had wonderful discussions with the students, especially during the Vietnam War.

Not everything is rosy, of course. About six months ago I had a setback. Margery broke her knee. She already had a colostomy and several other problems, such as a herniated esophagus which causes her to gag on her food. Well, I began to worry about what we would do. Maybe we wouldn't be able to remain here in our house. Although women come in during the week to help out, none of them are nurses. Would we have to go to a nursing home? Could we get in? What should I do? I was so upset that I couldn't sleep and was so nervous that I couldn't drive. Finally, I went to a counselor, thank goodness, and she told me that I must renew myself and keep open the world in which I had been active. I shouldn't stay home all the time worrying about Margery. I took the advice and was able to sleep and drive again.

Religion has always been central to my life. Although I was raised as a strict Presbyterian, we have been members of the Episcopal church here for more than fifty years. I know there are a lot of questions today about God, whether He exists or not. But I think He does. For many years, I have listened to the Temple Emmanuel Sabbath service on the radio. The prayers remind us of our connection with all of creation. In his book, *Celebration of Life*, Norman Cousins offers a similar message: we are all part of humanity, and one after the other we pass on life to the next generation. Eternity is doing whatever you can for others.

It may be fitting that I am still active, as I have been for forty years, as a director of the 200-year old community burial ground. When I visit the old cemetery I can't help but reflect on life and time and history. Twelve generations have been buried there. Each did its part. For me, that burial ground is a place of grace.

KIWANIS CLUB LEADER AT 92:
ORVILLE R. DAVIS

*I*n May 1993, NBC presented an
extravaganza called "Bob Hope:
The First 90 Years." Presidents
past and present joined an array of
entertainment figures in honoring
Hope, whose familiar profile and
quick wit belied his ninety years.
In a sense, the Bob Hope birthday
party drew national attention to
the phenomenon being documented
in this book, namely, the emergence of the active nonagenarian.

As millions of viewers looked at
Hope (and also at the much older
George Burns who was in the audience), they were being taught an
important lesson: that it is possible
to live a productive life at that age.
What many people may not realize
is that there are thousands of non-
celebrities equally as alive and well as Bob Hope.

One such physically and mentally competent individual is Orville Davis
of Orlando, Florida. Davis is involved in a busy round of activities from
writing articles and books on his word processor, to fashioning wood crafts
in his workshop, to arranging for guest speakers at Kiwanis Club meetings.

Nonagenarians are like the population in general. Some are extroverts, *others introverts. Some are loners, others gregarious. Some are reflective and philosophical; others live more in the present moment. Orville Davis is a blend of diverse characteristics, able to spend hours alone at his desk working but also very comfortable in social settings, typically taking a leadership role.*

For over thirty years, until his retirement, Davis was a secondary school principal in a pre-Disney Orlando. At the age of 66, he was called from retirement to serve as interim Superintendent of the Orange County (Orlando) public schools and was a key figure in starting Valencia Community College. In 1989, the school board dedicated the high school auditorium in his honor.

Not ready to rest on his laurels, Davis undertook to compile key documents and the recollections of many of the people involved in the establishment of the college twenty-five years before. At his own expense, he contacted former school officials, searched archives and old files, reproduced and bound the materials, and in his 93rd year was able proudly to hold in his hands a 400-page book. Although he has sold a number of copies, his primary goal is to see that libraries and other institutions add his work to their collections.

Since the age of 29, Davis has been active in the Kiwanis Club. The day I was to interview him coincided with the weekly luncheon meeting of the local group. He said that he had to get there early in order to be sure all the arrangements had been made and to welcome the guest speaker for the day, a sports reporter for an Orlando newspaper. Davis invited me to attend the meeting as his guest. It was a rare opportunity to see an active nonagenarian "in action." He drove his car to the meeting, interacted with the other club members, and smoothly introduced the speaker.

Last year I read a paper at our Methodist church on the value of devotions or prayer in the schools. I quoted the handbook of the Orlando school where I had been principal. It stated:

> Morning devotions are prepared and
> presented by students with the guidance
> of a faculty member. For a few minutes
> each morning after the ringing of the tardy
> bell, Edgewater High School is a huge

cathedral where more than a thousand people
are worshipping God in their own way.
Moving down the hall at this time is just as
inappropriate as going down the aisle in a
church during a prayer service.

I went on to argue that the decline in the quality of our schools began in the 1960's with the Supreme Court decision banning prayer in the public schools. I proposed that the churches mount an effort to get the court to reconsider. Well, last Sunday, one of the church members told me that a committee had gotten together with the ministers and had decided to take the issue on up the line to the Methodist Conference where they could get some action by the state body.

I'm going to do what I can to bring devotions back into the schools. Just yesterday, I got the addresses of the headquarters of ten major religious groups from the *International Almanac* and mailed off copies of my paper. No one may pay attention but I'm doing what I can. I'm like Johnny Appleseed.

I was born in Philadelphia. People ask if I was named after Orville Wright, but he didn't gain publicity for inventing the airplane until about 1908, long after my birth. When I was nine years old, my family moved to Miami and I've lived in Florida ever since. My dad was a carpenter and used to ride a bicycle to work. I was one of five children, three of whom lived to their 80's, but I'm the last.

My education included some time in a one-room schoolhouse just north of Miami. My college education at the University of Michigan was interrupted by World War I. After the war I went to the University of Florida where I received my B.S., M.A., and a Ph.D.-equivalent. After teaching for a few years, I became principal of a junior high school and then the senior high here in Orlando.

With my career underway, I married at the age of 32. My wife, Adelaide, and I had two daughters, both of whom live here in Orlando and work together in a program called Getting Well, which provides counseling and support to people dying of cancer and other diseases. They come over here once a week for a pancake breakfast.

My wife and I traveled all over the world and had many wonderful experiences together. The most memorable adventure occurred just after I retired as principal. For two years I served as liaison officer for a construction company building a port in Somalia. The port was a gift of the U.S. government on the occasion of Somalia's independence in 1960. Adelaide and I lived in Mogadishu. In building the port, except for the rock and soil, everything had to be imported. The country was desperately poor, but we felt proud helping them to become self-sufficient. Of course, recent events over there show that they never really became a stable, prosperous country.

Then I suffered the most terrible loss of my life. My wife was killed in an auto accident.

We had lived for many years in a large house in another section of the city, but about twelve years ago I sold that house and have been renting this smaller house ever since. It gives me greater flexibility. I don't want to be thinking about possessions. I see people worrying to their last breath about their house or their investments. That's no good.

I take care of the place myself, if you can call it that. I vacuum maybe every six months. Whenever something worries me, I do something about it. I'm old maidish in that I like things in order. If they get too much dust on them, I'll dust. I'm very happy here. It suits my needs.

Out back I have a shop. Most of the furniture you see here I made myself. When I need something, I make it. This table was made from a piece of driftwood that I found over at the beach. Five years ago, I saw a design for a boat in *Popular Science*. I sent off for it and built the boat. It was a 12-foot sailing boat. Just recently I dismantled it.

My health is good. When I passed the eye test for my driver's license last year the clerk said, "Do you realize that the next time you renew this, you'll be 100 years old!" My only problem is that I'm having difficulty remembering names. In fact, when we go to the Kiwanis meeting later, I may forget your name when I go to introduce you.

I need a project, otherwise I get so bored. I have my shop but run out of people to make things for. Also, I like to write, and since I have completed books on the two extinct junior high schools and one on the extinct Orlando Junior College, I'm now developing a book of memories for the old Orlando High School which was replaced in 1952 by two new schools. Last week I attended the fiftieth reunion of one of the classes and have the names of those still around. I'm going to contact them for their anecdotes.

Writing these histories of the schools has a social dimension for me. It keeps me in touch with people. When you get to be my age, all your friends are gone and the younger people are not interested in you. You have to create new ways to be involved.

About a year after my wife died, while I was interim executive secretary of the Heart Association, I became re-acquainted with someone whom I had known decades before. At that time, she was a student in the junior high school where I was principal. When our paths crossed again, she was a director of the Heart Association and a widow. We have been keeping company ever since. Charlene looks after me and I look after her. At least three times a day she calls me—checking up on me, I guess. I go over to her house most evenings and we have dinner together. She's my companion. We've been to Europe, Alaska, and many other places together.

Charlene is seventeen years younger than I. When we first started going together casually, I was hesitant because of the difference in age. Then she had a mastectomy and I said to her that that sort of equalized things. I was still healthy and here she was with cancer. Her son, who has died, said that I would probably outlive all of them. Seventeen years age difference seemed much greater twenty years ago than it does now. In any case, the relationship has been wonderful for me, and she says that it has been for her also.

My first health problem occurred shortly after my wife died. I took my daughter and granddaughter on a trip to Europe where I began to experience back trouble. When we returned, I found out that I had an enlarged prostate. I had it taken care of. That was when I was 70 and the first time I had been in a hospital in almost 40 years.

A few years after that, I had a quadruple by-pass but have had no problems with my heart since then. That same year I traveled to Thailand where my daughter was living with her husband who was in the service. I picked up an infection and had a lobe of one lung removed. Again, though, I've had no problems since. Well, I went on then for more than 15 years with no further health concerns until a year ago when I was experiencing terrific pain. I went to the Navy hospital and they removed six feet of my small intestine. Apparently it had closed up and twisted. I went down to about 120 pounds but am up to 140 now.

My father loved to sing, and although with his Welsh background had been a Presbyterian, when we moved to Florida someone invited him to join the Methodist choir, and we've been Methodists ever since. The man who sits next to me in Sunday school class is 95. He had been a school teacher also. A couple of years ago, the mayor issued a proclamation honoring us on our birthdays.

Frequently I take my bike when going up town. It's easier than finding a parking space for the car. When we are very young, we learn how to ride a bike, to swim, to skate. Then we forget about it for years. But later in life we take it up again and find that we can still do it. That's why I believe that children should be exposed to as many things as possible when they are young. What is learned in youth is never really lost.

THE FOCUS OF FAMILY GATHERINGS AT 96:
KATHRYN DONOVAN

*T*he elevated train threads its
way slowly up Broadway, as if
being careful not to touch the
aging buildings which line its route
through the Kingsbridge section of
the Bronx. Well-kept five story
walk-up apartment buildings on
streets with names like Review
Place, Bailey Avenue, and Sedgwick
Avenue are encrusted with the
memories of generations of
immigrants. To the North is Van
Cortland Park, an oasis between
New York City and Yonkers. To the
East is the Jerome Park Reservoir,
pointing to Fordham Road to its
south with the Grand Concourse to
the east. Kingsbridge is a working
class area, unintimidated by the
more affluent Riverdale section to
its west.

Here, in the early decades of the century, thousands of Irish immigrants
got their foothold on the American dream. In the evenings, they gathered
in the bars along Broadway and Kingsbridge Road. On Sundays, after
Mass at Visitation Church, young couples brought their American-born
children to Croake Park, where the rough and tumble games of Irish foot-

ball and hurling were played by ruddy-faced Sunday athletes.

Kathryn Donovan is one of the survivors of what was a stressful yet wonderful time in the adjustment of European peasants to the cosmopolitan world of New York. She has seen the neighborhood evolve from a center of Irish culture to one increasingly populated by a new wave of immigrants. The superintendent and maintenance staff of the building on Bailey Avenue in which she has lived for more than forty years are young men from Czechoslovakia. On a winter day they are shovelling snow and spreading salt on the icy steps. With warmth, they direct a visitor to the first floor apartment of the 96-year-old Irish tenant.

Three weeks ago I had a mild heart attack. The doctor wanted to put me in the hospital but I told him that if I was going to die I wanted it to be in my own home. But I didn't die! However, I haven't really felt right since then, but it doesn't keep me in. More limiting was a fall I had two years ago. Until then I was marvelous. You couldn't keep up with me running. I injured my back. There's a disc pressing on a nerve in my spine. They said I'd never walk again, but I fooled them. When I was being discharged my son-in-law called and said that he'd come down so that I could give him a kick with the bad leg! I use a cane when I go out but don't need it around the house.

I was born on a farm in Kilgarven, County Kerry. There were nine children. One of my surviving sisters is 91, and I have two other siblings in their late 80's. We live long in my family. My father was 86 when he died and my mother, 82.

I attended the Kilgarven National School until I was 14 when I stayed home to help my father on the farm. At 18, I came to New York and lived with my aunt in Manhattan while in nurse's training. I worked all my life as a nurse, mostly in a hospital but sometimes doing private duty. For the last 15 years of my work life I was in charge of a nursing home. I know what nursing homes are like and am trying to keep away from them. I love my own apartment and hope I can stay here until the end.

When I married at age 29, we moved to the Bronx and I have lived here ever since. It has been a pleasant place for me. When we were young, there was Croake Park and Van Cortland Park. I have always felt at home.

None of the buildings in the neighborhood has elevators. We never gave it a thought. Perhaps it was all the climbing of stairs which kept our hearts strong. We certainly never thought about exercise as such—or certainly not the women. Well, I was on the fourth floor of this building until ten years ago when it got to be too much, especially carrying packages up all those steps. Fortunately, this first floor apartment was available and so I moved downstairs. There are still some steps down to the sidewalk, but they're no problem.

My husband was a plasterer. When we married I discontinued work. We had our first daughter the following year. When I was pregnant with my second daughter, we went to Ireland on a visit. Well, my husband contracted scarlet fever and died a month after we returned. My daughter was born several months after her father died. I was married only three years and have been a widow for fifty-three.

There was no Social Security then and my husband had no insurance. For several years while the children were young, I was on public assistance; they called it child welfare at that time. But once the younger one was in high school, I went back to work as a nurse, retiring when I was 75.

I go to Mass every morning at Visitation Church. It's only three blocks away. I've been mugged a couple of times on the way to church but fight them off. A few years ago they tore my rosary beads apart. The boys were not from the neighborhood. This is a good neighborhood. I have a lot of friends. Upstairs is a very good woman. The two of us go shopping together. Also, my daughter brings me groceries every week. So, I'm never short of anything.

I have no special diet or medications. I don't exercise. When I had the fall two years ago, I spent five weeks in a rehabilitation center. They had me doing exercises because I couldn't walk. But now I can walk fine. I used to have a girl come in to do the vacuuming and am right now looking for someone to come in occasionally to help me, but basically I do everything for myself. There's just the three rooms.

Of course there's a heaven. I don't know whether or not I'll make it, but I'll try. Some people don't believe. There are many different views about life. Today we are supposed to be accepting of others; to live together; people of different races and nationalities. It used to be all the Irish stayed together. Now, it's a lot more mixing.

I've had a happy life. Even though I lost my husband young, I've made the best of it. I don't deal that much with people now. My sister who is 91 lives on the Grand Concourse. She comes here to visit. She can walk better than I can. I have five grandchildren and four great-grandchildren. Just today one of my grandchildren visited me with her husband and their son. There's always someone calling or stopping by. And we all have grand get-togethers.

As long as God leaves me my memory, I'll be all right. I wouldn't want to live to be 100 if that meant losing my faculties and being a problem for others.

Mrs. Donovan died two months before her 98th birthday after a short illness. Her daughter wrote, "Mom died as she lived — in charge.... At the funeral we played 'My Way' and she left the church to the sound of 'The Kerry Dancers'."

CONCERT VIOLINIST AT 92:
JOSEPH FUCHS

*I*n a lengthy article which appeared more than two years ago in The New York Times, *"Going on 90, Joseph Fuchs Goes on Playing Violin,"* the feisty Fuchs is quoted as saying, *"Look at these hands. These are not the hands of an old man. I'd like to go on playing for a while. I don't have any difficulties. When I do, I'll quit, simple as that. It's a matter of pushing against time, and I must say, time has been good to me."*

Time has continued to be good to a man who is as absorbed in music today as when he was a child prodigy 85 years ago. A flier for a concert, which he gave at New York's Carnegie Hall, refers to him as *"one of the great violinists of this century"* and notes that the 92-year-old musician had been invited by Leonard Bernstein to christen Philharmonic Hall and by Alice Tully to perform at the opening of Alice Tully Hall, both major New York concert halls located in Lincoln Center.

Deeply ingrained skills can be retained into advanced old age.

Psychologists refer to crystallized and fluid intelligence. Those skills which have become habitual or crystallized, remain strong, while new, fluid knowledge is more difficult to acquire and retain. Thus, someone who learns another language early in life is likely to retain it, while acquiring a language late in life is difficult. People who are continuously absorbed in practicing a skill, such as playing the violin, may not notice a decline in competence unless physical handicaps emerge. Hence, Fuchs' reference to his hands.

I don't think that being a music teacher and performer at my age is anything unusual. Some of the greatest inventions were made by older people. Picasso, daVinci, Casals were active and creative into advanced age. Wisdom takes time. By trial-and-error, you become what you are truly capable of being. If you can correct errors, something emerges.

In music, some of these 11-year-olds who are put on the stage are not really mature. They can play a concerto by Mendelssohn at age nine, but when they are 19 they have trouble with it. Yehudi Menuhin told me, "They put me on the stage too soon." The world is too quick to forget people who are doing things at an advanced age. The young have their years and the old have theirs. But society focuses on youth. You knock the baseball over the fence more often at 23 than at 43. You run faster at 18 than at 80. But if you don't run that fast, you have time to think. More importance should be placed on the constructive achievements of old people.

There is a young Japanese violinist, Midori, emerging from the prodigy class. I remember her when she was a student at Juilliard, perhaps twelve years old. She was having a problem with a particular movement, and her mother asked why she couldn't do it. I noticed that her thumb position was wrong and pushed it to where it was supposed to be. She was already playing Brahms. She is good, but such young people need more experience.

A house must be built on a firm foundation. But in the United States, the Barnum element is strong. Pull a rabbit out of a hat and you are guaranteed a large audience. Get a name and you receive a standing ovation before you play one note. I just gave a recital at Carnegie Hall. It was the largest audience I have ever had, and *The New York Times* didn't cover it. Big names and extravaganzas get all the attention.

To retire at 60, when a man is at the height of his ability, is foolish. In his late 70's, the conductor Eugene Ormandy was asked when he was going to retire. He replied, "To retire is to die."

I was born in New York City. My mother came from Czechoslovakia and my father from Austria. Like many Jewish people who lived downtown, my father worked in a shirt factory. Both my parents loved music. Without being educated, they had more musical taste than many people who had been trained in music.

One of my sisters, Lillian Fuchs, was one of the greatest viola players this country has ever known. We were very musical. They tell me that when I was three, if I heard someone singing off key, I would put my hands over my ears.

When I was four, a neighbor boy and I climbed onto a table. He threw me off and I sustained a compound fracture of the left arm. Hearing that I was musical, the doctor suggested to my parents that they buy me a violin for therapy. That's where my troubles began! At age six I was enrolled in the Institute of Musical Art, now the Juilliard School. My sister followed me shortly thereafter and then my brother, who became first cellist of the Cleveland orchestra. On a number of occasions, the three of us gave concerts together.

After graduating from Juilliard at age 19, I did a concert series in Europe. When I returned, I auditioned as concert master with the Cleveland orchestra. The conductor heard me play three pages of Brahms and said, "You're hired." I remained there for 12 years. When my elbow began to bother me they thought that I would never play again. But I had a transplant of an elbow nerve and it brought me back. Nevertheless, I felt it was time to move on. I resigned from the orchestra, came to New York, and resumed my career as a soloist.

Eugene Ormandy offered me the position of concert master with the Philadelphia orchestra, guaranteeing me a solo performance every year in Carnegie Hall. I said to his agent, "It's one thing to make an

entrance from the wings and another thing to get up from the chair."
I wanted to be on my own. Although I have played with many orchestras and gone on tours throughout the world, never again did I tie myself down to a particular orchestra.

When I was 46 years old, I returned to Juilliard as a violin teacher and have taught there ever since. Presently I have twelve students and see each of them for an hour a week. I am a firm believer that performers should teach; they should pass on to the next generation what they have learned. Teaching is the duty of every great artist.

Only an older person has the experience and wisdom when working with a talented student to know how far that person can go. There is something in the playing that reveals the unique signature of the young person. My role is to identify and foster that, not to force them to do it my way. There's a difference between skill and art.

The president of Juilliard said to me recently that I am probably the most important influence there. And it is not because I am old, but because I have been a successful soloist, someone who has toured Europe and played with many major orchestras, including the New York Philharmonic. Most of the other teachers have not had such a career. I set an example for the younger people. I teach not by method but by example. One student just couldn't get a particular theme. I took my violin and played it. Tears rolled down her face as she listened. She watched my form and from that she learned. Some teachers don't even bring an instrument to the lesson.

I married for the first time while in Cleveland. It didn't work. She was an intelligent, educated woman but tone deaf. She began to hate musicians. When I left Cleveland, that was the end of that.

We had one daughter. She is brilliant, a wonderful writer. She has two children, one a Rhodes scholar and the other also studying philosophy. I don't have any other children or grandchildren.

I married my present wife, Doris, nearly fifty years ago. She has accompanied me all over the world.

Besides the fact that my left arm was disfigured somewhat in the childhood accident, I don't have any physical problems. My bow arm is perfect. Without a bow arm there is no playing. Just look at what's involved in playing a violin. You have to raise your arm in order to bring it down. And your back is involved—many sets of muscles.

My memory is good but I'm having a slight problem with my hearing. Playing the violin requires infinitesimally refined finger placement in order to achieve the precise tone desired. As I get older, I have to be more careful to get the right pitch.

I read avidly, am interested in painting and politics, and keep abreast of new music. I'm continually exploring new ways to play on those four strings.

I don't worry about the beyond and am not afraid of dying. I was born Jewish, but my family soon realized that they couldn't keep that strict Hasidic thing and so they let it go. When I arrived in Cleveland, two temples wanted me to attend. I didn't go to either. Although I have never denied that I was Jewish, that's as far as it goes. I have tried to be as honorable and honest as possible.

I've made thirty-five recordings which are now collectors' items. The world goes on to other things. I've toured Japan and the Soviet Union. I've done a great deal.

I played with Pablo Casals when he was 89. I looked at his hands. They were like those of someone 35 years old. He died at 97. Nathan Millstein and I were the oldest violinists still playing, but he had to stop several years ago. He wrote to me and said, "The difference between us is that I am already a cripple and you are not."

Next year I will have a concert in the big hall at Juilliard—all American music. The old one is going to do new music.

DINNER DATES WITH
GENTLEMAN FRIEND AT 91:
EVELYN GOLBE

*T*he world of the well-elderly
often lies hidden behind tall
fences or guarded gates. Granted
admission, one finds hundreds of
men and women whose lives are
characterized by unsuspected
productivity and vitality. A
retirement community encompasses
substantial diversity and an often
unnoticed range of economic
activities. The diversity is found
not only in the age of the residents,
but in the variety of interests and
talents which they possess. The
economic activities include both
products and services, from crafts
and baked goods to chauffeuring
and sewing. Often the transactions
are of the nature of what
anthropologists call "generalized
reciprocity," one person does something for another with the expectation
that at some time in the future the favor will be returned. At other times,
as in the case of Mrs. Golbe, modest payment may be involved. For many
years, drawing from skills from her earlier life, she provided a sewing
service for other residents of her Lauderdale Lakes, Florida, community.
   The community also provides opportunities for leisure activities which

draw people into social interaction and which enhance physical and mental well being. It is almost impossible to be isolated. Although privacy is cherished and respected within the confines of one's apartment, just outside the door are companions and recreational facilities. Mrs. Golbe walks about 100 yards each morning to the swimming pool in her section of the community. Just beyond that is a plain but serviceable clubhouse with exercise machines, pool tables, a modest collection of books, and a large assembly room. Many evenings, she goes to the recreation center where men and women dance to the music which links them with other times and other places and other partners.

On occasion, for those who are fortunate and so disposed, the community also affords that special companionship which is the most precious gift of life. Love happens. The sun may be setting after a very long day, but it sets in glory; a glow suffuses the horizon and warms the soul. Mrs. Golbe has a "gentleman friend." There is no thought of marriage, no need of it, just the sharing of time each day, of meals, of music. Nonagenarians are not too old for romance.

How do I feel? Like an old woman, but I shouldn't complain. I can still take care of myself. I am very happy in my one-bedroom apartment. It's equipped with all the appliances and utilities and is very comfortable. This community consists of eight buildings each of which has thirty-two apartments. There are some couples, but most of us are widows. My husband and I moved in here nineteen years ago. He had six good years and then he passed away.

My friend next door moved in at the same time. She is a year and a half older than I am and still has her husband. *[Actually, the neighbor came in during the interview, "to borrow a stamp," but obviously really to meet the man who was interviewing "Evey" and to give her views on longevity. She said that both of them had lived to "a nice age" and attributed it to God's will and good living. She was very friendly and robust and greeted me with a hug and kiss. When Mrs. Golbe jokingly commented on her kissing younger men, the neighbor said, "Why not, I like men better than women."]*

I was born in Russia almost 92 years ago. My family came to this country when I was 13 years old. I had five brothers and two sisters.

My parents did not want my brothers to serve the czar and so were planning for years to leave. I attended school in Europe, of course, and can still speak and write both Russian and Yiddish, but only with the words and expressions that a child would learn. An adult's vocabulary is different and many new words have been added.

Over here I went to school and learned to read and write. But after two and a half years, they threw me out and I went to work. We lived in an apartment on Myrtle Avenue in Brooklyn with the elevated train running right outside our windows. My father was supporting us all and could use my help. It wasn't easy, but we lived respectable lives. Both in Russia and here, I always had enough to eat and clothes to keep me warm.

After he got established, my father began buying houses, fixing them up, and renting them out. One was a four-family house, and it was there that I lived even after getting married when I was 21. My parents lived in the basement apartment while my husband and I had the parlor floor.

My life's work was sewing—fancy work. I even made my own wedding dress. While my children were young I stayed home, but when my son was 15 and my daughter was 10, I said to myself, "What am I doing at home?" We were still living in my folks' house. My mother was there; my father was there. So my husband and I decided to go into business. For years my husband had been a fur salesman in a ladies specialty shop. He was bright and ambitious. We had a little money, so we set up our own fur business. I became the furrier while my husband was the salesman and buyer. I did a man's job. I stretched skins; I nailed them; I cut them. I was making and repairing the fur garments.

Then my husband began to have health problems, a heart attack, hernia operations. I had to run the business myself. We moved to a smaller apartment; we tried to manage, but I knew he wouldn't last long in New York. The winters were terrible for him. Eventually, I couldn't go to work at all. He needed me for everything. I had to shave him, bathe him, feed him.

Well, my brother-in-law, who was already down here in Florida, saw this retirement community being built, called me, and said, "Evelyn,

I've found you an apartment." That was in December. In February we came down. All they had so far were models, but I took one, went back and sold the business, and we moved. I knew it was the only hope for my husband to have any more life. He was too sick for us to drive down from New York, so I sold the car and we came by plane. I planned to get my Florida license and buy a car, but my brother-in-law said, "Don't bother. When you need a car, it's only a phone call away." But he played us a dirty trick; he died a year later.

Until last year I used to sew. I made dresses. I altered clothing. I could do anything with a needle. But then the arthritis in my hands reached the point where the needles were falling out of my fingers. I still make my own clothes and do my own cooking. I can't complain.

I like swimming. Some people walk up and down in the pool, but I swim. I do ten laps. That's enough. I float a little bit. I enjoy myself. I do it each morning, unless the weather is bad.

I used to walk more. Now I find that I get tired. I rest on the sofa a couple of times a day. I have some sewing there and something to read. I should be educating myself but I read trash, romances. When I told a friend that I should be learning something new, he said, "If you learn something, what are you going to do with it?" But I can see OK and like to read. Hearing is my problem. I keep away from crowds, because my hearing aid picks up every sound that's around. When I go to a show and there's comedy, I miss the punch line!

Tuesday I shop and get all the things I need to cook a big meal for Wednesday when Saul, my gentleman friend, comes for dinner. I cook enough that I have the leftovers for the rest of the week. I put it in freezer containers.

Saul wanted to get married, but I told him that neither of us needed it. He cooks for himself and has a woman come in to clean and do his laundry. He has plenty of money. I don't want to marry him and become his chief cook and bottle washer. I do things for myself; that's enough. It's very good the way it is. I have him here for dinner every Wednesday and he takes me out to a restaurant every Saturday. It gives me a reason to have my hair done, to dress up, to have something to look forward to.

He's 88. He had a beautiful wife, but she was bedridden and he had to have women come in every day to help him care for her. Well, one chilly morning several years ago, I saw him sitting on a bench all bundled up. I said, "Saul, what are you doing sitting there. It's better to walk." So we took a walk. Every day after that, there he was waiting for me. We became very friendly. We were friends long before his wife died. They were customers when I was doing sewing. Now, I am altering all his clothes. He had an operation and lost fourteen pounds. Even his underwear was falling off him.

I'm not a religionist. I believe in the Ten Commandments, the law of the land, and in people. That's my religion. There's a beautiful temple for those who want to go. I don't have a kosher kitchen. I feel that the dishwasher cleans and sterilizes everything, and that's kosher enough. The community here is maybe 15% or 20% non-Jewish; most of them are Italians. Jews and Italians get along well.

My son lives in New Jersey. His mother-in-law is my age and had to go to a nursing home because she couldn't care for herself anymore. My son is concerned about me, but I am not going to make any changes or worry about it. As long as I can take care of myself I'm happy. What will be, will be.

I have grandchildren and great-grandchildren. They move into the world as we move out.

WRITING PLAYS FOR COMMUNITY THEATRE AT 95:
HARRY GRANICK

L aSalle Street divides two social worlds. On one side stand towering low income apartment buildings, what most New Yorkers would simply call "a housing project." On the other side of the wide, clean street is Morningside Gardens, a privately owned co-op apartment complex of 21-story buildings for middle income people.

In the 1950's dilapidated tenements stood on the land, an outcropping of blight on the westernmost end of Harlem's 125th Street. A few blocks to the south stood Columbia University, one of the world's most prestigious institutions. Already buttressed from Harlem on its eastern flank by Morningside Park, now it would be protected by housing for stable, middle class people. Bulldozers leveled the tenements and Morningside Gardens emerged.

Sensitivity to the local community was not lacking. It was agreed that in the new buildings 40% of the residents would be white, 30% black, and the rest from a variety of other racial and ethnic groups. Also, permission for the middle income housing was granted by the city on condition that *an equal number of public housing units for the poor be constructed on adjacent land. Thus was born a neighborhood that for more than forty years has been racially and socio-economically integrated.*

Several active nonagenarians live in Morningside Gardens. On many days, one of them, Harry Granick, can be seen walking around the block, passing the guarded off-street parking lot and the well-kept gardens.

Tomorrow is my 95th birthday. The pension plan to which I belong sent me a congratulatory letter. Perhaps they just want to be sure that I'm still alive!

When my wife and I moved into this two-bedroom apartment ten years ago, I learned that there was a theatre on the lower level of the building where a residents' group presented plays. When I went to see a show, I found that all the performers and everyone in the audience was white. I decided to do something about it. Since then I have written several one-act plays for the theatre, in all of which the cast has been racially integrated and the audience as well.

I still write. Sometimes I sit at my table by the window where I can look out and see the George Washington Bridge. Until a new building went up, I could see the Hudson River as well. More often, I work in my den which doubles as a guest room. My best friend lives in Hollywood now but visits me several times a year and sleeps there.

These buildings are beautifully managed. The 2,000 residents are more than the population of Bethel, Vermont, where my wife and I had a summer home for more than forty years. On this floor are four white families, two blacks, one Chinese, and two Latinos. And because we are all middle class, we fit. Our behavior toward one another is respectful. On the other side of the street, where people of a less fortunate heritage live, there is not the same high regard for education and less concern for disciplining children. Yet, we have had very little trouble. We consider this one of the safest neighborhoods in the city.

Three years ago I had a setback when my wife died a few days before her 90th birthday. Her death upset me and I spent a week in the hospital. When I returned home, I had someone stay with me day and night for about a month. Since then I have been able to take care of myself. Social Services downstairs did insist that I wear this beeper. It's like a wristwatch. If I'm in trouble, all I do is touch it and a signal goes to security. An alarm sounds in this contraption on the table and then a voice asks if I'm OK. If not, they come right up. They also have the names of three people to be contacted in an emergency. Well, the first day wearing the beeper, I triggered it accidentally and thought that the sound I heard was the fire alarm. Within minutes two guards were at my door. It works!

As far as housekeeping is concerned, I employ a cleaning lady who comes in once every two weeks to give the house a run through. But I manage my own affairs and do all my own grocery shopping. My black neighbors are afraid to shop in Harlem. But there's a good fish store there, so when I go, I get extra fish for them. The people on the floor are very helpful. When someone cooks something special, they will bring me some and when I have something, I reciprocate.

I try to get out every day. If I don't have errands to take care of, I walk around the perimeter of the development. It's the equivalent of eight blocks. If I go to the post office or the fish store, I'm going fifteen blocks. If my grandson is here or some of the other younger people I know, I might walk another ten blocks along Riverside Drive with them.

I was born in Russia. This is a portrait of my maternal grandparents who never left Europe. I can still remember my grandfather with whom I lived for a year. I recall riding with him on horses and that he had a water mill.

My father, who was a tutor for the children of wealthy people, had to flee the country because of his revolutionary activity. It took him two years to earn enough money to send for us. I arrived here at the age of seven, speaking only Russian. We were intellectuals and did not speak Yiddish. When we arrived in the United States, our relative said, "What, you are running away from the czar, yet you speak his language!" So we began to speak Yiddish.

More children were born here until we were seven in all. My mother devoted her life to us, but when she was 78 she began to paint and continued until she died at 84. She produced 250 canvases and was written up in *The New York Times* and art magazines. I have many of her paintings here on the walls. They are similar in some respects to the work of Grandma Moses.

My formal education ended and I went to work after only one and a half years of high school. However, it was in the process of leaving school that I first knew that I was a writer. I wrote an essay about how difficult it was for my father to earn enough money to feed our large family. Composing that essay so delighted me that the desire to write was born, and I still have it. Whatever I know was learned from my work. For example, I read a lot of science when preparing documentaries for radio and television.

But that was not to be right away. For several years I held various jobs. In one place, when I was demoted because the boss said I was too young to have authority over older men, I quit in anger. I felt betrayed and spent time in the country recovering from a nervous breakdown. First I had been deprived of an education, now of my chance for advancement at work. I was embittered at society. I couldn't even get in the army during World War I. They turned me down because of my eyesight.

Then, since I was a Zionist, when the Balfour Declaration called for a Jewish homeland in Palestine, I joined the British Army and served for two years in the Jewish Legion for Palestine. There were some 10,000 of us from all over the world. I think I'm the last survivor.

I was raised an agnostic and am still one. I've never been near a synagogue. I've seen men die; I've seen cattle die. I believe that once you're gone, you're gone.

When I left the army, I bummed around for a year. It was a valuable growth experience. Then I was ready to go to work and to marry Rae with whom I was deeply in love. I was 26; she was 25.

For a while I worked in sales in order to support Rae and our son, David, who was born two years after our marriage. But I was not content. So, when I was 30, Rae and I agreed that she would do what she was interested in and I would do what I was interested in. From then on I was a writer and she was a librarian. I never had any pension plan but am the beneficiary of the annuity my wife accumulated through her many years in library work.

Everything was equal between us. I would pay the rent; she would pay for the food. We worked out this arrangement early on and lived that way the rest of our lives. When I was busy and couldn't get away, she would vacation on her own. She was a very independent as well as very beautiful person. She retained her maiden name while she worked. After retirement she became Mrs. Granick.

Our son was a professor of economics at the University of Wisconsin for 35 years. He died last year at the age of 68. I have three grandchildren. The oldest is a full professor of chemical engineering at the University of Illinois. His sister is a librarian and his younger brother, a policeman.

Writing has been my life. In 1947, my book *Underneath New York* was published. It is about the network of tunnels, wires, and pipes beneath the streets of the city. I knew nothing about such things and so went to the engineers who did and said, "Look, I don't know anything about it, so explain it to me in simple terms, and I will do the same for my readers." The book was well received and I was interviewed on the radio. Well, two years ago, Fordham University Press published a paperback reprint of that book. It turns out that what's underneath the city hasn't changed much since the 1940's!

I have written in every form of the word. My short stories have been included in anthologies. I've had two concerts of my tone poems in Carnegie Hall. It's funny, but my youngest brother played the violin for Toscanini for 18 years and never had his name on the marquee, and here I was with my name on the billboard because I had written the words for scores. That brother is 82 now and still plays with the Mostly Mozart group. I have a sister who is 91 with not a wrinkle on her face and is very active in volunteer work.

The bulk of my work was for the theatre. Years ago I was one of ten young men selected to study under the tutelage of a master playwright. Lawrence Langford, the head of the Theatre Guild, stopped by and said to us, "You don't know how to write a play until you've written twenty." That was discouraging, but I've written about twenty now, so evidently I'm about ready to really write a good one!

My plays were produced in many regional, university, and stock theatres. In recent years I have been writing one-act plays, five of which have been performed in the little theatre here. I have directed as well.

One of the plays, *Florabelle for President*, is about an 11-year-old black girl who is told in school that she could be president of the United States. She comes home and tells her folks that she's going to be president. Her parents are irritated with the teacher for telling the girl that. But she goes all over the city. Everywhere she goes, she wins votes.

The theatre, the friends I have in the building, my writing, all these keep me alive. It's an environment in which someone my age lives and thrives.

More than a year after the interview, Mr. Granick sent me a copy of a poem he had written, "A Rumination at Age 97." It includes the lines, "So glad I am to be alive / Alive and resonant still. / I would not have it otherwise."

AUTHOR AND INVESTOR AT 92:
LEON F. HOFFMAN

*M*any of the nonagenarians have a "social safety net," people they can call upon for aid in an emergency. It might include a spouse, a son or daughter who lives nearby, or close friends. Those who live in a retirement community can rely on a staff that is trained to respond to the needs of residents. However, there are a few, frequently men, who live alone and have no one close at hand to whom they might turn. They are proud of their independence but very vulnerable. Leon Hoffman is such a person. Although in excellent health and kept busy with his writing and investments, he is increasingly isolated in his apartment in a densely populated, anonymous neighborhood of New York City.

Like many of the nonagenarians who have never experienced serious illness, Hoffman does not give much thought to his vulnerability, confident that he can take care of himself and not willing to be dependent on anyone. Although it is difficult to fault a man who remains strong and self-reliant, it would be better if he had someone who might check on him regularly.

One woman said that she was registered with a Senior Citizen telephone contact program. Each morning a volunteer calls her and chats for a few moments just to be sure that she is well.

I was brought up in an intensely religious atmosphere. My father was a prominent rabbi, and my mother's family was the richest Jewish family in Philadelphia and very philanthropic. At one time I had wanted to be a rabbi myself. Also, I spent many years in Palestine working to establish a Jewish homeland. However, when the Holocaust happened I lost my faith. How could there be a God who allowed his chosen people to be wiped out for no reason? A friend counseled that everyone had doubts, that it was important not to lose hope. But I have never changed my mind. So, the first half of my life was one of devotion to God, while the second half has been devoid of faith.

I was born in Philadelphia almost 93 years ago. My father was a lawyer, although he was very unhappy. He wanted to be a rabbi but felt that at thirty-five and with a family, it was too late. However, my mother encouraged him, and so while I was an infant, the family moved to England where my father undertook rabbinical studies.

When we returned to the United States, his first pastorate was to a congregation in Indianapolis, but they wouldn't pay him. The people felt that, since he had been a lawyer and his wife was from a wealthy family, he didn't need any money. We then moved to Newark, New Jersey, where he spent the rest of his life as rabbi of the Oheb Shalom Congregation. It was in the shadow of that synagogue and of my intellectually and morally powerful father that I grew up together with my two brothers and two sisters. I was the youngest except for Hannah who is the subject of my book, *Ideals and Illusions*, which was published earlier this year.

All of us attended Columbia University except for Hannah who went to Smith College. But since my three older siblings had gone to Columbia, when it came my turn my father said that he could not afford it. I wanted to go and was able to get a four-year scholarship. I have a copy of a letter from the dean which says that I would lose the scholarship if my grades were not high enough. But I was able to maintain them.

When I graduated from college I went into business, a very low prestige road to follow. To be a professional—a lawyer, a doctor, a rabbi—put you on a higher plane. I decided that I would make a million dollars in a few years, retire, and devote the rest of my life to Jewish institutions. But it didn't work out that way.

My first position was in the women's clothing business in the showroom. Models would parade before the buyers in new coats. My job was to help them on and off with the coats, under which they were not wearing very much. I must have attracted some of the models, because several of them would suggest that we go out together after work. And here I was, a rabbi's son, working with models who were entertaining the customers and propositioning me. Also, it was crazy. After four years of college was that the best job I could get?

I moved up the ladder and got increasingly more responsible positions in several businesses, mostly in department stores. Another time I worked in real estate sales and was making good money. However, I learned that they were engaging in shady business deals. When anyone asked questions about it, they would say, "How can there be anything wrong? One of our salesmen is a rabbi's son." I had to give that up.

In 1932 I went to Palestine. One reason was to try to convince my fellow Jews that they must make friends with the Arabs and gain their consent to establish a Jewish state. This was not a popular idea, but it seemed reasonable to me, and I hoped that I might make some contribution. Also, I brought to Jerusalem $125,000, collected in the United States by the United Synagogues of America and the Women's League, for the erection of a Jewish center. I gave the money to a group of influential men and they used it to build a synagogue, the largest in the city at the time. I served on its board of directors for many years.

Although the Depression was at its deepest here, the economy was prospering in Palestine. I worked as controller of the Loan Bank in Jerusalem for three years and traveled around to all the branches.

My sister, Hannah, had gone to Palestine in 1925 and lived for two years in primitive conditions in a kibbutz. My book about her is largely the letters which she wrote home. By the time I arrived in Palestine, she had moved from the kibbutz, having grown tired of the ideological bickering. But she married a man whom she met there, and helped by my father the two of them lived there for the remainder of their lives. They had two children who were the first generation of Jews to span the period between the old British mandate and the establishment of the state of Israel in 1947.

While in Palestine I married an American scientist who was conducting cancer research at Hebrew University. Her father set me up in a retail refrigeration and radio store. During World War II, concerned that the Germans might conquer North Africa, we moved to the United States.

That marriage ended. There were no children. Then in 1949 I returned to Israel where I married a second time. Our only child, a daughter, was born prematurely in Israel, and we were advised to go to New York for proper medical care. We stayed in the United States after that.

I bought a wholesale candy-packaging plant in Brooklyn, which I managed until I was 68 years old when I was mugged and sustained head injuries that almost proved fatal. Following my recovery, I performed accounting work for various companies until my final retirement when I was 87.

My second marriage ended in divorce about ten years ago. My wife was German and had fled Germany during the Hitler period. Well, it just so happens that she died two weeks ago. Our daughter took it badly. She was very attached to her mother.

Since the divorce I have lived alone in this apartment and manage fine. I have more than enough to live and am still banking money. Much of my time is spent managing my investments.

A woman comes in once every two weeks to clean. Apart from that, I do everything for myself. My car is what makes it possible for me to get to the bank and the stores. My only physical disability is walking any distance. There's a hill leading up to my house here. When I walk up it, I have to stop two or three times. But I guess when you get to be 92, you have to take it easy.

I worked on my book for several years. I had to gather documents from Hannah's children in Israel and from other family members. People ask me what I do with myself now that the book is finished, but I have no trouble keeping busy. I have some lady friends. One was in my sister's class at Smith. Another is a woman who was my first girl-friend over 70 years ago. Our paths have crossed several times over the years. She lives in Manhattan and I see her quite frequently. Through the accounting jobs I had, I got to know some other women, younger women, but I've had to cut down. It's getting to be too much of a struggle for me traveling on the subway in New York. I used to like to attend the opera and concerts, but my desire is fading away.

I see a doctor once a year. He wants to see me every three months, but there's no need for that. He says I am borderline diabetic. I take some medicine for that and something to thin the blood. Apart from aspirin, I don't take other medication and don't have any dietary restrictions.

This is the first year that I found it too far to drive to the Catskills for vacation. There's a resort there where I have gone every year. It's a lovely place on the top of a mountain. My mother and father went there on their honeymoon.

A year after the interview, Mr. Hoffman moved to what he called "a large, luxurious home for the aging" in a suburb of Washington, D.C. Recently, the now 94-year-old Hoffman gave a lecture to the residents titled, "A Rebel Looks at the Prospects for Peace in the Middle East."

RELIGIOUS FORMATION LEADERS:
ANNE (93) & GRAYSON (95) HOLT

P opular wisdom would have it that people become more religious as they age. The inevitable decline in strength and the accumulation of health problems underscore the undeniable fact that no one lives forever.

Social science research has not found this common sense belief to be true. The fact that older people are more religious than younger people does not suggest a movement back to God as the years accumulate, but rather that the habits formed in youth are likely to be maintained. If this be true, then today's less observant young adults are not likely to become more devout in their old age.

What about the religious beliefs and practice of the active nonagenarians? Interviews with more than forty nonagenarians did not uncover anyone who said that religion had become more important with the passage of time. In fact, two said that they had abandoned earlier *religious convictions. Leroy Campbell had been a Protestant minister but subsequently drifted away from religion. Leon Hoffman, raised in a devout Jewish home, had considered becoming a rabbi but lost his faith after the Holocaust and has not been near a synagogue since.*

Ironically, anti-religious sentiments were more convincingly articulated than were pro-religious feelings. The views of Catharine Wright, coming from a Protestant background, of Lena Wulf, from a Jewish heritage, and Tonio Selwart, from Roman Catholicism, are impressive formulations of philosophies of life which do not include traditional religious beliefs. The fact that they dissent from the prevailing belief in the existence of God and of an afterlife may have forced them to hone and refine views, which they have been challenged to defend on numerous occasions.

Even those nonagenarians who attend church seem to do so out of habit rather than conviction. For example, Russell Wilson admits quite candidly that he participates in his church not out of faith but because of the social life it provides.

This dearth of religious commitment in active nonagenarians raises the intriguing possibility that part of the "secret" of longevity might be the ability to move beyond traditional religious categories. In fact, some theories of the stages of moral development suggest that the capacity to transcend denominational and culturally-imbued perspectives characterizes the highest levels of human growth. Those rare men and women who climb above the clouds of religious ethnocentrism may be the most spiritually healthy. And spiritual health promotes physical health.

Having said this, it must be recognized that some of the nonagenarians are deeply religious. Sister John Baptist has given her life to the service of the church and her joyful manner springs from a deep faith and an active prayer life. Eugene Curry is a fervent believer as are Edward Corcoran, Peter Comerford, and Nida Neel. However, none of the interviewees are more enthusiastic about religion than Anne and Grayson Holt. As people experienced in speaking publicly about religion, they spent the first twenty minutes of our time together explaining their work with the lay renewal movement of the Methodist Church. The manner in which they smoothly and respectfully alternated sharing their perspectives reflected not only a long history of shared religious ministry, but certainly as well the 73 years which this 95-year-old man and 93-year-old woman have lived together as husband and wife.

Anne: The Methodist church in Grayson's town here in Virginia hosted a youth convention which I attended as an 18-year old delegate. His job was to meet people at the train station. Well, when I stepped off the train in my closely fitted dress with perhaps an inch or two of leg showing, he was so taken with me that he suggested that we go to a local restaurant for lunch. We were attracted to one another immediately and had a delightful time. When lunch was almost finished I asked Grayson when the other delegates would arrive. He said, "What delegates?" He had completely forgotten about the other people he was supposed to meet.

At the time, I had finished a year of college and came and taught school for a year in Grayson's town. We courted, of course, and were married two years later. I had to discontinue my work because at that time married women were not allowed to be teachers. We set up house and started our life together on an income of $125 a month. I still have the record books. He was the banker but I kept the family accounts.

Grayson: I was born 95 years ago in Chesterfield County, Virginia, just south of Richmond. My father was the general manager of a textile mill in a small town. When the mill was sold, my father moved to county government as deputy commissioner of revenues.

A few years ago we buried my mother's sister. She was 98. Mother herself lived to be 92 and my father 87. I had a grandfather who died at 94. Two of my sisters are still alive.

My entire career was in banking, although I got into it accidentally. After high school I thought I would attend Randolph-Macon College and either teach history or become a minister. However, I went to work in my uncle's jewelry store. He would send me twice a week to the bank across the street with a deposit. One day a bank officer said that they had been observing me, liked what they saw, and wondered if I would like a job. My uncle suggested that I try it to see if I liked it. I did and remained with it for over 50 years.

Anne: We have always been active in the Church but in 1968 were introduced to the lay renewal movement which is a weekend program conducted by a trained team. The team is invited to a church and has a set approach to helping the congregation examine both their individual and their community's spiritual commitment. It is evangelical and calls people to reawaken their faith in Jesus. It's an updated version of the revival meetings they held in tents in the old days.

Grayson: There are sessions for children, young people, and adults. Every weekend begins with the question, "What do you want to happen in your church this weekend?" This is followed with, "What would you like to see happen in your own personal life this weekend?" That, of course, is a sort of trick question, because nothing could happen in the church unless it happened first in their personal thinking. The program is not holier-than-thou, but it's holy. It's practical, like taking an inventory. I was in the banking business all my life, and each year I had to report whether the bank had made progress or not. That's what we try to bring to people. Are you really church or are you just playing church? We get into some real good discussions on these questions.

Anne: We were approved by Church headquarters as team members and have participated in programs in hundreds of churches all over the United States, including Hawaii and Alaska, and have gone to England and Panama. Last year alone we were on six weekends. One was at an Episcopal church near Washington, D.C. Many of the participants were generals, business executives, Ph.D.s, even the Lieutenant Governor of Virginia. At the final service in their large church, those who wished to renew their commitment to Christ were invited to come forward. Well, everyone in that church swept forward, surrounding the pulpit. There must have been a thousand people.

Grayson: When we go with a team we stay in the homes of local people. It's very interesting but also tiring. We begin on Friday evening and end on Sunday afternoon. Maybe people know how old we are or maybe they don't. They just seem to want us. We eat whatever is served and with staying in all those different places have never even so much as taken a sleeping pill. We've traveled with younger people who have pillows at their back and all sorts of aches and pains. Not us! It's no bed of roses but we have seen such marvelous results that we are continuously drawn to the program. We will continue our ministry as long as we are invited and able to do it.

Just recently someone asked why we had lived so long. I said that I didn't know, that they'd have to ask the good Lord. My friend replied, "Well, there must be something that He still wants you to do and is giving you the chance to get it right."

Anne: I was born 93 years ago. My father's father came over from Germany and with his wife traveled West. Well, they were going up the Ohio River when my pregnant grandmother said, "This is it." My father was born right there in the middle of the river. The family settled in rural Virginia and raised peanuts and horses. I had one brother who died a few years ago at age 98. My older sister who lives here in Richmond is 98. My mother lived nearly to 100, but my father died of a heart attack in his late 70's.

We had two children. Our son lives in Florida with his family and our daughter lives near us with her husband and their three children.

At times, while I was raising the children I worked with Grayson in the bank and have always been involved in the church. I've traveled extensively all over the world. When I was 74, the youth group invited me to go with them to Mexico for a youth ministry program. We were grinding corn for eight hours a day. I slept in a sleeping bag for ten days. Everyone in the group got sick, even the minister, except me.

On my eighty-fifth birthday, I was in Jerusalem with a church group. When they found out it was my birthday they gave me a bouquet of 85 yellow roses. At dinner I went around and gave one rose to each person.

Grayson: We've lived in this house more than 35 years and have no trouble taking care of it ourselves. I still drive. You may have noted that there is no car in our driveway. That's because just last week two young men in a pickup truck ran into me right in front of the house. They destroyed our car and their truck. My shoulder and knee bother me some, but x-rays and other exams have not turned up anything serious. We have to get a new car, but in the meanwhile, church members are forever calling to ask if they can take us anyplace.

I am a charter member of the local Rotary Club. About 100 members meet every Monday. I lead them in singing, even if off key at times! I am invited to speak at various meetings around the state, especially of Ruritan Clubs, which are Rotary-type groups in rural areas. I was one of the founders and organizers of Ruritan.

I have a house full of bowling trophies and was president of the bowling club for thirty years. I still bowl, but not as regularly as I used to. For nearly forty years, I bowled every Monday night.

Since the first Senior Olympics in 1979 I participated regularly and have won a dozen gold medals. Every year I won the mile walk for my age category and also awards in the 100-meter dash and softball throwing for distance and accuracy. Three years ago was the last time I participated, because it was held too far from Richmond.

Not long ago, I had a physical examination. The doctor said that he couldn't find anything wrong with me. He said, "I want to know what your parents fed you and what your wife is feeding you. They must have done something right for you to be in such fine shape." But I think it can be summed up in one word: moderation. I have never smoked or drunk alcohol. My only health problem is some difficulty with hearing when I'm in a crowd and everyone is talking.

Anne: We don't take any medication. We know people in their sixties and seventies who have all sorts of health problems. I don't say these things to brag. It's just that we have lived active lives and have done so many things. There is no reason to stop. We just live; there's so much to do. We get a great feeling of accomplishment working with people.

In 1994 the Holts celebrated their 75th wedding anniversary and continued to participate in the Lay Renewal program. In a December letter they listed all they had done during the year, concluding with the comment, "otherwise we have led a normal life dealing with everyday problems as best we could."

COMMUNITY TREASURER AT 90:
SISTER JOHN BAPTIST HULL

*I*n recent years committing one's
life to religious service as a nun
has lost much of its appeal and the
number of women in Roman
Catholic religious communities has
been declining. Sister Eleace King,
who edits the directory of men and
women in religious life, when releasing the 1993 edition referred to the
drop in new women religious as
"frightening, stark, sobering." The
decline in women in initial formation was down 23 percent in just
four years. Recruitment into communities with hundreds and even
thousands of women has virtually
dried up. The average age of
American nuns is now about 60
and there are more sisters over 80
than there are under 30.

*Not only are fewer women entering religious life, but many of those
who had been nuns for many years have left, undertaking new lives as lay
women. Those who remain in the convents during such a period of crisis
have had to reassess their own vocation and to base their commitment to
their vows on a deeper understanding of themselves and of the Church.
Perhaps Sister John Baptist can serve as a model not only of an active*

nonagenarian but of a woman who continues to live joyfully as a nun in a turbulent age.

I'm delighted to be ninety because I'm well. The Golden Years are only golden if you're healthy, if you don't have some life-threatening disease, which most people seem to have. My experience or my interpretation of my experience has been different. I remember a Jesuit on a retreat some time ago said that when he died he would say to God, "Lord, I'm glad to be home again, but the trip was wonderful." That's how I feel. In fact, just recently on retreat I said to the priest, "Nothing has happened to me in my life but good things." Later I wondered what made me say that. I've had some terrible things happen to me, like my mother dying when I was twelve years old. But looking back, I see that I would not be a Catholic today if my mother had not died of TB when I was a child.

I was born Eleanor Elizabeth Hull 90 years ago in Flatbush, Brooklyn. A month later I was baptized in St. Paul's Episcopal Church. My father was a non-practicing Catholic and my mother, a Protestant. I was an only child, and my mother suffered from TB all her life and that was before there was a cure. We traveled all over the country in search of a climate that would help her.

My father was a self-trained mechanical engineer and eventually had a rather lucrative business making the metal caps for glass preserve jars. Father was descended from a family that came to this country from England in the 17th century. St. Francis de Sales says not to boast about your family, but I could be a Daughter of the American Revolution. My father enlisted in World War I eleven days before he would be overage because there never had been a war in which a Hull had not served. Patriotism ran high.

Perhaps I have lived so long because when I was a child they were so afraid I would contract TB, that I was examined frequently and given the best of food. When mother was at Saranac Lake for treatment, I attended a school that met outside in winter on a porch. We children were all bundled up and had our little feet in a warmer. I once said to a doctor that it might have been such experiences that toughened me up. He said, "No it's in the genes. You have good genes."

Through the seventh grade I was in public schools. I figured out that I was in eleven different schools. Each time mother would go away because of her health, I would go with her. We lived in Texas, in Seattle, in Denver. Denver was the best. It was while we were there that I became a religious maniac. I went faithfully to the Episcopal church, but I also went with two little friends to the Baptist church. I loved to see baptism by immersion. Then in the evening I would go to the Catholic Benediction service with my mother's Catholic nurse.

Mother's final days were spent in St. Anthony's Hospital in Queens. She was so attracted to the kindness of the Little Sisters of the Sick Poor, who staffed the hospital, that she converted to Catholicism shortly before her death. She was 36 and I was 12. I decided to join my mother in faith.

Father and I then went to live with my grandparents. The family sent me to St. Joseph's Academy, a boarding school in Brentwood, Long Island. It was felt that this was the best way for me to learn about my new religion. I boarded there for five years, right through high school. Every Sunday father came all the way from Brooklyn to visit me. He was a wonderful father...father and a mother.

After high school I went to the College of New Rochelle run by the Ursuline Sisters. When eventually I decided to enter the convent, the Ursulines were surprised that I joined the Sisters of St. Joseph. I told them that it would be like turning my back on my mother not to join the Josephites because they had mothered me from my very first days in the faith.

I didn't enter the convent until six years after graduating from college, even though I knew since my high school days that I had to be a nun. I remember saying to a seminarian who became a priest and who has since died, "I have to become a nun in gratitude."

But first I enjoyed being a young woman during a very exciting time in history. Those were the days of the Charleston and Prohibition. It was a crazy decade, much too nice to miss. I went out with the boys quite regularly. There was one I could have married. He was a doctor. He practiced for six months and died. My father said he was sure he died of TB because he had interned in a TB hospital in Washington. But my father didn't like him. Will, my boyfriend, said, "I don't think your father likes me to come to see you." I said, "Did you come to see my father or to see me?" Father sat in the next room the whole time and heard what was said and must have said something to Will. The next day I received a letter from Will saying that he hoped I would have a very happy life. I knew that it was the end of our relationship. I was so angry that I gave father and everyone else the silent treatment for the whole summer.

But something good came out of it. I knew all along that I should enter the convent but was resisting it tooth and nail. Now I had no excuses. In 62 years as a nun, I have not regretted it for a moment.

For six years I taught in public schools and then at age 28 finally entered the community. When I made my first vows after three years, they sent me to Washington, D.C., to get my Masters in English at the Catholic University. When I came back I taught for eleven years at the academy where I had attended high school myself. It's some of the "girls" I taught then, now women in their sixties, who have remained close friends. Very special relationships are established in a boarding school that don't happen in a day school.

Then, forty-seven years ago, I was sent here to St. Joseph's College in Brooklyn. So all my years as a sister have been spent in only two places. At the college, I taught English and speech. When the President of the college asked if I would like to get a Ph.D., I said that I was too old. I was in my forties! Also, at that time it was awkward participating fully in the academic world as a nun. With the habit we wore then it was awkward acting in a drama or even making stage scenery. Today we look and live like real people, but at that time there were many obstacles.

After eleven years on the faculty, they made me academic dean. I was in that position for 13 years during which time I had a hysterectomy and a gall bladder operation. I said that there was nothing the matter with me that couldn't be cut out and thrown away and I go on as usual!

When I was 67 years old I resigned as dean but continued on the faculty until my official retirement at age 76. After that I did a considerable amount of tutoring: people from other countries who wanted to learn English and also American students who needed help with speech. Also, I took courses here at the college including all the religion courses, all except the morality course. I felt that my presence might inhibit the young students.

For years, a priest faculty member and I would get the same spiritual books and have a monthly discussion of the book we had read. When he became a pastor, I began to knit or crochet something each month for a raffle in his parish. I'm working on one now.

Over the years I have traveled extensively, usually with groups of students, and I've been to most states visiting friends. They say, "Enter the convent and see the world!" But now, most of my contemporaries have died. There's only one person I know older than me, and she has Alzheimer's disease. My friends from boarding school days are very good to me. This weekend some are coming to pick me up and take me to their homes on Long Island for a couple of days. I tell them, "If you want to see me, send a car."

When I was in my mid-seventies, I was made treasurer of the convent here, responsible for all the accounts. There were 26 sisters at that time. Now there are 22. As of yesterday, I gave up that job. I kept saying, "When I'm 90, someone else has to take over." I'll be working with the new treasurer until she learns what has to be done.

So I guess I'm finally fully retired. But they don't want me in Maria Regina, the community retirement home. They have enough people out there. The general superior said at one time, "If you can take care of yourself, stay on your local mission." It's much less expensive for the congregation. So I guess I'm here until I can't take care of myself anymore. I'm full of arthritis, but it doesn't hurt, and I've had two bad falls this year. Once I banged my knees so hard on the bathroom floor that they had the design of the tiles on them. The other time I twisted my hip and fell. They were sure it was broken, but the x-rays were negative.

How do I spend my time now? Every day I take a walk and with so many sisters in the house there's always someone to talk to. Also, we have a chapel where the Blessed Sacrament is reserved. With fewer duties, I have more time for prayer. It's wonderful. I'm not a holy Moses, but I do love the Lord.

I have a long and interesting past and a miniscule future. But I'm very happy.

The following year, Sister John did move to the sisters' retirement home, located on the same campus where as a high school girl she had first dreamed of being a nun. She died there at the age of 92.

SENIOR CITIZEN CLUB PRESIDENT AT 90:
ANN JORDAN

*A*lthough senior citizen clubs are available in virtually every town and neigh-borhood in the country, provide a wide range of activities, and enroll hundreds of thousands of older men and women, very few of the active nonagenari-ans expressed any interest in them. *In fact, besides Ann Jordan, who is the leader of her local club, only three of the people interviewed participate—Sheila McGuth, Chapman O'Connor, and Rose Roubian. Most of the others expressed no interest, insisting that they were too busy or that they didn't really identify with the people who belong to clubs. Nevertheless, the clubs are an important dimension of the lives of many older people.*

About twenty years ago, my research for a Ph.D. in Sociology at St. John's University involved interviewing members of several senior citizen clubs on Long Island. The resulting dissertation, "Senior Citizen: A Study in Competence," was an effort to measure the impact of club participation on the lives of members. In particular, did club participation contribute to "successful aging?" Successful aging was defined in terms of the concept **competence** *which was viewed as having three dimensions:*

l) **Competence** *as* **effective social-role performance***. In America, the aged are vulnerable to being labeled as incompetent because, in general, work and family roles have ended. The objective was to determine what social roles senior citizens held and how well they perceived themselves as performing them.*

2) **Competence** *as* **ability to cope***. This psychological view of competence focused on the mechanisms and processes used to deal with problems and new situations. Senior citizen coping styles, the ability to use a variety of resources, and effective reality testing were explored.*

3) **Competence** *as* **experienced mastery***. Finally, feelings of personal power, of the ability to influence one's environment, and of self-determination are characteristic of the competent person. Did club members feel that they had control of their destiny, that their actions influenced what happened to them?*

In the interviews conducted two decades ago, it was found that the club members were indeed competent. However, it proved impossible to establish whether competent people tended to join clubs or whether it was the clubs that instilled or enhanced competence.

While listening to the words of Mrs. Jordan and other nonagenarians, these facets of competence might be kept in mind.

By coincidence, the club of which Ann Jordan is now president was one of those included in my study twenty years ago. Mrs. Jordan, at the time 70 years old, was already a member of the club and knew the people whom I interviewed, all of whom are now deceased.

Mrs. Jordan's older sister, Marie, also a club member, was present and participated in the interview. She seemed to be as lively and active as her sister, although she has not taken on leadership roles or developed the range of interests that characterizes her "baby sister."

At 90 I'm the baby of the family. Marie is a year older and we have a sister, 93, who lives in Florida with her husband. He's 94.

Marie lives just a mile from here in the house where our parents spent their final years. Marie never married and took care of Mom and Dad. I lived here in my own house with my husband who died about 10 years ago. My sister and I spend a lot of time together but prefer to live alone. She has her ways and I have mine. Both of us have drivers licenses and cars, although I only drive occasionally to keep in practice. Usually people pick me up for meetings.

Look at all the pictures I have of myself, especially as a bowler. I've been bowling for about fifty years and have gone to many bowling conventions all over the country. I still bowl regularly.

Three weeks ago I had a fall at a senior citizen club meeting and hit my head and knee. You should have seen the black eye! I didn't bother going to the doctor, but a few days later my informally adopted son, Ronnie, insisted that I go, just to be sure. The x-ray showed that I had a cracked kneecap. My son asked the orthopedist if it was all right for me to bowl. The doctor advised against it but then asked me if I had bowled since I fell. When I said that I had, he threw up his hands and said, "Go ahead!" It wasn't the knee I have to bend when releasing the bowling ball.

Other pictures are of my installation as president of the Senior Citizen Club at St. Joseph's Church. I've been a member for more than thirty years and president for almost twenty. No one else wants the job. I conduct the meetings, making sure that the hall where we gather is in order and that new members are welcomed. I plan club activities, such as arranging for luncheons in restaurants. Next month we are going on a five-day trip upstate. There are lots of details, although I appoint people to take care of the kitchen and to make sure the coffee is made. We have a membership of 135 but only 70 or 80 come to any given meeting.

Sometimes someone will call and ask me, "How can I get my mother to be more active?" I tell the son or daughter to bring her to the meeting and that I will introduce her to the people at the different tables. Usually they feel right at home. If a man comes, I say, "See all these ladies? You can have your pick!"

We were born in the Bronx but moved to Maspeth, Queens, when we were children and attended the local Catholic school. Our parents were immigrants from Switzerland. They had been sweethearts over there. First my father came to America, and when he had the money saved he sent for my mother. Father was a cabinetmaker. Mother made all our clothes and cared for the vegetable garden. She even went up on the roof and painted the house.

We didn't go to high school. I remember my sister and I working in Woolworth's on Saturday afternoons to make fifty cents for spending money and in a doctor's office counting pills. Later I went to business school and became a secretary. I worked for a New York City utility company for thirty-five years, even after moving out here to Long Island.

Since neither my sister or I had children, we worked as secretaries continuously throughout our lives. Marie cared for our sick mother for six years and then for our father for twenty more. She worked in a local real estate office and could go home for lunch with father.

I was 24 when I married John Jordan. He worked for the Gulf Refining Company in Brooklyn, and when we moved out here he became a school custodian. John belonged to the club also and was very skilled in marquetry. His work was displayed all over and some of it decorates the walls of my house here.

Although I have no children, a very interesting thing happened about twenty years ago. My husband and I met a young man in church who sort of adopted me as his mother, and his children adopted me as their grandmother. He stops by almost every day. He keeps telling me to slow down and to drink lots of water. *[The "adopted son," Ronnie, came in while we were talking and joined the conversation. It is obvious that he is an important part of Mrs. Jordan's "safety net."]*

For my 90th birthday, my family and friends threw a big party at the Marriott Hotel. To me, 90 is just a number. It doesn't make me feel any older. *[Marie interjected, "When anyone asks me how old I am I answer, 'My baby sister is 90.'"]*

I've always been active in politics and am a committee woman for the Republican Party. Our present county executive used a picture of me with him in his campaign literature last year. At church, I'm on the council and am a member of the Catholic Daughters. I go to Mass but am not overly religious.

I have no health problems and don't see a doctor regularly. Once when I was feeling dizzy, I did go and asked the doctor what caused it. He said, "I really don't know. Good-bye." Ronnie, here, is my doctor. He is always after me to take care of myself.

For the few years that my husband was sick before he died, I was somewhat limited in what I could do, but I didn't let it stop me. It was awful losing him, but as my mother used to say, "You have to live with the living."

Marie and I are happy in what we are doing. We don't worry. We play cards. When she comes here, out come the cards. When I go over there, out come the cards. If we go to a meeting and we don't like what they are doing, we play cards.

When people ask me how I keep going I say to them, "If you have a rocking chair, don't sit in it. Just keep going."

At age 92, Ann Jordan was still active in the Senior Citizen club but was written up in local newspapers because she had enrolled as a freshman at Dowling College on Long Island. Although taking history and creative writing classes, she was quoted as saying that what she most enjoyed was bowling. At Dowling, she was named honorary captain of the college's bowling team.

ENJOYING SECOND MARRIAGES:
JACOB (99) & RETA (91) LASKY

*F*lorida is the
*prototypical
retirement world
with 17.7% of its
population over age
65. Not only is this
the highest rate of
any state in the
nation, but with the
continuing movement
of older people to
the Sun Belt, the
projections are that
the graying of Florida
will continue to
outstrip that of the
country as a whole.
The Internal
Revenue Service, which tracks population movements by the addresses on
income tax returns, reports that from the mid-1980's the number of people
moving from the Northeast to Florida increased each year. It is the lure of
the warm weather, of course, but also of the lower taxes and less costly
housing. In January 1993,* The New York Times *analyzed the living
costs of two hypothetical couples moving to Florida from New York. One
couple with a retirement income of $112,000 could purchase for $95,000
a home in Florida that was equivalent to their $300,000 house in New*

York. The couple saved nearly $20,000 per year by making the move. The other couple with a more modest income of $24,000 could save nearly $5,000 by relocating. The savings could be invested in an improved standard of living.

Understandably, most of the nonagenarians interviewed in Florida are former Northerners. However, since they are so old, they moved to the Sunshine State decades ago. They represent a wide range of income levels and housing arrangements, from a luxury Palm Beach apartment to a modest mobile home in St. Petersburg. Even the retirement communities reflect that diversity with some people living in modest buildings with few amenities, while others enjoy breathtaking water views in park-like settings. The Laskys live in the Century Village development in Boca Raton, which is aimed at the middle range of the retirement population, with comfortable apartments and a variety of community services but without the design features that would signal affluence.

Jacob Lasky: I was born 99 years ago in Elizabeth, New Jersey. I don't have a birth certificate but my World War I discharge papers give my date of birth. We live in a very warm and loving house here which has a monthly residents' meeting. Well, ever since I was 90 years old, the month of February has been dedicated to me. Recently, when I turned 99 all the residents signed this poster, which has photos of me at different stages of life from my baby picture to my wedding to my 75th birthday party to last year.

There are approximately 10,000 residents of Century Village, all of them over age 55. There are five four-story buildings in our section and each building has seventy-two apartments. Most of us have lived here many years and, since we meet regularly, tend to know everyone.

Without my advice or consent, when I was less than a year old my family moved to London, England. My father had a brother there who wanted my father to join him in manufacturing caps. Apparently they didn't get along because after three years my family moved to Liverpool where we stayed for seven years and then returned to the U.S. I was the first born, but by the time we came back there were six children.

I started school in Bayonne, New Jersey, but when I was fifteen we moved to Newark. Three more children were born there, so we were nine in all. There are only four of us left. We're all old; the youngest is close to 90.

I'm a dropout. The high school in Newark was so large that I got lost there and, since there were nine of us, I decided to go to work. After working in odd jobs for a few years, I got the wanderlust and took a trip to California. When I came back, my brother asked me to go into the printing business with him. Well, I settled down and worked in that business for 40 years, retiring at age 63.

Reta Lasky: I am eight years younger than Jacob, only 91. I was born in Philadelphia where I remained through college at the University of Pennsylvania. After college I married my first husband. You see, this is a second marriage for both Jack and myself. We were both widowed. Most of my life with my first husband was spent in New Jersey. I was a social worker with a graduate degree from the New York School, which is now the Columbia School of Social Work. I had two sons. Jack had one. We go north twice a year to visit family, and when they can, they come here. The grandchildren, who are adults now, come more frequently than do our children.

Jacob and I knew each other since the 1930's; we lived in the same area of New Jersey, but we are married to each other only twenty years.

Jacob: I was 79 when I proposed to this lady.

Reta: My first husband and I had vacationed for many years in the Florida Keys and moved to Miami Beach in 1966. The congregation of one of the synagogues there decided that they wanted to have a professional, rather than the rabbi, do the counseling, so I worked for several years until my husband got sick and I had to give it up.

Jacob: She's still counseling people, although not for money. Sometimes they don't even know her background, but they know she is a good listener and a wise counselor.

Reta: Jack and I moved here from Miami Beach about a dozen years ago when this building was new. A man named Levy had the idea that he would like to create what he called "a way of life for senior citizens." So he developed Century Villages, the first one in West Palm

Beach, the second in Deerfield Beach, and this is the third. There's a fourth in Pembroke Pines.

Jacob: He sold a lifestyle.

Reta: We have a very active community here. There are indoor and outdoor Olympic-size pools as well as the smaller ones in each area. There is a gym. Almost every night there is entertainment in the club house. Much of it is not of interest to us, but there is a monthly chamber music series that is very good. There are movies. Tonight we are going to see "Unforgiven" for fifty cents!

In addition to that, there is a marvelous program for older people at Florida Atlantic University. They call it the Lifelong Learning Program for Senior Citizens. It has developed to the point where they are raising money to build their own center at the university. About 10,000 people participate. Jack and I have taken courses in oceanography, Highlights of History, and physiology. By myself I am taking an ongoing course in sociology. Recently we were discussing gender and the issue of gays in the military. Earlier we had done a study of retirement and the ghettoizing of older citizens. Personally, I feel it is all right to live here, but it's necessary to get away from the ghetto and mix with the broader community.

Jacob: I have stopped taking the courses because I was falling asleep in class. I find I am getting tired and have to take a nap frequently. Also, the medication I take for an enlarged prostate, Proscar, makes me sleepy. If I was twenty years younger they might operate, but I have a heart valve situation also. I feel OK but behave myself. I do what they tell me. I've slowed down in the past few years.

When I was 92, I turned in my driver's license. Apparently they appreciated it because they sent me a congratulatory letter. Also at 92 I stopped playing golf.

Reta: I can't drive anymore either. I have macular degeneration. But Century Village has a transportation system and also there are a number of men here who get restless and like to earn a little extra money, so they drive for a fee.

Except for my eyes, I don't have any physical problems. My mother lived to be 93 and was playing bridge almost to the end of her life.

In the final months she had to be in a nursing home. Her only complaint was that the people were so old!

For years we attended the Chautauqua program in upstate New York. It's the great granddaddy of Elderhostel in which we participated also. Chautauqua is a nine-week program and each week has its own topic. They bring experts from all over the world. In addition, Chautauqua has its own resident symphony orchestra, an opera company, and a ballet company. But there's a rich cultural life right here in Boca Raton, including the marvelous symphony orchestra. For the opera, we go to Miami on the bus.

I take a yoga class three times a week. It's the most invigorating thing I could possibly do. After the hour of yoga, I come back so relaxed.

Jacob: Now she's lifting weights also. It's beginning to worry me!

Reta: Well, it's that I found some of the yoga positions required more strength in my arms than I had so it was recommended that I lift weights. Now, before the class I spend a half hour in the gym. My arms definitely have gotten stronger.

Jacob: I was a mountain climber in my youth. This is a picture of me after I climbed Mt. Ranier. Now I do calisthenics every day. You have to to keep limber.

Reta: I'm active in several community groups. You can see that I have worked out activities which I do by myself, as well as others which Jack and I do together. Even in the apartment we have room for privacy and separateness. We use the second bedroom as a workroom where one of us can be alone when that's needed.

Jacob: Being old is OK until people find out your age. I used to play in a foursome. We never talked about age. Then one day the topic of age came up, and I told them that I was 90. Well, on the next hole, after I had putted and it went into the hole, they wouldn't allow me to pick up the ball. They pushed me away and insisted that one of them get it. And one guy took my arm to help me down to the next hole. When I go out today, people take my arm. I don't mind. It makes them feel good. They don't want me to trip or anything.

Reta: There are a lot of people in their sixties here. They jog, play

tennis, skate. In a community like this, they are "the younger generation" and people like Jack and I are "the older generation." We're the
elder citizens in this house.

Jacob: Sometimes I can use my age to advantage. When people call
on the phone trying to sell something, I tell them that I am over 90
and wouldn't be interested. Once I got a call and was about to use the
same story when the guy said that he represented a funeral parlor!

Reta: Actually, we have been looking at total care communities.
There are several in Boca. The apartments are lovely and a range of
health services are available. Here there is nothing like that. If we
needed nursing care, we would have to move. Marriott is building
such a facility, and we are waiting to receive information. We've very
comfortable here, but there is that question: If something were to happen, where would we go?

Jacob: But you have to keep in mind that the people in the house
are already talking about a big party for my 100th birthday. Willard
Scott on NBC television each morning mentions the birthdays of people who are 104, 107. It's encouraging!

*A few months after the interview, Reta Lasky wrote to say that "Jack did
not quite reach the century point. He died quietly, peacefully at home." In a
letter eight months later she wrote, "I have been putting the pieces of my life
together again. I have returned to my former activities and shared in some
joyous family occasions."*

HARD PHYSICAL WORK AT 92:
MAGNUS A. LUNDSTROM

*M*any of the active nonagenarians are immigrants and others are the children of immigrants. They come from Ireland, Italy, Russia, Germany and, in the case of Magnus Lundstrom, Sweden. This should not be surprising once it is recalled that in the later part of the last century and in the early decades of the present century, millions of people came from Europe in one of the greatest migrations in the history of the world. The story of the various waves of immigrants has been told over and over again. Images of poor, frightened people being processed at Ellis Island in the shadow of the Statue of Liberty and within sight of the fabled New York City skyline are part of the folklore of the nation.

It is generally agreed that the development of the United States into a world power could not have been accomplished without this influx of young, energetic people. Some brought professional skills, such as Giuseppe Maltese, one of the nonagenarians who arrived from Italy a trained physi-

cian and was of great value to the Italian immigrant community. Joe Mishkin came from Russia with a good educational foundation and became a prosperous pharmacist. Tonio Selwart arrived from Germany a highly regarded actor and soon became a leading man on the Broadway stage. Lena Wulf also arrived from Germany with a good education and became a physical therapist.

However, the majority of the immigrants brought little more than strong bodies and a determination to succeed, even if that meant working long hours at low wages in menial tasks. So, Frank Regan, who came from Ireland, went to work in an automobile manufacturing plant, and Sheila McGuth, also from Ireland, went into domestic service. That was a long time ago for these nonagenarians, but they look at their children and grandchildren who are solid middle class Americans and have no regrets about the great adventure of their youth—leaving their native land and starting a new life in America.

Magnus Lundstrom is a prototypical immigrant, a man of great physical strength and even greater determination to succeed. At 92, speaking with a pronounced Scandinavian accent, he relives with enthusiasm the story of his long career. If it is said metaphorically that the immigrants built this country, then it is true literally in the case of Lundstrom, who for half a century was a home builder on Long Island, New York. He made it a point to give me a yellowed business card which read, "M. Lundstrom, Builder and General Contractor."

I feel fine, although I had a real scare in the spring. A truckload of topsoil was delivered to the house for use in building a flower garden. I shoveled the soil into a wheelbarrow and pushed it back to where it was needed. Well, I put some of the dirt into a five gallon pail, and when I went to lift it, there was this terrible pain in my back. At first I said that I wouldn't let it stop me, so I lifted it again, but the pain was too great. I couldn't bend over. In fact, I went to the doctor in my pajamas because I couldn't dress properly. He x-rayed me and said that I had damaged three vertebrae. I said to him, "I guess I'll be crippled for the rest of my life." He said no, that I should be OK again in a few weeks. But it took longer, almost three months. But I have no pain now.

Magnus A. Lundstrom

I was born in a small town in Sweden 92 years ago. My father was the strongest man I ever met. He could pick up two men by their hair and bang their heads together. When he took off his shirt, his muscles rippled over his whole body. He was a partner in a local brewery, which made deliveries with a team of horses but eventually switched to trucks. The partnership had problems. As my daddy said, "Partnership is the poorest ship you sail."

I had three brothers and four sisters. All my brothers are dead. The oldest had a big farm in Sweden, was never sick, and died at the age of 87. One of my sisters is still alive. She's two years younger than me and was living by herself out in the woods in Sweden. Her son lived about 100 miles to the south and was very concerned. He said, "Mom, I can't come up here and look after you. Sell the house and come live near me." Well, those old Swedes are stubborn. Once they have a home, they don't want to sell it. But finally, she did move and now lives in beautiful housing built just for senior citizens.

Once I left Sweden, aside from a brief visit after seven years, I didn't see my family again for fifty-three years. I was sailing the oceans and making a new life for myself to the extent that I almost forgot my family.

In high school I learned carpentry and then went to work. I built many things, including the complete harness and yoke for a horse. This woodcarving here represents me at age 14 with the horse equipped with the tackle which I had made. I was very good with wood.

When I was 21, I left Sweden because there was no future there for me. I had been working as a deck hand on my uncle Victor's boat, but it didn't pay much. He liked me and offered to send me to school to be a seaman. He said that in time I could work my way up to be a first mate. But I was young and impatient. I felt I would be old before I would make any money, so I left for America.

I always heard about the United States although I had no one here. I worked my way on a ship and, after one return trip to Europe, I landed in Baltimore where I jumped ship. This was risky business because the police raided the bars where the guys went at night and arrested those who were illegal. I went on to New Orleans where developers were building houses. There I met a Frenchman who had a business making windows and doors. I had no money but asked if he would sell me the business. He agreed. I left a small down payment and went to work in order to make the rest of the money. I took a boat up river and worked at crushing rocks, dirty work. The dust was always like a cloud around us. I made good money at that but twice as much by selling bright colored shirts to the black people. I would buy the shirts for $0.75 cents in New Orleans and get $3 or $4 for them up river.

In time, I saved enough money and bought the business which I improved substantially. Everything was going well until one day a policeman came and asked to see my papers. That was it. They shipped me back to Europe. That was the worst thing that happened in my life. I was 29 years old by then. I worked in Holland for nearly a year until I got the papers to return legally to the United States, where I had left everything.

When I arrived back in New Orleans, I found that the bank had taken all my property. The man whom I had left in charge had disappeared. I was 30 years old and had a darn good start, but now it was all gone.

I was so discouraged that I started drinking night and day. Every bartender knew me. As long as I had money, I was well liked. I was treating everybody. But then the money ran out. I was sick and decided that I couldn't keep that up or I would drink myself to death.

Pulling myself together, I got a job pumping oil on a rig off Venezuela. All we had to eat was oatmeal and water. It was so hot that we slept on the open deck and when we woke up in the morning there was a pool of water around our bodies. I did two three-month periods out there, but the third time out I got malaria and was taken to a hospital in New Orleans. It was bad. They kept pumping out my blood and it was black as tar. The doctor said, "You have a strong constitution. When they brought you in here, I never thought you would live."

It was then that I moved North and have lived here ever since. At first I worked as an estimator for a cabinetmaker in Brooklyn. I brought in so much work that the boss couldn't handle it all.

In less than a year I moved out here to Islip, Long Island. For a time, I worked for builders to learn the business in this area. Although I had some good job offers, I was determined to have my own business. Well, I became a builder and general contractor and worked at it for half a century. I built my own house and worked out of an office there. All my houses were built with the best materials and great care. The town inspectors were happy when I had a job because they knew it would be done right.

I was always looking for a woman who was smart and strong. When I was 42 years old, I finally found her. A plumber working for me told me about this woman with three sons whose husband had died suddenly. I married her, and we raised her three boys but didn't have any children of our own.

My wife died fifteen years ago and two of my stepsons have died also. The one who survived lives not far from here and is very good to me. About ten years ago, I signed over my house to one of his sons and his wife. The agreement was that I could live there as long as I wanted to. It didn't work out, so after staying a while with my stepson I found this place and have been very happy.

I saw an ad in the newspaper, "Room for rent." I called and the woman said they really wanted a woman, but she invited me to look at it. We hit it off. I've been here for nine years now and they treat me like one of the family. There are two school-age girls who consider me their grandfather. I have my own bedroom, but full use of the house and I have taken responsibility for the garden.

I thought I could do anything. All my life I have been physically active. When I hurt my back, I learned that I can no longer do everything. I was thinking that I was twenty years younger and much stronger than I am. But my health is good and I don't see a doctor about anything.

While working on my own, I never declared my income and accumulated no Social Security credits. But I did work in Washington as foreman on a construction job for several years during World War II and that's how I earned enough credits to qualify.

I have some good friends. Although there's a local Senior Citizens

Club, a few of us have formed our own informal club. Every Wednesday we get together for a pancake breakfast. A man across the street takes me out at least twice a week. We go to the club or to a restaurant. He saves my life.

I wish I could take you on a trip around this area to show you all the houses that I built. Also, about twenty years ago I built the Church of the Nazarene from the ground up. I did it with volunteer help from the church. It was difficult. You couldn't count on people. Some days it would be just one other man and me. It took three years, but we finished it. I always finished what I started.

ATTENDING DAILY MASS AT 90:
SHEILA McGUTH

The risk of a hip fracture increases dramatically with age, especially for females. After age 50, the rate for women is double that of men and it is estimated that, by age 90, one in three women will have sustained a hip fracture. The cause is osteoporosis or bone loss which occurs with age, especially in post menopausal women. Several things can be done to lessen the risk. The Johns Hopkins Medical Letter "Health After 50" urges menopausal women to consider hormone replacement therapy (HRT). In addition to alleviating hot flashes and vaginal dryness, HRT offers the long-term advantages of preventing bone loss and of providing protection against heart disease. The earlier a menopausal woman begins HRT, the more it will help her.

Exercise programs also are recommended, compensating for the more sedentary lifestyle of most people today. Studies show that weight-bearing exercise not only builds bone but also increases muscle mass, which can protect against fractures by absorbing the shock of a fall. Even women in their 80's can stem bone loss by regular exercise. Helpful activities include walking, cycling, aquatic aerobics, dancing, stair climbing, weight training, and treadmill exercises.

Still other preventive measures include minimizing risks in the home, such as improving lighting and installing grab bars at the toilet and tub or shower. Also, attention should be paid to a nutritious diet, especially adequate amounts of calcium and vitamin D.

Many aged women who are managing very well, find their lives abruptly changed by a fall. Although frequently modern medicinal procedures can restore the hip fracture victim to near normal living, as in the case of Sheila McGuth, a long, costly, and worrisome period of rehabilitation may be required.

I was born in County Kerry, Ireland. Next month I will be 91 years old. All I had was a grade school education, which wasn't at all unusual at the time. We were poor; my father died young and I was needed on the farm. We all worked hard but seemed to accomplish very little.

At age 18 I boarded a ship and came to New York, where two brothers and a sister had preceded me. Two other sisters and a brother remained in Ireland. It was what all the families were doing. The farms were small and the families large.

Long life runs in my family. My mother lived to be 91 and my older brother died at 90 a couple of years ago. Another brother lived very close to 90. Others were in their 80's. My older sister is 93. She lived in her own home here in New York until two years ago when she moved to New Jersey to be with her daughter. She was unhappy about leaving her house but she had trouble with her hearing.

For ten years I worked for several wealthy American families as a domestic, cooking and doing whatever I had to do. There were many of us in service in those days. We lived with the families for whom we worked, and so although we were not paid very much, we were safe and taken care of.

When I was 28, I married an American-born man of German descent. We lived on West 108th Street in Manhattan until we bought this house in Queens. That was 50 years ago now. At the time, this area was being developed. Row after row of attached brick houses were constructed and sold very reasonably. The lots are only 20 by 100, but there are three bedrooms upstairs and a nice garden in front and back. The neighborhood has not changed that much and I have no thought of moving.

My husband drove a delivery truck for Horn and Hardardt, a restaurant chain noted for its automats. Shortly after our marriage I had a daughter, but she died at birth. I went back to work for a time and then our son, who's now 58, was born. I stayed home with him until he finished school then went to work as a lunch room attendant in a public school. Unfortunately, my husband got sick and for two years was in and out of the hospital. There was no Blue Cross and whatever money we had was soon gone. He died on our 30th wedding anniversary. So I was married for 30 years and now for more than 30 years have been a widow.

Since I was already working in the lunch room, I just kept on working until I was 70. My husband had no insurance or benefits. It was difficult. We had a car, but when he died I sold it. Somehow we managed. My son went to college and then had a 28-year career in the Air Force. I visited him in each place that he was stationed, all over the country. He's married and lives near Washington, D.C. He and his wife had no children. I would like to be a grandmother, but it wasn't meant to be.

My son is mad because I don't come down to visit him, but my cat, Tabby, is old and I don't like to leave him. *[The cat died a few months later. Mrs. McGuth was heartbroken for a time but got over the loss.]*

I worked hard but took care of myself. Good plain food and enough sleep are important. Besides taking some vitamins when I think of it, I am not on medicine of any kind.

The only setback I have had was when I fell down the stairs here a year ago and broke my hip. The man next door came in and found me. The doctor said that I had very fast-healing bones and was strong. I was in the hospital just a few days and had someone come in to the house for about a month until I was able to manage by myself again. When I go out, I use a cane but don't need it around the house or going across the street to church.

Everybody says that I don't look as old as I am, but what good is that? You're here and you hang in. I'm very independent. No one comes in to help me. The boy next door does the lawn and shovels the snow. If it's raining, neighbors will bring me things from the store, but usually I can go myself and bring groceries in my shopping cart. This is a wonderful neighborhood. I know so many people and we watch out for one another.

My son wants me to come and live with them, but it would be very hard. Old people don't make friends as easily as young people. My life has been here. Everything is convenient and there is always something going on at church. Most mornings I attend Mass and always meet some friends. I belong to the Golden Age Club and Rosary Society at church and work on the card parties and flea markets. I look out my living room window here and see the church and parochial school which my son attended. There are many memories attached to the church. It has always been the center of my social life as well as of my religion.

I haven't noticed any change in myself from age 70 to 90, besides breaking my hip. When I go to the bank, I take a cane. You're old! So, what the heck! I come from a healthy family. I have a friend who is 85, but she is always complaining. She's stiffened up and stays in the house. Now she has pains in her elbows because she doesn't move enough. I don't do any exercise as such. Walking and housework are enough.

A long time ago I signed the house over to my son. He pays the taxes and the water bill. I take care of the telephone and other things myself. For instance, a couple of years ago I had new windows installed. My only income is from Social Security, since neither my husband nor I had a pension and I never could save much. But I have enough.

I do a lot of crocheting—afghans. I make lap robes for the people in the nursing home. Some of those in wheel chairs are not dressed that well, so when they go downstairs they can use the lap robes. Also, when a baby is coming, I make a carriage blanket.

As soon as I could, I became a citizen and vote regularly. I follow politics in the newspapers. Clinton says he's going to do this and that. Where is he going to get the money? You can be sure it will be from higher taxes.

I talk on the phone, have people in, meet the girls, watch the Mets on television. You have to keep busy. You can't feel sorry for yourself. Sometimes on long winter evenings I feel lonely, but in the summer time it's not bad because you can be outside more. I think: I'm here and have to keep going.

PHYSICIAN AND OPERA-GOER AT 94:
GIUSEPPE MALTESE, M.D.

*W*ith rising life expectancy, it is projected that one out of every five marriages will survive to celebrate a 50th wedding anniversary. A number of the active nonagenarians have had that experience, several having moved beyond the 60th anniversary. Nevertheless, the majority of nonagenarians are widowed. In the present study, eight of the men are married and thirteen widowed. Of the women, four are married (all to other nonagenarians), fourteen are widows, and three never married.

Numerous studies have established a relationship between marital status, life satisfaction, and longevity. On average, married people are happier and live longer than their single, widowed, or divorced counterparts.

With marriage so important, how do widowed nonagenarians cope with the loss of a spouse? One might read the interviews with special attention to this question. And as is true in other aspects of life, great diversity will be found. However, women tend to have more social skills than men, equipping them to move smoothly into informal social networks, *that is, groups of friends who provide much of the support and companionship lost through widowhood.*

Widowers, on the other hand, are more vulnerable to isolation and loneliness and even, stereotypically, to be unable to take care of basic needs, such as meal preparation and laundry. Fortunately for men, they have a much greater likelihood of finding a new partner than do women. Of those people age 75 or older, 70 % of men but only 22 % of women still have a spouse, meaning that there are more than twice as many widowed women as men.

Of special interest might be the experience of those nonagenarians who have developed a close non-marital relationship with someone of the opposite sex. One of the women and three of the men have such relationships. Evelyn Golbe has a gentleman friend for whom she provides wife-like services, including altering his clothes. Orville Davis and Joe Mishkin maintain close relationships with women as does Giuseppe Maltese, the subject of the present interview. Marriage is not found to be necessary for any of these nonagenarians. All have separate homes from their companions but spend a considerable amount of time together and insist that the relationship is a major source of life satisfaction.

I am 94 years old and a physician. I still see a few patients but don't go to the hospital anymore. It's too strenuous. Actually, I discontinued my practice about a year ago. My daughters didn't want me to work anymore. I see patients because they want me to attend them but I don't take any money. They are friends.

I was born in Sicily. My father was a "sculpalino." In Italy there are many old churches and monuments. My father's job was to replace the decaying stones. He would take out the old ones and make new ones that were identical. He was very talented but not able to make much money.

When my oldest sister got married, she needed a dowry. Father borrowed the money and then went to the United States in order to work to repay the loan. In two months here, he was able to make all the money he needed, whereas back in Italy he could never do it. Anyway, once here, he decided to stay and brought my mother over also. I was about 14 at the time and remained in Italy to complete my education. The teachers wanted me to stay there because I was a good student.

All my education was in Italy, including my medical training. Also, after my mother left for America, World War I broke out and I had to serve in the Italian army. Even so, I was a licensed physician at the age of 22. I had been able to complete the six years of elementary school in four years and the five years of high school in four.

It was always my intention to follow my family to America and I did so when I was 23 years old. Shortly after arriving in New York I passed the basic English exam, and four months after that I passed the tests of the State University of New York and was licensed to practice medicine.

I settled in Brooklyn, living for many years on Montrose Avenue, Williamsburgh. Eventually I bought a house in Forest Hills, one of the best places in the United States. We lived there until I was 63 years old when the stress of working just knocked me out. Three times I collapsed in my office from fatigue. I was making fifteen, twenty house calls a day—up and down three and four flights of stairs in those Brooklyn houses. I just couldn't continue. I said to myself that if I kept that up, I would go to an early grave. So, I sold everything and moved here to Long Island. My wife's sister lived nearby and found the house for us.

Since I was already in my sixties and we had enough money, I retired and thought that I would just take care of my roses for the rest of my life. Well, as it turned out I was to practice medicine for another thirty years. People started to come so I opened an office downstairs and started my practice again.

I never took much money from people, $10, $15. I know that they charge much more but money wasn't important to me. And I would spend time with people. I was more like a counselor. I don't know how many marriages I saved telling husbands to be nice to their wives.

I love books and have thousands of them. I just finished the new life of Jackie Kennedy. And I'm always reading a volume of Dante in Italian and can recite by heart many passages from the *Divine Comedy*. At times I stay up until three in the morning reading.

Opera is a passion. For several years I took singing lessons and love to sing arias, not in public, but at home. *[Dr. Maltese sang one for me in a rich, strong voice.]* I have a thousand recordings of classical music. These antique vases were collected over the course of some sixty years. I love beauty. Some of these paintings are very old. One of them I bought for $0.75. Recently it was appraised for $1,000.

My life is not like that of other people. If you interview people my age, you won't find many like me. I travel. A few months ago, I went to Quebec with my daughter who lives in Maine. I take a lot of pictures. Here are boxes of slides from recent trips to Florida and Las Vegas. I drive and take care of my own affairs.

The woman I married had been born in a town near me in Sicily, but I didn't know her over there. She came here as a child. We had two daughters, both of whom are married and have children. My wife died on New Year's Day twelve years ago. Here are pictures of her when she was young, beautiful. And here is a picture of us on our fiftieth wedding anniversary.

A very nice lady is my closest friend now. She is about 58 years old and has a doctorate in education. When my brother-in-law was president of the local school board, he got her a job in the district. We see each other every day and have dinner together. This evening we are going to a party. She has her privacy and I have mine, but we do many things together. It gives me joy having her and sharing so many experiences.

I brought my grandmother here from Sicily when she was 87 years old, and she lived until she was 99 and a half. That's why I'm 94! Also, since childhood I have eaten very little. My stomach is small and I don't get hungry. I used to work for two or three days without eating. My wife would have to call me to eat. I have no desire for food. Another thing is that when I was working in Brooklyn, I'd be going up and down stairs all day long. Today people are out jogging. House calls was my jogging and I didn't know it!

I'm a Catholic. All Italians are Catholic. When I was a kid, you couldn't get inside the church it was so crowded. Later, when I visited Italy, I would attend church with the woman with whom I stayed. The church was empty. It's all over. Religion is not felt anymore. Aside from close-knit sects, people are not religious today. Nevertheless, I think that religion is necessary. If people would think about burning in hell, like in Dante's *Inferno*, they wouldn't do so many bad things.

The last time I was to Italy was three or four years ago, but I don't plan to go again. All my friends are dead and their wives are dead. I correspond with their children, but they are a different generation.

People afraid of death are stupid. Everyone has to die. Sometimes death is a liberation. When I was a kid, I had an aunt who was a nun. When she would visit dying people she would have them say, "Jesus, Mary and Joseph, I give you my heart and my soul."

DAILY GOLFER AT 94:
JOE MISHKIN

*M**any of the responses to my "Author's Query" in* The New York Times *came from friends and relatives who "nominated" nonagenarians for the book. I was always curious to see if the glowing account of vitality given in the letter was matched by what I experienced in the subsequent interview. The letter on behalf of Joe Mishkin of Miami, Florida, is a good example of what people wrote.*

"Joe, age 92, my Mom's 'boyfriend,' plays golf every day, volunteers time at a hospital pharmacy on weekends, and recently leased a new car because: 'Why buy when you know you're going to be trading it in in three years?'

"My mother and he travel extensively. They're going to Israel to attend a family wedding in early November, then flying to California to spend Thanksgiving with his daughter, followed by two weeks at a Mexican spa after the New Year and, well, I'm getting exhausted thinking of it all.

"What's more, Joe has a vibrant personality, a delightful sense of

---

humor, and is a kind and loving companion to my 78-year-old mother.

"Personally, I can't imagine a book on active nonagenarians that doesn't include Joe."

It was six months after receiving this letter that I was able to interview Joe Mishkin and meet his "girlfriend." I was concerned that perhaps during the intervening period he might have had a setback. What I found was that not only was he still going strong and had taken all the trips mentioned in the letter, but that, rather than 92 years old he was but a month shy of 95.

I was born in Minsk, Byelorus, which later became part of the Soviet Union. Since I was Jewish, I had to wait two years to be accepted into the gymnasium, the equivalent of high school here. There was a quota: only 10% of the students could be Jewish. So all the gentiles were admitted first. While I was waiting, my uncle visited us from America and suggested that I go to America for my education and then return to Europe. I liked the idea, but my father, who was a prosperous pharmacist, objected. Druggists didn't send their children to America; that was the workers, the poorer people. However, I begged him and was allowed to go. I arrived here at the age of 16.

My family remained in Europe. During the Russian Revolution, they took away my father's business. He died in his sixties. I'm sure it was from a broken heart. My mother lived longer, but the Nazis got ahold of her. When they came into our town, they took my mother, my brother, my sister, my nephew, and they did away with all of them.

During the First World War, I served in the American army and was awarded the Silver Star for bravery and the Croix de Guerre from the French Army. My bravery was that I was continuously repairing telephone lines under heavy shellfire.

After the war, I returned to my studies at the Columbia School of Pharmacy. Not only was my father a pharmacist but so also were my father's brothers. They had done their apprenticeship in my father's drugstore in Europe and then came here.

My career as a pharmacist in New York was very successful. By the time I retired, I owned a dozen stores. In the early years I worked day and night. In fact, when I suggested to my son that he go to pharmacy school, he refused. He saw how I had worked and didn't want to do the same thing.

While I was a student, I had met a beautiful nurse and we got married shortly after I graduated. We had two children. My son, who is now 65, retired as Assistant Dean at the Albert Einstein Medical School. My daughter is 69 and retired also. She was a prominent psychiatric social worker and had taught at Stanford University. My children don't worry about me. They know I can take care of myself.

Let's see. I was 67 or 68 when I sold my business, retired, and moved to Florida. Already, my wife was not feeling well. At first we lived on the Gulf coast, but it was very windy and affected my wife. A doctor recommended the East coast and so we moved over here to Miami. It helped her for a time, but a few years later she passed away.

This is a very nice community. There are 17 six-story buildings, five swimming pools, a golf course, all sorts of facilities. You have to be 55 and no children or pets are permitted. The only trouble with this community now is that not everyone is as fortunate as I am as far as health is concerned. People came here in their sixties when they retired. Now that they are in their eighties, their health is failing. You see many in wheelchairs or with nurses, not able to take care of themselves.

Golf is part of my daily routine. I get up at five-thirty and leave the house at 6:00. I tee off at 7:00 or 7:15, as soon as it's light, play nine holes, and am home by 9:30. It gets too warm after that. I've golfed here so long that they give me a free electric golf cart and don't charge me green fees. Look at this plaque I received several years ago. It says, "Congratulations on making Par 90 when you are 90."

In the summer I don't stay here. It gets too hot. Sometimes I go to the mountains. This year I'm planning to go to North Carolina for June, July, and August.

This lady you met goes with me. I'm very attached to her. We do everything together. Later this month we are going on a Caribbean cruise for ten days. When my wife died, I didn't want to get married again, but I welcomed the companionship. At our age, there's no need to get married. The children are not conservative. They realize that we both need companionship.

We live in our own apartments, but from the moment we get up we are practically always together. The minute I come from golf, I call her up and tell her I'm home. I take my shower and we decide what to do. We have lunch here or at her place. Then I take a nap for an hour or two; I get up so early and get tired. I have to break up the day. But then I'm ready for the rest of the day. We go shopping or to a matinee. Then we get ready to go to dinner, the theatre, the opera, whatever is planned.

People say they can be alone. I can be alone too, but when I go somewhere or do something, I want to have someone with whom to discuss it. Otherwise you come home, you hit the four walls, you don't have anyone to ask, "Did you enjoy the concert?" "What did you think of the play?" I couldn't take that. I'm very fortunate to have someone so compatible. It's an arrangement that means a great deal to both of us.

We're out all the time. Almost every evening we go some place. I have season tickets to the opera and the philharmonic and to the playhouse in Ft. Lauderdale. I drive a car. I think for a man 95 years of age I'm doing pretty well!

Last year, the head of the pharmacy department at Hollywood Memorial Hospital asked me to help out, so I volunteer one day a week. The system is different from when I was a pharmacist. Today they have what is called "dose dispensing" instead of unit dispensing. If the doctor prescribes one teaspoon of cough medicine every four hours, you send up one teaspoon to the nurse. I go in on Saturday and work for five or six hours, as long as they need me.

Besides a little rheumatism in my arms, I don't have any health problems. You know what annoys me? I go to my doctor and I say, "Dr. Silverman, I can't hold my golf club with the strength that I used to." Right away he says, "What do you expect at 95?" When I go to my dentist and complain to him about something, he says, "What do you expect at 95?" I went to my eye doctor. He removed a cataract. Now I have 20/20 vision, but I said to him, "Sometimes at night there's a certain glare when I'm driving." What does he say? "What do you expect at 95?" They never offer any help or suggestions as to how the condition might be improved. I know nothing can be done, and I am grateful, but I'm tired of hearing that line.

I smoked until I was about 48 when I began having trouble with my throat and went to a dear friend of mine, who was an ear, nose, and throat specialist. He looked at my throat, scraped it, and said, "You know, Joe, you haven't got a throat; you've got a chimney." He said I had to give up smoking. I said, "Doctor, I can't give up smoking, because I must have a cigarette in my hand for everything I do. I can't think without one; I can't write without one." He said, "If you can't do without cigarettes, you can do without me. I'm not your doctor anymore." I took him seriously. I threw away a package of cigarettes for which I had paid $0.19. It broke my heart. I suffered for two weeks or so, but I haven't smoked since.

I'm not a drinker but I have a scotch every day, and when we go out to dinner, I have a glass of wine. I don't eat steaks or heavy chops any more. I prefer fish or chicken. I've put on a little weight so have to watch the fat in my diet.

As far as religion is concerned, I'm a freethinker. I'm not religiously inclined. My father was religious, but I wasn't home long enough for it to become part of me. Religion is largely a matter of habit, so to speak.

I don't know why I have lived so long. No one knows why some people have good health and others get sick. A positive attitude helps, no doubt about it. I read; I'm interested in politics. Life has to be meaningful to me. Once I lose interest in things, I might as well close my eyes and call it a day. The only arrangements I've made for the future is that I'll be cremated. I'm ready to go as soon as my mind or my body doesn't work any more.

A year after the interview, Joe Mishkin wrote that he had been in every state except Hawaii and that he was going there the following month—at the age of 96.

COUNSELOR TO YOUNGER WOMEN AT 97:
NIDA NEEL

C ows graze in the pasture
between the road and the
central Connecticut house where
Nida Neel has lived for more than
forty years. Three-foot-thick walls
are reminders that in the eighteenth
century, the building was used as a
fort to protect settlers from Indians.
Ceilings are low and doorways
narrow. What had been a dirt floor
storage area looks incongruous
with modern washer and dryer.

Mrs. Neel, 97 years old,
moved to this farmhouse with her
husband when he retired from his
West Virginia garage business. He
had been one of the earliest auto
mechanics in the Huntington area
and was successful enough to sell
his business and move North to be
closer to a daughter, who lived in New York City. Retirement years were
spent renovating the house and attempting various uses for the rolling
acres, which offered more beauty to the eye than profit to the economy.
Paul Neel died last year at the age of 93.

Nearly every afternoon two or three women come here for tea. The other day one woman drove up, but when she saw two cars here already, she turned around and left and came back the following day. She felt it would be too many people. There are six or seven neighborhood women who like to come. They are old. No, wait! I forget that I am nearly 100. They are in their fifties and sixties. They say that I'm a good listener. Years ago I had thought to go back to school to become a therapist. But I have no training; it just comes naturally. They trust me and share their concerns. It must be helpful; they keep coming.

How did I get to know them? Well, as a little girl, one of them used to play around this old house. She's now married and has a family of her own. She comes at least once a week for tea. She will bring a friend or tell someone about me and that person will just come by on her own. Everyone has a story to tell and if you can listen to that story and appreciate it, well, you've done something important. I can't remember everything they say, but I listen. I'm like a mother confessor. We sit at the table in the kitchen for an hour or so—nothing fancy or special. If I have a hobby, it's people.

This is the oldest house in the area and I guess I'm the oldest person. Several years ago my daughter, Jean, and her husband moved here to be with Paul, my husband and me. They built an annex to the house and so had their own private quarters. They felt that at our age we shouldn't be alone. Well, Paul died last March and just a few months later so did my daughter's husband. And then the dog died. So we've had three losses in the past year. But we are managing just fine.

I was born 97 years ago in Franklin, West Virginia. My birth certificate is in the bank safe deposit box, but I have this book in which my father recorded the birth dates of all the children. I was the oldest of nine, and seven of us are still alive. One sister is failing and in a nursing home, but the rest of us are still busy doing things. My youngest brother is 82 and continues to practice medicine in Franklin.

My father was president of the bank in town, although we lived on a farm. Father was very active in public affairs, serving as a trustee for one of the state normal schools and for many years as Collector of Internal Revenue for the state of West Virginia. Father insisted that all his children have a college education. He started out by sending us to a boarding school. After high school I attended Lewisburg Seminary and Greenbriar Women's College.

My mother was a homemaker but also an avid reader and a devout Christian woman. We were Presbyterians. My grandmother came from Northern Ireland. She and her brother came to teach and to preach to the natives of Virginia. Grandmother lived with us. Queen Victoria was her queen. When I was growing up I used to think that it would be wonderful to have known Queen Victoria, that she must have been a wonderful person. That was a childish thought, but one that has remained with me.

I had wanted to be a nurse, but my father objected. In those days, the profession of nursing was, what shall I say, frowned upon. It didn't have the prestige it holds today. So after college I taught in a district high school. The president of the college received a letter from the principal asking for two graduates to teach, one for music and one for home economics. The president chose me for the home economics position. I can still remember how pleased and proud my father was when the letter came. My father said that if I didn't like it I could then go into nursing but urged me to try it for a year. I did and taught there until I got married when I was 27.

Shortly after I began teaching I met the man who would become my husband. He was just getting ready to go off to World War I and was driving down the road when he saw me and another girl, who also was a teacher. He offered us a ride. It was one of the first cars in town. Well, as Paul used to say, I got into his car and he hasn't been able to get me out since. He went on to the service and I went on teaching.

When he returned he went to business college for two years. It was after that that we got married and went to live in the West Virginia town where Paul had a job helping the president of a coal company. Our first daughter was born in the hospital in the coal fields and our other daughter a few years later in Huntington, West Virginia, where my husband had bought a service station and sold tires. He loved cars.

At that time I used to drive. I drove for my father who had one of the first cars in our little valley. The roads were mud and clay. I was always so happy when a week went by without rain, so that the road wouldn't be mud. I continued driving after I married but gave it up years ago. Paul did all the driving.

I have a deep religious faith and still remember the childhood catechism questions; they were the foundation. "Who made me?" "God made me." "Why did God make me?" The answer to that question was "because He loved me." That answer has been so consoling to me. I then went on to study the Bible. In the seminary, which was a Presbyterian school, we had to have three years of Bible study before we could graduate.

I'm also a believer in Dr. Norman Vincent Peale and his message of positive thinking. My husband and I just didn't feel at home in the little Congregational church here in town, so we soon stopped going. But I listen to the Sunday morning service on TV and every morning I read Dr. Peale's book *Guideposts*.

Although both my husband and I had been raised on farms, neither of us had any experience in farming. Well, when we came here, Paul decided that we would have some sheep. To me it was the most distressing thing in the world to see those sweet little lambs being born and then people coming, sticking one in the back of their car, and taking it away for an Easter feast. I said to Paul, "No more of this." Then Paul decided to get some cattle and goats. That worked out fine, and so we cared for animals for many years. Now we rent the pastures. There are twenty-one head of cattle out there.

Like my mother, I am an avid reader. I enjoy the stories by the veterinarian, James Herriot. They are about England and, since I was never able to travel to other countries, the stories are a way for me to experience people in other countries. And just recently I finished *Mrs. Mike*, an old story about the mounted police in the northern part of our country. Also I read the biography of Mary Baker Eddy, founder of the Christian Scientists. What a fake she was!

I read the newspaper every morning, column by column. I think President Clinton is trying to do a good job, but I don't know how it will turn out. Politics has always been important in our family. My father was a southern Republican, but I am a Democrat.

Rug hooking is one of my hobbies. This rug is a picture of Jonah and the whale. Both my girls are artists. They draw designs on burlap and I work on it.

Just the other day I was looking at the stack of cards I had received for my 97th birthday. I put them in the back of the box to make room for the ones I will get soon for my 98th birthday!

Besides medicine to keep down my blood pressure, I don't have any health problems. Laser surgery cleared up a problem I had with one eye. My hearing is good. That reminds me, I had a letter recently from my sister-in-law in West Virginia. She said that my brother, the doctor, had just gotten a hearing aid and that now he can hear, whether he wants to or not, the old women complaining and his wife snoring!

My bedroom is upstairs and I'm up and down several times a day. I have a cane but don't have to use it yet. Perhaps I've lived so long by not thinking about it and by following Dr. Peale's message of positive thinking. Before I go to sleep each night, I say the prayer I was taught at my mother's knee, "If I should die before I wake, I pray the Lord my soul to take."

Recently, Mrs. Neel wrote to tell me about the books she had been reading and that she was looking forward to becoming 100 during the coming year.

SQUARE DANCING AT 90:
CHAPMAN O'CONNOR

A series of letters can introduce a man who was interviewed in St. Petersburg, Florida, as he made preparations to close his mobile home for his annual trip north for the summer months.

On the occasion of his 80th birthday, Chapman O'Connor had written a five-page letter to his twelve grandchildren, which he titled, "How does it feel to be eighty?" Some excerpts from that letter can be compared with his situation more than ten years later:

My birthday, falling on the day after Christmas, is usually ignored, but this was an exception. So I have decided to write a little note and have copies made and sent to each one of you.

I was born on 124th Street and Morningside Avenue in Manhattan and baptized in St. Joseph's Church on 125th Street, one of eight children. From the time I was very young I was lucky enough to be able to spend my summers

*in Vienna, Virginia, with my grandmother and
grandfather, my mother's parents. I can still
remember at night sitting on my grandmother's
lap and going to sleep with her singing lullabies
to me. She had many grandchildren, but I was
always her favorite.*

*My father was sick with asthma and often
unable to work. As the oldest boy, I had to leave
school to help support the family. I can still
remember my first job thinning corn in the fields
for 25 cents an hour, backbreaking work in the
hot sun.*

*How does it feel to be eighty? It feels wonderful.
Although my hair is gray and falling out, my
teeth getting loose, and I can't run as fast as I
used to, I am still able to bowl, fish, etc. I find
life very interesting, spending summers along
the Jersey coast and winters in Florida.*

*Ten years later, certainly having forgotten the letter of a decade earlier,
Mr. O'Connor's daughter, Jane, wrote to me about her father:*

*My sisters and I have just celebrated our
Dad's 90th birthday with a huge family
gathering to which we invited his many friends.
He still bowls—winning trophies until very recently,
plays bridge, square dances, attends the marriages,
graduations, baptisms of all our new family
members. We consistently look to him for
emotional, intellectual, and inspirational support.
He still manages to help his many younger friends,
navigates his own boat, and drives—with no accidents
on his record for many decades. He gave us an
example of the meaning of long-term commitment
by providing full-time personal care for Mother
during the last years of her life, which ended
five years ago.*

Then, in response to my letter requesting an interview, Mr. O'Connor wrote in a clear, steady hand similar to that of the letter he wrote to his family when he was 80:

> *I would be happy to give you any information about myself. I live alone in a mobile home and enjoy it very much. I am still quite active, prepare all meals, handle my financial obligations, drive, bowl, square dance, and fish.*

Finally, on the eve of his 92nd birthday, Mr. O'Connor wrote to say that he was "still going strong. Bowling, fishing, square dancing, bike riding. Since I saw you I have been to Ireland, Hawaii, Oregon, etc."

Just before you arrived, I was talking on the phone with my insurance agent. I have to take my car here in Florida off the insurance and put it back on the one in New Jersey. There's a lot involved with spending half the year down here and the other half up north. When I leave here next week, I just close up the place and leave it until I come back next fall. This is a resident-owned mobile home park. It's old but comfortable and the people are very nice. We watch out for one another. There are a couple of retired nurses. They make it a point to check on people if they notice anything unusual, like the newspaper not picked up.

I had a lot of trouble getting my birth certificate. In 1907, New York City put records before that time in dead storage. My record was on microfilm. I needed it to get a passport. We are going to Ireland in August. One of my granddaughters has been trying to construct a family history. She has been to Ireland twice but has not been able to track down precisely where my father came from.

Because of family financial problems, I never finished grammar school. After a variety of short-term jobs, I went to work for the Railway Express Agency and was with them for thirty years as a clerk in the supply department. We used to distribute stationery, typewriters, and other supplies needed by the various offices all the way from Montreal to Cuba. The company was having all sorts of problems, so in 1959 I quit. Eventually they went bankrupt.

I then sold and installed aluminum windows until I officially retired at age 66. Although I worked most of the time in New York, we lived in New Jersey. When I retired, we moved from north Jersey to Long Beach Island in southern Jersey. I still have that home and spend every summer there. That is, when I'm not off some place with the family. Last year I spent Christmas in Houston and August in Portland, Oregon. I have grandchildren all over the world, and they include me in all the special occasions. Most of the time I travel by myself.

One of my sisters lived to age 89, but aside from that no one in my family lived to an advanced age. Perhaps it is that when I was a child I spent most of my time with my grandparents and they grew their own vegetables and had a cow. The only meat we had during the winter was rabbits, squirrels, partridges, and other animals that we would hunt. Meanwhile, the people back in New York were living on pork and store-bought food. I think that early nutrition was a factor in the good health I have experienced.

Actually, my health was wonderful up until this year when I began to fall to pieces. For eighty-nine years I had been in a hospital only once, for an abscess on the rectum. Then, in December I started passing blood and was in the hospital for three days with prostate trouble. They removed part of the bladder and the testicles. I got over that quickly, but then in February while I was on a cruise, I caught a virus and that sort of knocked me out for a time. Other than that, I have no health problems and I still bowl and dance.

My wife and I had a very nice life together. We were married over 60 years and had four daughters. For the last five years of her life Mildred was very sick. For the first two years, I drove back and forth to New Jersey with her and her wheelchair. I would have to take her to the ladies room. It became quite an ordeal. Then, I tried to care for her here. I rented a bed and had a hydraulic lift to get her in and out of bed. But it got to be too much, so for the last two years, she was in a nursing home.

I stayed here those two summers and visited her every day. The cost was terrible. That was six years ago and at that time I was spending $2,200 a month. In two years almost all my savings were consumed by the nursing home. We didn't have any insurance. Now you can get insurance for nursing home care. I don't have it for myself. At my age it would be prohibitively expensive, assuming I could get it at all.

Many times when one spouse dies the other is helpless. One advantage of my wife being sick so long was that I had to take care of cooking and everything, so I got used to it. Some people can't write a check, don't know how much money they have, what their operating costs are. They're lost. I had a transition period.

Having two homes requires that I be on my toes mentally as well as physically. For example, after a recent storm, the insurance company canceled the flood insurance on my house in New Jersey, so I had to find another company. And, although Florida does not have state income tax, there is a tax on assets: 1% on stocks, bonds, CDs, and the like, up to $100,000 and 2% over that. So there's paperwork involved all the time.

If I have any worry, it's about money. My savings were in CDs. They generated about $400 a month interest, which supplemented my other income to enable me to maintain my standard of living. Now, with rates so low, I have to be more careful. In fact, I have had to withdraw some of my principal.

Yesterday twelve of us went for a smorgasbord dinner at a Chinese restaurant. There's lots of social life here. The social hall in the mobile home park has dances on Saturday night and movies. When you're in a place like this for a time, you get to know everyone. The problem is not things to do but to be able to do them. There are quite a few people who can't drive or get around very much. But people are very solicitous for one another. There's always someone to take you shopping or to the doctor's. Fortunately, I am able to manage everything for myself, from shopping and cooking to taking care of the house inside and out.

In New Jersey it's quite different. I have tenants in the house. They go to work during the day so I'm by myself. But I have a boat in the water nearby and go out fishing, either by myself or, if someone else is around, with them. Up there I play a lot of cards with one group. Another group, called Senior Islanders, meets every two weeks and plans a number of activities. So, although it's not as social as here, I have enough to do up north also.

Besides going to Mass every Sunday, I'm not very religious. I used to count the money in the parish up north, but down here I haven't gotten involved.

Family is very important. I'm the oldest member of a large network of people. However, the grandchildren are scattered and have different interests from me. My daughters used to come to our house on the coast for summer vacation, but it's not the same with the next generation. They are more interested in cruises and expensive vacations. But we have wonderful reunions.

I never take a nap in the afternoon, but my legs bother me if I walk very far. It's a circulation problem. So I ride the bike more than I walk. Also, perhaps surprisingly, my legs don't bother me at all when I square dance. Which reminds me, we have to end this interview now because I am scheduled to go dancing. Four people are needed for a square, and you have to let them know a day ahead of time if you can't make it. I don't want to disappoint them.

PROMOTING ART AT 91:
DOROTHY REDFIELD

*I*nfluenced by such French artists as Claude Monet, a number of late nineteenth and early twentieth century American artists formed the American Impressionists School, producing dazzling landscapes and haunting portraits. The best known American Impressionists are John Singer Sargent and Mary Cassatt. One of the most productive members of the group was Edward Willis Redfield (1869-1965), who for many years would complete one painting a day, anxious to capture quickly the feel and mood of a scene in his native rural Pennsylvania. Although Redfield's paintings are included in museum and private collections all over the world, he has not gained extensive popular recognition.

His daughter-in-law, Dorothy H. Redfield, is attempting to change that situation by actively promoting the work of her father-in-law. She has produced a video which tells the story of his life and displays his work. She has had prints made for the first time of many of his paintings and has created full-color and black-and-white stationery with an assortment of Redfield's

---

The Emergence of the Active Nonagenarian 167

impressions of life and nature around New Hope, Pennsylvania, in the days of horses and sleighs, of pristine brooks, and crystal lakes.

It is perhaps appropriate and certainly striking that an artist who lived to his 96th year has a nonagenarian as his one-person public relations firm. Today, Dorothy Redfield lives in a studio apartment in Heritage Towers retirement community in Doylestown, Pa. She selected the one-room unit over one with a separate bedroom because the large room was more appropriate for displaying many of the scores of Redfields which she owns. Not only does her apartment look like an art gallery, but she treats it as such, welcoming visitors and inviting them to sign her guest book.

Promoting Pop's paintings is my life. The best way to begin would be for me to show you the video I made recently in which I narrate a tour of his work. Pop started as a portrait painter but gave it up because he wanted to paint what he saw, not what the subject wanted to look like. He felt that each day was a different picture and painted in what he called "one go," never returning to a painting in his studio. He worked outdoors in all sorts of weather, walking miles to a location, and then when it was dark, carrying home his easel, paints, and the day's finished product.

Pop never wanted to have prints made of his work, but we think it is so wonderful that we have just about completed arrangements for the production of a limited edition. Then people who can't afford an original will be able to enjoy possessing his work.

This large wood chest was decorated on all sides by Pop. He gave it to me as a gift for my first birthday after my marriage to his son. He painted my name and birth date in the lower corner. Pop produced works of art in all sorts of media. For instance, he made these chairs and hooked rugs. When he stopped painting on canvas, he would paint on serving trays. This one he did when he was 92 years old.

My own only claim to fame is this booklet "Highlights of History through 50 Years of Acrostic Greetings." Every Christmas from 1942 to 1992 I composed and sent an acrostic to our friends. The one for 1992 reads:

For all these years I've tried to say
In varied acrostic rhymes
First, know God loves you night and day,
Then, He's with you at all times.
Your prayers, faith, trust and love are cherished by God above.
Your footprints left as on you trod
End as you help another.
All that you do shows love of God
Renewed aiding a brother.
Such joy it's been greeting you, fifty years seemed all too few.

It's amazing how the history of those years is portrayed in the annual greetings: wars, the atomic bomb, the first trip to space. The more recent ones are done in calligraphy. I hadn't learned it yet when I did the earlier ones.

I was born in Philadelphia 91 years ago, almost 92 now. My father was an osteopath who had offices in different towns around the area. When I was about five, he decided to settle here in Doylestown. I have lived here ever since—more than 85 years. Dad built a combination house and twelve-bed private hospital. It was my home until I married, and even then I was there every day working with my father. After high school I went to business college because I was going to work with dad, which I did seven days and four nights a week for forty years. I was my father's right hand, taking care of the books and doing all the purchasing and hiring for the hospital. When my father went to a medical conference, I would go with him as his secretary.

When I married Laurent, who repaired and sold lawn mowers—a far cry from art—he used to come to the hospital each day for lunch. Then when our daughter was born, she was brought over, and my mother took care of her and taught her many things. Our own house was just across a family-owned field from father's hospital.

God bless my husband. It was only after my father died that I realized that I had put my father ahead of everything else. My husband never indicated that it should have been otherwise. And here I am now devoting my life to Laurie's father the way I did for so long to my own. Each was a great man, well worth whatever I could do for him.

When we married—I was 24—Laurent and I bought an old house with three acres of land. We called it "The Barn" and over the years fixed it up, and it became the center of a busy social life. We entertained artists and people interested in art. I would have as many as twenty-five to a sit-down dinner. I did everything myself. How I loved that place! We lived there for sixty rich and stimulating years.

At that time, I just couldn't imagine living in a retirement home like this; there couldn't have been anything worse! Then Laurie had a stroke. For a year and a half I had twenty-four-hour help but came to realize that I couldn't keep up the place by myself so put it on the market. It sold in about six hours. We had bought it for $6,000 and sold it for $375,000.

We came over here seven years ago, and you know, I don't give a thought to the Barn any more. I drive past and don't even remember it's there, although its only a block and a half away.

My husband was ill for five years. During that time, he was kind and loving and unselfish but did not realize that he was married. It gave me time to adjust to a different stage of life. I happen to be religious enough to believe that that was God's way of helping me.

We took an apartment here in Heritage Village that overlooked the shopping center. I felt it would give Laurie something to look at. But, even here, he got so bad that I couldn't take care of him myself, and he was moved downstairs to the health center. It's like a nursing home. That's where he died two years ago. Both of us have donated our bodies to science. I feel that when all that is left is the body, you might as well do someone else some good. Also, I'm very parsimonious and it saves a lot of funeral expenses!

My daughter is 65 years old and lives about a half-hour from here. One of her daughters spent several years with the Peace Corps in Nepal. Her letters were so interesting that I would like to see them published. Now she is teaching the emotionally disturbed and the deaf in Santa Fe, New Mexico. For Christmas she sent me two books by Torey Hayden, a teacher of the emotionally disturbed. I enjoyed them very, very much.

Heritage Towers has many activities for residents, but I never take part. I am perfectly content to be by myself. All morning I write at the typewriter and in the afternoon I read. I have my own car and every Sunday drive to the Episcopal church. The residence provides bus service to stores, banks, and the post office, but it does not operate on Sunday so I have to keep my car. It's about the only thing I need it for.

Dinner is included in what we pay here. *[In 1993, for a studio apartment in Heritage Towers, the entry fee was $32,800 and the monthly service fee for single occupancy was $887.]* I like to eat early and so go down about 4:00 p.m. I make arrangements a week in advance to eat with particular people. The dining room is very nice and the meals excellent. It's not required, of course, but everyone dresses for dinner. It's nice to have a reason to dress up and go out, even if it's only downstairs.

A couple of years ago a retired Baptist minister, who is a resident here, conducted a Bible study group. About 10 of us attended. He could explain everything so clearly. People of all Christian denominations found his answers to questions very satisfactory. He said that you might as well believe, even if you have doubts, because if there is an afterlife at least you will have believed and have a chance of attaining it.

A friend of mine is downstairs in the Health Care Center. Each day I visit her; she has gotten very bad—on oxygen and gasping for every breath. It is when you see things like that that you wonder about God's plan, how He lets people suffer and go on when there's no hope. I believe in euthanasia. When people reach a point like that, they should not have to continue to exist. I have signed a living will indicating that I do not want any life support. I think you should be able to choose to die when you are no longer active mentally or physically. I believe that God decides when one's life is over, but I would not want to be kept alive artificially.

My health is good. I've had high blood pressure since I was in my 20's but with medication keep it under control. I go to the doctor every three months and I'm as good as you can hope for at 92.

I said to someone the other day that I feel a little guilty because I am so completely content.

At age 93, Mrs. Redfield fell and broke her wrist, shoulder, and foot. She wrote, "I took it very nonchalantly." She uses a walker but still manages "to get to all the local and some not so local art shows."

WORKING OUT ON EXERCISE
MACHINES AT 93:
FRANK REGAN

*F*rank Regan retired when he was 70 years old, an age that would seem reasonable enough and indeed was eight years older than the average age at which American men today retire. The only trouble is that twenty-three years later, Mr. Regan is still healthy and for all these years he has not really done very much. Since childhood, work had been his life. He developed no hobbies, belongs to no organizations, has no friends, and has never considered volunteer work.

Why do people retire? There are many reasons, of course, but the following are the most frequently cited:

1) health problems make it impossible to continue working;
2) workers are involuntarily retired or laid off;
3) the work is unsatisfactory, either too stressful or too boring;
4) the desire to devote more time to an avocation or to develop new skills or interests;
5) workers are made to believe that they should retire because of their age.

Frank Regan

This final reason is the one which led to Frank Regan's retirement. His family convinced him that he was too old to be working and that he "deserved" to be able to take it easy. The argument was offered, "Why work if you don't have to?"

A dramatic change has taken place in the participation of older Americans in the labor force. Whereas in 1947, 47.8% of men over the age of 65 were employed, 40 years later, in 1987, only 16.6% were still working. And it must be remembered that in the earlier period, many workers were in positions covered by mandatory retirement, whereas today that is seldom the case.

Two developments in American life facilitate the retirement of men and women today: the improved financial status of the elderly and the emergence of the leisure ethic. Despite fears about inadequate income in retirement, most workers find that pensions, savings, and Social Security enable them to retire while still enjoying good health. And they have accepted the cultural message that they are entitled to a prolonged period of leisure after decades of gainful employment. Life is viewed as consisting of three stages: Training, Working, and Resting. Thus, forty years of working might be sandwiched between twenty years of training and twenty years of resting.

For a different perspective on work, it would be instructive to read the interviews with Anna Cassidy, Edward Corcoran, Joseph Fuchs, Al Ross, Harriet Strachstein, and Russell Wilson. These nonagenarians are still employed, find great satisfaction in their work, and have no intention of retiring. In none of these cases are the people working mainly for financial reasons. They are working because they can't think of anything else they would prefer doing.

I was born in County Roscommon, Ireland, 93 years ago. I have made a number of trips back to the old country, including one earlier this year but never seriously thought about returning there to live. There were ten children, although one died very young. My oldest brother and sister lived well into their eighties, and I have a younger sister who is 91 and a brother 89. Another sister is 85, but she's not doing very well.

I attended the National School until I was 12 or 13 and then went to the secondary school for four years. At that time, very few children in the parish went to secondary school. It was possible for me because, despite the large family, we were fairly comfortable. My father was in the cattle business and there was profit in cattle around the time of World War I. If you bought a beast today for ten pounds, tomorrow you could get twelve. From 1912 to 1920 we prospered.

Actually I didn't finish secondary school. I was anxious to get out on the road and make money with the cattle business. I went back to the farm and let my younger brothers and sisters go to school. We planted corn, potatoes, carrots, and cabbage—enough vegetables for the year. Twice a year we killed a pig for bacon and we bought fresh meat for Saturday and Sunday.

When the cattle market declined, I knew that I was in trouble. I asked myself, "What am I going to do here for the rest of my life?" Even if you inherited the place you could hardly live on it unless you had something else to do. So at the age of 24, I came out to this country.

After landing in New York, I traveled by way of the Erie Railroad to Cleveland where I had aunts and uncles. There I got a job in an automobile plant starting at $0.45 an hour, which wasn't bad. I learned to do body striping, making those thin lines around the wheels. I practiced and practiced. The boss said to me, "Do that an hour a day, and as soon as you learn it, I'll give you the job." I went from about $45 a week to $120 in three or four months. It was piecework—so much a wheel. Cars were selling. We made about ninety a day. Then the Depression came in 1929 and the auto industry went to hell altogether.

I went from plant to plant for a time but in 1931 was laid off. They were laying them off left and right just the way they are now in the auto industry.

It was a turning point in my life all right. I took a trip to Paris for the ordination of my brother as a priest. Then we went to Ireland where we spent a couple of months.

When I returned to America, I remained in New York where a friend got me a job in the grocery business. I started as a clerk but in a few years worked my way up to manager. Safeway had an excellent management training program. I learned so much that, when I was in my early 50's, I decided to go into business for myself.

I bought a saloon in the Bronx. Many of the Irish ran bars. What else could we do? I was successful, but it was long hours and the clientele wasn't the best. So the family talked me into getting out of it. Anyway, I was past 70.

It was when I was a store manager that I was finally in a position to think of marriage, and so when I was 39 years old, I married an Irish woman who was a hairdresser. We had two sons. One of them is a priest, a Columban Father. He's stationed in Ireland as head of the order for six years. The other son is in sales. I live with him and his wife here in Greenwich, Connecticut. Their children are grown and gone.

My wife died while the boys were still young, 12 and 14. My sister-in-law, who worked for Safeway as a check-out clerk, was living with us at the time and stayed on to help me with the boys. When she moved out, a niece, who came from Cleveland to get a teaching job in New York, lived with me. She stayed for nine or ten years at which time she married and moved to New Jersey. So, I always had a woman in the house to take care of things. As far as marrying again was concerned, you'd be looking but afraid to venture.

When my niece left, my son didn't want me to be in the house by myself. I was in my 80's. So I sold the house and moved in with him. I have my own room and the run of the house. They both work, so there's no one here but me during the week. On Fridays a cleaning lady comes in.

My daily routine is quite simple. I get up about 10 or 11 and read *The New York Times*. Then I walk to the village or work out on the exercise machines in the basement. I spend a half-hour on the treadmill and rowing machine. Not a day passes that I don't get some good exercise. In the late morning I have juice, oatmeal, toast, and coffee. That's breakfast and lunch. I make my own supper, except on weekends when my son and daughter-in-law are here. What I do is put a lot of cabbage, carrots, celery, onions, and potatoes in this big pot and pressure cook them. I don't eat much meat anymore.

I've never belonged to organizations. When you're in the liquor business, you don't have time. It was seven days a week. The only hobby I ever had was the working hobby. Up here I haven't joined anything and don't know the neighbors. I'm not much of a one for a lot of people.

Maybe once a year I see a doctor, but nothing has turned up yet. I eat well and have no trouble walking. There are three stories to this house and I'm up and down several times a day. I've never had any health problems.

I go to church most of the time and generally live by the law, but I am not particularly religious.

There's not much to living to be ninety. A lot of people today live to be 100 and don't think anything of it. They're talking now about living to be 120.

Some time after the interview, Mr. Regan's daughter-in-law wrote to say that they had held a big party for Frank's 95th birthday, that he had spent the previous summer in Ireland, and that he was "still exercising, cooking and doing chores."

NEWSPAPER PUBLICIST AT 91:
AL ROSS

*A*l Ross works full time at a job that requires that he travel all over his hometown of Palm Beach, Florida. He puts 12,000 miles a year on his Cadillac, golfs every Saturday and Sunday, and looks and sounds more fit than most people twenty years his junior. Like all active nonagenarians, Ross takes great pride in his competence and accomplishments and insists that he has not experienced any age discrimination.

Ross showed me a list which had appeared in a newspaper of famous people who had been active at an advanced age. The list included Grandma Moses, who was painting at 100, Bertrand Russell, who was active in   inter-national peace drives at 94, George Bernard Shaw, who wrote a play at 93. After Eamon de Valera, who served as president of Ireland at 91, Ross had inserted his own name in the list: "At 91, Al Ross was the public relations officer for a number of publications." After himself, the list continued with Pablo Picasso, who was producing drawings at 90.

In each of the letters Ross sent me, he wrote "I am not retired" and *included his business cards, one for the* Palm Beach Daily News, *the other for* Palm Beach Life, *a monthly magazine. For both publications he provides "promotion services," which means that he sees to it that the publications are available at the many special events and meetings which take place in Palm Beach. More than that, with his wit and skill in salesmanship, he talks to people and makes sure they remember not only the newspaper and magazine but also Al Ross.*

At the Chamber of Commerce annual awards dinner the other night, I was taken completely by surprise when I was called up to receive the Board of Directors' Special Award for my work in protecting the dignity of amputees. They say I have the gift of gab, but I didn't the other night. Here's the article about it with my picture that appeared in yesterday's paper.

My interest in amputees originated with my service in World War I of which I am the youngest surviving veteran. By forging my father's signature, I was able to enlist at the age of fifteen. I served aboard the training ship USS Richmond at Norfolk, Virginia. Here I'm 91 years old and the baby of the veterans. But there are enough of us in the area to have the only World War I color guard in the U.S. We're all in our nineties, of course, but we proudly carry the flag at parades and memorial services. The numbers are declining rapidly, but there are still thousands of World War I vets around. By the year 2000 just about all of us will be gone. Since I'm the youngest and in such good health, perhaps I'll be the last surviving veteran of what used to be called The Great War.

As to the amputees, in the 1950's while I was a businessman in New York, I read an article about the National Amputation Foundation, an organization composed of veterans whose handicaps are permanent. I had long been an avid golfer and got the idea that their handicaps should not keep these veterans from playing golf. My first project was to get the equipment these men needed. I wrote, telephoned, and visited hundreds of sporting goods companies and appealed for clubs, balls, bags, anything but cash. I estimate that over all I collected more than half a million dollars worth of equipment that was distributed to about 20,000 amputees all over the country.

Then I got the idea of a pro-celebrity type golf event for amputees. One purpose was to raise the consciousness of the general public to the extent to which so many of our young men had been maimed defending their country. Because of the nature of the conflict, the number of soldiers who lost their limbs or the use of them in the Korean conflict, and later the Vietnam War, was much greater than the toll of the World Wars. Well, the dream came true in 1962 when I chaired the first of many pro-amp tournaments. Celebrities like Jimmy Durante and Perry Como, together with many pros, joined the disabled vets.

My interest in helping handicapped people play golf continued when I moved to Florida twenty-four years ago. I established a chip and pitch course at the Palm Beach Spa and worked as pro there for more than ten years. I have golfed all over the world and have made four holes-in-one. To show the importance of control and concentration, I would demonstrate one-handed shots and two-handed shots while on my knees. I have taught blind people to play. Handicapped veterans gave up some of their normal lives for their country. The more I saw of them, the more I wanted to do something for them. I believe that if you're doing good for others, you're doing good for yourself.

I was born in the Williamsburg section of Brooklyn. My father owned small businesses, candy stores, grocery stores. He would hold a store for three or four years and then sell it and move on, so I lived all over Brooklyn. Although neither of my parents or my brothers lived to be 90, I heard that my grandparents lived to nearly 100 and that they didn't die; they were killed in Europe in the war.

I had quit school to join the Navy and I never went back. After the service I worked for many years for a group of magazines, eventually becoming circulation director. As good will ambassador for the magazines, I traveled to every state and major city in the country. We were doing well until the Depression. Then people didn't even have the nickel or the dime that the magazine cost. It was a terrible time. They were selling apples on the street; desperate. I myself sold candy out of my car. I would go up one side of the street and sell the candy at the regular price. Then I would go down the other side and sell it for half price so that I wouldn't have to bring any home.

Eventually, through my brother-in-law I went to work as a salesman for a chemical company. I was so successful that they offered me a partnership. In time I bought out the others and became the sole owner. It was very successful; still is. When I was 68 I turned it over to my daughter and her two sons who still run it.

Frankly, I was ready for a change. Some relatives were developing housing down here in Florida and urged me to come and manage a site. I was to have a lovely apartment, etc. After a year the development flopped. And I had an investment in it. Now what to do? Well, I was riding my bike past the Palm Beach Spa and saw a vacant lot across the street. I spoke to the manager of the spa and he spoke to the owner, John D. McArthur, who gave me the go-ahead. So I built a driving range and putting green. It became extremely popular. But when Mr. McArthur died, his property was sold. So once again, now in my 80's, I had to find something else to do.

It was then that I got involved in the local newspaper business and have worked full time at it ever since. My work is similar to what I did for the magazines back in the 20's, not exactly sales but public relations, promoting the product. They consider me very important, because I know everyone in town and am effective in getting the paper and the magazine out there and into people's hands.

My beloved Etta and I have been partners now for 68 years. No one could have a more supportive wife. She puts up with all my antics. Unfortunately, Etta, who's 88, fell recently and hurt her leg, so she's somewhat handicapped. I have to do the shopping; I don't like that, but I've got to do it. Most evenings we eat out. We have this lovely apartment just a block from my office and right near the restaurants and shops, so it's very convenient.

I've always golfed. When I was 70 I was scoring in the seventies. When I was in my 80's I began to score in the eighties. Now that I'm in my 90's I'm scoring in the nineties. I'm looking forward to scoring in the hundreds.

I've never been sick a day in my life or lost a day of business because of illness. I did take off some days to play golf. Do I notice any changes in my health? That's not the way I think. I don't let myself think that way.

I belong to a temple. We go two or three times a year for the holidays, but religion is not important to me. It never has been. But I'm proud to be Jewish. Back in 1939 and 1940, I was Brooklyn Unit Director of the American Jewish Youth, which was affiliated with the Jewish War Veterans. At that time there were Nazi meetings in New York. We would go to them and try to break them up. Some of the fellows got hurt.

Sports have always been part of my life. I played semi-pro baseball in Brooklyn, originated basketball on rollerskates, and just recently won a bicycle race for seniors. I was on the radio the other day with the woman who runs the Senior Olympics down here. She had just jumped from an airplane at age 88. We were talking about the possibilities for physical activity for people our age.

When I was 80 I tried to become a model. I had a professional photographer make up a portfolio of pictures. My resume' said that I was 80 but looked like 55. Well, I didn't get many calls. They wanted someone who was bald with a pot belly.

I'm not going to bore you with all the things I've done, like winning an essay contest a few years ago on why I'm proud to be an American and receiving the "Workaholic of the Year Award" from a national business organization. I just get up every day, go to work, look for chances to help people. I'll never retire. To force a man to retire is to issue him a death warrant. If they fired me, I'd step right out and get another job.

My philosophy of life is best expressed in a brief statement I read a couple of years ago when I received the Timex "You're Still Ticking Award."

> Aged wine is best to drink;
> aged wood is best to burn;
> aged authors are best to read;
> aged friends are best to trust;

an older person is best to employ
if you want a job well done.
The older you are the better you work.

More than a year after our meeting, Mr. Ross, now age 93, wrote in his inimitable style: "So many things have happened since your interview. Parades. Honors. Standing ovations. You name 'em."

ON THE GO WITH A WALKER AT 96:
ROSE ROUBIAN

*A*fter interviewing Mrs. Roubian in her Chatham, New Jersey, apartment, I phoned her daughter, a woman in her sixties, and asked if she could indicate changes which had taken place in her mother during the past six or seven years, that is, since her mother's 90th birthday.

The daughter said that until her mother was 92 she was just fine, doing her own shopping, managing her own affairs, and living her own life, which included active involvement in Senior Citizen groups. Then, the mother suffered collapsed vertebrae. Although the mother says that the problem was caused by a fall, the daughter believes it was that the vertebrae fractured and then she fell. In either case, the mother was incapacitated and lived with her daughter for five weeks. However, Mrs. Roubian was anxious to return to her apartment. She did so, but her mobility was restricted by the need to use a walker.

A few months after that, the mother broke her wrist. The woman's two daughters began to think that it was the beginning of the end, that mother

---

would not be able to live alone much longer. Much to their surprise and relief, aided by several modifications, their mother has been managing just fine.

She had only one telephone, in her bedroom. They got one for the living room as well, so that she would not have to hurry to the bedroom when the phone rang. They bought her a television set with a remote control and a very simple-to-operate microwave oven in which she could heat meals and not have to spend so much time on food preparation.

When the mother broke her wrist, she couldn't sign checks. This led to the daughter acquiring power of attorney for her mother and assuming responsibility for paying bills. Since the mother lives on the second floor and cannot easily get down to the mail box, mail is delivered to her daughter's house. The daughter says that her mother is relieved not to have to worry about such things.

The most recent innovation was getting a monitoring device with an alarm button. The program, PromptCare, is connected to a local hospital from which medical assistance would be dispatched in an emergency. If the button is pushed, the hospital telephones in order to ascertain if it had been pressed accidentally. One day, the mother was outside with her granddaughter and great-granddaughter and inadvertently activated the alarm. Since she was outside, she didn't hear the phone when the hospital called back. Within minutes, the EMT team was hurrying up the walk. This false alarm convinced the daughter that the system worked.

Not wanting to get trapped into a pattern of worrying every time there is no answer, the daughter does not call her mother each day, Also, although she lives nearby, ordinarily she sees her mother only on Sunday. Each woman has her own life and wants to maintain her independence.

Soon I'll be 97. I hope that I can make it because each year takes its toll. You lose a lot of energy as you get older and you have aches and pains. And I must have allergies because I was reading the newspaper now and started sneezing. Maybe it's from the newsprint.

Every Sunday my daughter and her husband pick me up for ten o'clock Mass, and then we have brunch and dinner at her house. In the evening she brings me back here. This has been our routine all the years that I've lived here. She's very busy so I don't see her much at other times.

Several years ago, I fell on the grass outside the house and damaged three vertebrae. Since then I have been using this walker. It has wheels, and it gives me just enough support to get around more comfortably when I go any distance. I don't always use it here in the house.

I was born in Brooklyn. My maiden name was Agnello; that means "lamb." My mother and father had come from Italy several years before that with my three oldest brothers. I lived in Brooklyn my whole life until I came here to Chatham. In fact, I lived in the same house on Avenue J for over fifty years.

I was the oldest daughter of nine children. In Italian families, the mother used to depend on the daughter to help her with the chores, so my schooling was interrupted several times and ended with grammar school. I was sixteen when I finished.

We didn't have indoor plumbing. There was an outhouse in the yard. But my mother didn't want the girls using it, so she had a carpenter build something like a throne in a room off the kitchen. That was just for the girls. The boys had to go outside.

Outhouses were not unusual. In fact, my husband and I would go to the Catskills on vacation and when we stopped along the way, it was outhouses. I remember my daughter complaining how smelly they were.

While still a teenager, I got a job in a department store. Although I didn't have any real training in bookkeeping, I was given responsibility for keeping the records of people who had charge accounts—the adjustments department. After three or four years I got a job with Western Electric taking care of employee deductions. After the First World War, I was transferred to the research department, where they were working on the early stages of developing television. I took care of the records.

I enjoyed my work, but it ended with my marriage when I was 26. My husband was an Armenian, born in Turkey. He was very well educated, graduating from Central Turkey College, an English-language school. He came here as a young man and worked as a photographer all his life, eventually having his own studio. He took wedding photos but mainly did portrait work.

My mother was concerned about me marrying a foreigner, especially someone from Turkey. I explained that he was a Christian, a Congregationalist, like the people who ran the college he attended. Almost all my brothers and sisters married people of different nationalities. We were a League of Nations. We were very assimilated. The neighborhood in which we lived was mixed, Irish and Italian, so we tended to meet many people who were not Italian.

We had two children, daughters. The first was born in the 1920's and the other during the Depression. But also, I had a brother who lived with me. His wife died of cancer, leaving him with a year-old baby, so I raised that child also. My mother said to me, "If you can't take care of your own, what good are you in this world?" I had a good husband and was able to do it, but it wasn't easy.

I was so busy with my home and my family that I didn't get involved in much else. I did a lot of gardening and belonged to a gardening club. I met a lot of nice people through my husband, who was very much part of the photographers' world.

When my husband died twenty years ago, the fiftieth year of our marriage, my bachelor brother came to live with me. I was so happy. I had someone to cook for and to keep me company again.

Long life seems to run in my family. My mother was 86 and my father 82 when they died. All through my marriage I went and helped my mother, who continued to live in the house where I was raised. Today, women are career-oriented. I was more family-oriented. My second oldest brother lived to 91. My younger sister is 92 and lives in senior citizen housing. She's not doing that well. Just before you came, I was talking with her on the phone and hope to visit her next week when they take me to visit my daughter on Long Island.

It was about 17 years ago, when I was 80, that the family convinced me to move here to New Jersey to be near my younger daughter. These garden apartments are not senior housing. There are people of all ages. Right below me is a young couple with a baby. He's a school teacher. It's very expensive. I pay over $900 a month rent, and none of the services available in housing for the elderly is provided. But I love it and wouldn't want to be any place else.

I belong to the Chatham Seniors. We meet twice a month. Speakers come or people show slides of their vacations. We also have a lot of good experiences on the day trips they are always sponsoring. If I didn't join the Seniors, I would have been stupid; I'd be sitting here doing nothing. I'm now the oldest member of the group.

But you know, I've never been in a plane and you couldn't get me to fly. I'm afraid. And I never drove a car. My husband and the girls took me everyplace.

Before I fell, I used to love to go out every day. Now I'm not able to do it unless someone takes me. Three times a week, wonderful people come in a van from the Senior Resources Center and take me to one of the churches where they serve a meal to the senior citizens. They take my walker down the stairs and help me in and out of the van. I really look forward to getting out and being with people.

I may not be as strong as I used to be but I still enjoy eating and I don't have any food restrictions. It's really funny. My daughter and her husband take me out to dinner and they are the ones not able to eat this, not able to eat that. I eat everything. My daughter bought me a microwave oven. At first I didn't want it, but now I love it.

A couple of months ago I was feeling tired, so my daughter took me to the doctor. He did a blood test and said that I was fine. I take two pills every morning with breakfast, one for my heart and one because my legs sometimes get puffy. Besides my back, my only problem is that I can't fall asleep at night. I might be watching television and feel like I'm sleepy, but then when I go to bed, I can't sleep.

I try to be a good Catholic. Every day I say the rosary, especially since Mother Teresa asked us to pray for people with AIDS.

When I came here I had many friends, people my own age. But I've buried fifteen or twenty of them and the rest are in the same condition I am. It's one of the consequences of living so long. Right next door lived a woman, a dear friend, who got Alzheimer's disease. How I enjoyed her company. It was terrible to see her get more and more disoriented. She would wander around the street in winter with no coat.

I don't think about why I've lived so long and don't worry about death. However, I hate to admit this, but lately when I go to bed, I wonder if I'll wake up or if I'll die during the night. It's because some of my friends have died in their sleep or have been found dead on the floor. I don't want to die. I still have a little zest for living.

More than a year later, Mrs. Roubian's daughter wrote to say that her mother, now 98, had fallen again and was living in the nursing home section of a life care community. "Her mind and spirit are willing, but her body just isn't able."

YOGA INSTRUCTOR AT 92:
MORRIS RUBIN

*"**P**eople who fear diseases are the ones who get them."*
James Allen

To be an active nonagenarian means to have a body free enough from disease and disability to function with a reasonable degree of independence. What is it that enables some 90-year-olds to remain physically robust, while others are frail? Is it genes, or diet, or exercise? Or is it "mind over matter": a happy disposition, positive outlook, or peaceful personality? As much as a definitive answer might be welcome, the key to healthy longevity is not that easily found. It appears to be a combination of several factors blended into the unique fabric of individual lives. Most nonagenarians can point to relatives who have lived to advanced age, but so can many people who do not live to an advanced age. Most do have a cheerful attitude, but so again do many who die young. Some exercise regularly; the majority do not.

In recent years there has emerged in America a pronounced concern for physical fitness. Health clubs have proliferated. Pictures of public officials jogging have become commonplace, almost a requirement for election it would seem. One of the first things President Bill Clinton did when he assumed office in 1993 was to install a jogging track outside the White House. Bicycling has grown in popularity, and in warmer climates like Florida and California, senior citizens can be seen pedalling to the super-market or post office on their three-wheelers. Swimming pools and exercise rooms have become standard equipment not only in hotels but in apart-ment buildings, housing developments, and retirement communities.

In the 1993 Public Television series, Healing and the Mind *with Bill Moyers, one segment featured a 90-year-old tai chi instructor who not only was strikingly healthy-looking himself but has several nonagenarian stu-dents. Tai chi is a graceful, slow-moving form of exercise practiced by millions of Chinese. The word "chi" means "life force" and it is believed that the meditation-like exercise enhances one's "chi" and wards off dis-ease.*

Another ancient form of Chinese exercise/meditation, one which has gained considerable following in the United States, is yoga. Morris Rubin, age 92, practices yoga on a mat on his living room floor each day, teaches it in nursing homes, and has made a video demonstrating how it is done. Like the Chinese Tai Chi Master, Mr. Rubin is extraordinarily limber, muscular, alert, and energetic.

See this list of names and phone numbers? It's of thirteen elderly women whom I take care of. After practicing law for 56 years here in Bloomfield, New Jersey, I retired and became a one-man social services agency. I help the women in many ways. They know they can call on me at any time. I rake leaves, bring out the garbage, and take them to doctor appointments. One woman I helped to be admitted to a nurs-ing home. I visit her regularly. Of course, the women are good to me also. These plastic bowls in my freezer contain soups and other foods, which they have prepared for me. They want to be sure that I remain in good health!

When I was getting started in my law practice, a woman came in and asked if I needed a secretary. I told her that I was in no position to pay her very much. It was the Depression. I told her I'd give her $4 a week and that some weeks she would make more than I did. She said, "When do I start?" I answered, "You just did." She was with me for thirty-four years until her health would not enable her to continue. I found her a less demanding job, then put her into a nursing home and finally buried her. During all that time, I managed her affairs and saw to it that all her needs were met. Her family had died or moved away. I was like a father to her.

But the yoga.... Every morning I spend 30 minutes on this mat on the floor in my living room and go through a program. When I get up in the morning I'm the rambling wreck from Georgia Tech, but when I finish the yoga I'm lubricated. Let me demonstrate. I used to stand on my head, but not anymore. It's not dignified for a man of my age! But I can bend backwards and sit in a lotus position and do most of the other movements. It's because I do it regularly. The last thing I do is press my body against the wall as hard as I can in the West Point posture: the back of the head, the shoulders, the backside, and the legs. Then you walk away and you're inches taller. You're either a winner or a loser by your posture.

The Lions Club made a video of my whole routine and is going to market it. Better me than Jane Fonda for older people. I don't take money for anything I do. Thank goodness, I don't need it.

It's the yoga that keeps me going. My doctor took an echo picture of my heart. He had me sit down and look at it. He said I had the heart of a younger man.

After the yoga I walk to a park at the end of the block. There, I sit on a beam and just remain quiet for a few minutes. Then I come home and have a good breakfast and read the paper.

After that I get in my car and drive to the local McDonald's for the meeting of the Northend Coffee Klatch. There are no dues, no tuition, and no one under 75. I cheer them up; have a joke ready each day. For example, Pat is dying and he calls over his friend Mike. "Mike," he says, "I'm dying. I have a bottle of scotch under the bed. When I'm dead and covered over would you do me the favor of pouring it on my grave?" Mike answers, "Of course, Pat. But would it be OK if I filtered it through my kidneys first?" And another one is especially meaning-ful to the elderly. Pat is dying. The priest comes in and asks Pat, "Do you believe in the hereafter?" Pat replies, "Why of course I do, Father. I go into a room and ask myself , 'What am I here after?'"

I was born in Russia. My father bought trees to be sent to a lumber mill. I remember logs from shore to shore on the Dnepr River and in winter the river frozen so solid that it was used as a road. But the pogrom of 1904 forced us to flee. First we went to Germany, but after a year the anti-Semitism forced us to move again. The Jewish Immigration Society waved its magic wand, and we crossed the ocean. There were five children and another was born here. I remem-ber arriving in New York harbor. They gave each of us a large orange with an American flag stuck in it. I'll never forget the taste of that orange.

The people who brought us over put Papa in a candy store on the lower East Side. We lived in a tenement over the store. From that, we had bread on the table. Next we bought a newsstand on 125th Street in Harlem. After a few years, Pop got a job in Bayonne, New Jersey, col-lecting the premiums for life insurance policies. Finally, he bought a delicatessen. But then Pop got sick and died of cancer at the age of 54. He was a chain smoker. I had just finished high school and worked for five or six years in the deli to help support the family.

At age 24, I went to New York University but was forced to leave after two years because I couldn't afford to buy the textbooks. It was back to the deli. But I knew that I wanted to have a profession. My brother was already a lawyer, so I went back to NYU and studied law for three years, working part time delivering tea and coffee. By good luck I passed the bar exam on the first try but didn't practice law right away. I was getting $35 a week on the coffee route, and that was too good to give up! This was in the depth of the Depression.

I was 30 years old when I finally started to practice law—from a desk in the back of a real estate office for $5 a month. But they kicked me out. They didn't like the way I was practicing law; I was ambulance chasing. Eventually I established a successful practice and became very active in the civic life of Bloomfield.

Several families from the same place in Russia used to get together every Sunday to socialize. Well, I was attracted to one of the girls and eventually married her. But she was supporting her mother and I was supporting mine, so we had to wait several years before we could establish our own home. We had only one child, a daughter adopted in Canada when I was 47 years old. By then I was doing very well and my wife, who had quit her job, was anxious to raise a child. I now have three grandchildren and two great grandchildren.

At age 67 I retired, but wouldn't you know, a year later the younger man who took over my practice died suddenly so I had to get involved again for a time straightening out his estate.

Mae, my wife, was a gifted poet, an Emily Dickinson. She died of lung cancer seven years ago at the age of 86. We were married fifty-six years. I wouldn't put her in a hospital where she would be all alone. I had round-the-clock help here. It cost $150,000. But it was the way I wanted it to be. She died in her own home.

My mother taught me to do the wash and to iron. I've always been very domestic. Besides having a woman come in once every two weeks, I do everything for myself. I'm the champion homemaker. I'm sure you will agree that the house is neat and well kept. The man next door is very kind. He shovels the snow for me.

Upstairs is my favorite room in the house, a library. Look how the walls are lined with the portraits of great people: Einstein, Toscanini, Stephen Douglass. Here is my Abraham Lincoln corner. I have the works of Shakespeare. I've read all of Mark Twain several times. I just start at one end of the set of books and go to the other.

I have angina and take pills for survival. When I experience stress and have that feeling, not exactly pain, more like a pressure, I take very deep breaths from my stomach. It sends the blood to my brain and the discomfort passes.

For 50 years I've been taking vitamin C and E. I heard Linus Pauling speak and since that time have been taking them faithfully. I don't know about the actual value of taking vitamins, but if you think it's doing you some good, it's doing you good.

Fifty years ago my wife and the director of the library started a

Fortnightly Club which reads and reviews books. This Wednesday we are discussing *JFK: Reckless Youth* by Nigel Hamilton. Its a long book. I read it in small segments but stay with it.

I've belonged to the Lions Club for over 50 years and am the self-appointed chairman and only member of the old clothes committee. People bring me used clothing and I take them to the mental institution. I've been doing that for more than 30 years. They gave me a certificate of recognition. I have a lot of awards and proclamations. In the basement of my house is a room filled with them, for what they're worth.

As far as religion is concerned, I'm Jewish but so reformed that you can hardly call me religious. I can't seem to visualize a God. It's so insubstantial. I welcome any excuse not to have to go to temple. This week I will go because they are going to read off the names of my wife and my brother-in-law for the anniversary of their deaths. They do it every year.

My religion is to help others. We pass this way but once.

COMPOSING LIMERICKS AT 96:
TONIO SELWART

The Biographical Encyclopaedia *and* Who's Who of the American Theatre *lists dozens of theatre, film, and television productions in which Tonio Selwart appeared, performing in German, Italian, and French as well as English. His debut was in Munich in 1927 and his final performance in Orson Welles' 1975 film,* The Other Side of the Wind.

Members of a profession tend to form a close-knit fraternity. Selwart's friends include prominent actors and others associated with the theatrical and music worlds. He considers Al Hirschfeld, the Arts and Leisure caricaturist of The New York Times, *his best friend. Regularly, Hirschfeld and*

his wife send a car to pick up Selwart to take him to their home for dinner.

Other members of the New York arts community take him to concerts at Carnegie Hall, just a few steps from his West 57th Street apartment. Although retired for two decades, Selwart still vibrates with the pulse of the world to which he had devoted his working life and which has not forgotten him.

New York's Central Park is two blocks away. Here he can be seen walking with his cane on a warm day, meticulously dressed and groomed. When Selwart starred in The Pursuit of Happiness *at the Avon Theatre during the 1933-34 season, he was billed as a new matinee idol. The ad for the play in the now defunct* World-Telegram *had a banner across the top which read, "New York Has Gone Completely Selwart!" A picture of a handsome young man adorned the display together with a quotation from a critic suggesting that, inevitably, Selwart was Hollywood-bound. As he strolls through the park today at the age of 96 much of that striking profile remains, and although his piercing blue eyes are now blind they still have the sparkle that befits a matinee idol.*

I have a bit of laryngitis from being out in the cold air yesterday. This isn't my real voice; I have a better voice. The other day I went to the League for the Hard of Hearing, but my hearing aid was not ready. The hearing is not that good, but I can understand someone who speaks clearly. My main limitation is that for the past few years I have been legally blind—glaucoma. When I saw an eminent eye specialist in London he said that it was inconceivable that doctors here had not diagnosed it correctly, because with drops it could have been arrested. I did have a major operation, but unfortunately I see less. But these things happen. It was not the fault of the doctor.

I try to be as independent as possible. By using an electric typewriter I am able to maintain an extensive correspondence with friends in Europe. Since I might type the wrong numbers, someone does address the envelopes for me.

I live alone. Much of the furniture is what I brought over from Bavaria when I came here in 1932. Above my bed are boxes with the texts of all the plays and films in which I appeared. Since I have been in this same apartment, which, thank God, is rent controlled, for more than twenty-five years, I know where everything is and can feel my way around all right.

I don't worry about something happening to me. Perhaps I'm a fatalist. A neighbor has a key and the landlord has the name of my lawyer. I try to get out every day. I suppose if they didn't see me, someone would come to check.

My memory is good, both of recent and distant events. Perhaps it is because I was always exercising my memory in learning scripts. Also, my knowledge of languages may have helped. I get Talking Books from the Library of Congress in English, French, German, and Italian just to keep fresh with all those languages.

Recently I have begun composing limericks just to keep my mind active. It started in a very funny way. A woman sent me some soup. She said it was lentil soup. I tried it and didn't think it was lentil soup. I gave some to José Ferrer who lives on this floor also, and he said it wasn't lentil soup; it was pea soup. So I wrote to the lady, "One doesn't have to be mental to distinguish a pea from a lentil." So I started to write good-natured limericks about my friends. I wake up during the night and make up little stories about their idiosyncrasies, all in good fun, of course. My friends are amused and it's a way to exercise my mind.

Friends frequently take me to concerts. There are so many people who are kind to me. One friend comes every Saturday and takes me for a walk and to lunch. A woman who comes in to do some housework will take me shopping or wherever I want to go. Unfortunately, today she told me that she just got a job in a bank. I'm happy for her; it pays more, but now I will have to find someone else.

I was born in Bavaria, Germany. After graduation from the gymnasium in 1916, I served in the German Army with the rank of lieutenant during World War I. I was in the cavalry and used to like to ride horses.

After the war, I married Claire Volkhart, a sculptress. Our only children were twin boys, but they died of a blood disease as infants. Today, they could be saved. Claire herself died of pneumonia in 1935, and I never remarried. I did have a wonderful woman friend for many years. She died of cancer more than twenty years ago. Those are the sad things of life. But I have beautiful memories.

In 1919, just at the time that I got married, I entered the University of Munich with the intention of becoming a doctor like my father but felt that I wasn't cut out for that profession. The theatre and music were of greater interest to me. When I told my father that I wanted to become an actor, his wonderful laconic answer was, "It is much less dangerous to become a bad actor than a bad doctor." What an understanding parent!

After school, I played on the stage in Munich and in Switzerland. An American friend convinced me that I could be a success here, so at the age of 36, I decided to give it a try and was lucky enough to make my New York stage debut the year I arrived. The following year I had the lead in *The Pursuit of Happiness*. That established my reputation. I was in demand as leading man in regional and summer stock theatres all over the United States and Europe. I never had trouble getting work. Wherever I went, I was billed as the star of the Broadway hit, *The Pursuit of Happiness*.

I played with Helen Hayes both in the theatre and on radio, with Burgess Meredith, and so many others. What a shame that Audrey Hepburn died recently. I played with her in *The Nun's Story*. This profession has resulted in my meeting so many interesting people.

One of my friends was Orson Welles. I had an excellent part, that of the Baron, in his film *The Other Side of the Wind*. When the film was finished, he wrote me this note. I keep it always with me in my wallet:

> Dearest Tonio,
>
> I'm sure you will be very happy to be liberated from this palm-fringed prison camp [Hollywood] to be free to fly back to your home and friends. But for me this is a sad occasion. I find myself wishing that your part in this film would go on forever and that we could meet night after night doing more and more new scenes. Indeed, it's with the greatest difficulty that I resist the temptation to write just one more page of dialogue for the Baron. You have contributed an extraordinary performance to our picture. I will be forever grateful to you for that as I rejoice in our friendship.
>
> Yours ever, Orson.

Every summer I fly to Italy and spend two months with friends. I get a wheelchair at the airport. For my 95th birthday, twenty-one European friends came to visit me in Italy. I think they were pressed to come by an English friend who said that it might be the last time they could see me. Well, I went again the following year and plan to do so again this summer as well. When I'm there, I swim because there's a pool. Here, I was a member of the New York Athletic Club. But now I can't see well enough to go. But I was always exercising, using the stationary bicycle and other equipment.

I'm Catholic but not very devout. Faith is difficult. As a child I was very religious. But I don't believe in an afterlife. It must be wonderful to believe that we are going to a better life. But I haven't got that faith. Rose Kennedy believed and so she could bear the loss of her children. It's wonderful to believe, but you cannot force it.

When I dream, and I dream a lot, it is happy dreams. There is always warmth, no angry relations in my dreams. If dreams reflect our conscious life, then it is true that I have had a happy life. To God or whoever it is who is responsible for it, I can only be grateful. If I died today, I could say only that I had lived a very beautiful and charmed life. Even when it looked at times like something bad had happened, it soon turned back again to something positive. Even the loss of my eyesight, although difficult, did not make me bitter. I figured that at my age I have to expect something and remembered all those poor people who suffer from cancer and are in terrible pain. I say to myself that I may have trouble seeing, but I don't suffer any physical, mental, or emotional pain.

Actually, I don't think about my age that much. When a birthday comes around I say, "Is it possible that I have lived this long!"

At age 98, Selwart sent a personally typed letter in which he said that he was well and had spent two summer months in Italy "using my brain conversing in four languages."

PLANNING INTERNATIONAL
ART TOURS AT 90:
ELOISE SPAETH

A picture window looks out on the lush green of a golf course in East Hampton, New York, one of the most beautiful and presti-gious areas of Long Island. On a lectern in the living room of Eloise Spaeth's spacious home is a large album with dozens of birthday cards. Each is an original drawing or painting by a different Long Island artist. The birthday being celebrated was Mrs. Spaeth's 80th, ten years ago. The tribute was for her decades of service to the artist colony, which uses the Hamptons as its summer gathering place.

On a wall of the same room is a framed collage in the shape of a tree, titled "Spaeth: the roots, branches and twigs." It contains photos of Mrs. Spaeth and her husband on their wedding day in 1924. Above these roots are pictures of their four children together with numerous grandchildren and great-grandchildren. The collage was assembled by a friend on the occasion of Mrs. Spaeth's recent 90th birthday.

Art and family are the pillars which support the life structure of an elegant lady.

I was born in Decatur, Illinois, but when I was six we moved to Oklahoma City. At ten I went to the Visitation convent school in Dubuque, Iowa, and stayed there until I graduated from high school. I went to college for about a year but really wanted to go on the stage. So, I moved to New York; I had to give it a try.

I got some small parts, walk-ons mostly, in several plays. I modeled hats but wasn't the right type, physically, to be a model; I was too short. After a year, my mother called and asked me to come home saying that my father, a lawyer, was sick. When I got there, I found that he wasn't all that sick. It was her way of getting me back. It worked out well. In fact, I had a very good time. I was the girl who had been on the New York stage and so was very popular.

Very soon I met Otto Spaeth and we were married when I was 22. After a honeymoon in Cuba, we moved to St. Louis and lived there for about fourteen years. My husband was a very successful businessman. He would buy a business, develop it, and then sell it. Business really got good during World War II. We moved to Dayton, Ohio, where my husband produced a machine which set type. Shortly thereafter, photo offset was introduced and that killed the typesetting business. But Otto was very enterprising and was able to move on to something else.

My life during all this time was that of mother and homemaker. We had a daughter shortly after marriage. Then, when we didn't have another child for four or five years, we adopted one. But as fate would have it, we then had a son. After he was born, I felt that it wasn't right to have the adopted child squeezed in between our own two, so we adopted another child. Over many years, I was busy with the four children.

After the war we moved to New York where we lived in an apartment on Park Avenue for many, many years. In fact, I gave it up only last year. Art was always part of our lives. My husband and I had fun collecting together. Many of the works I have here were bought decades before Otto's death twenty-five years ago.

Long before that I had gotten involved in the art world and continue to be active today. My first major role was as a board member of the American Federation of Arts. They soon asked me to be chairman of traveling shows. The Federation would send paintings and sculpture to museums all around the country. My position, which was as a volunteer, required that I visit museums all over the country in order to talk to the directors to find out what they wanted. It was time consuming, but stimulating and enjoyable.

Later I got involved with the Archives of American Artists, an organization which saves the papers and memorabilia of American artists. So, for example, if you wanted to write a book on Winslow Homer, you'd come to us, and we'd have his papers, biographies, and anything else which would help you understand Homer better. I'm now Chairman Emeritus of the Archives, which used to be in New York but has become a branch of the Smithsonian in Washington. There are collecting units in various places in the country. People go out and interview artists and acquire their papers.

Earlier yet, the archives were located in Detroit and Mrs. Edsel Ford supported it very generously. When she died, her children were not interested in it. So fund raising became necessary. Well, I got the idea of taking groups of our members on trips to art galleries and museums abroad. I should have taken out a patent on the idea because now every museum in the country does it. In fact, we had two museum directors on our first trip. They went right home and started the same kind of trips themselves. We've been all over the world and were the first ones into Russia after it was opened up. This fall we are taking a group of people to Germany and Austria.

For twelve to fifteen years, I did all the planning myself. Now I have a partner but still prepare the copy and send out letters. Effort is made to arrange private showings for our group. Also, I try to get the names of collectors in the foreign cities so that we might visit them as well. It makes it more personal and memorable to meet with people who can, as it were, take us behind the scenes and show us work not available to the general public. In connection with my work for the archives, I make several trips to Washington each year.

Although I lived in Manhattan, I had this vacation home in East Hampton. For many years I was active in the art world here during the summer, especially Guild Hall. I still have many friends here. I've voted out here for many years, believing that my vote counted more here than it did in the city.

About a year ago, at the prompting of my children, I gave up my Park Avenue apartment and moved out here full time. My daughter lives here with me. It's very convenient for both of us since both of us were alone.

I still go into New York frequently to meet people and to attend meetings and functions. There's a young man who drives me or I take the Hampton Jitney, a very nice bus service between the Hamptons and the city. I'm a member of the Cosmopolitan Club, so when I'm in the city, I get a room there and have dinner in the club restaurant. It's convenient for me.

My health always has been very good, perhaps that's why I have lived so long. I do have an inclination toward high blood pressure, so the doctor recommended that I not eat red meat. My eyes are not as strong as they were, and so I am selective in what I read. It's the better part of wisdom not to overdo it. Also, I have trouble sleeping through the night and get more tired than I used to. But I can't complain. Oh yes, on a trip to Washington about a month ago, I did take a fall in the airport; really banged myself up. But I've never broken any bones.

I was raised a Catholic and my husband was a Catholic. I go to Mass every Sunday but can't say that my thinking on religion has changed very much with time.

Family is very precious. I have ten grandchildren and sixteen great-grandchildren. When I lived in the city, I saw them more often than I do since I moved out here. But there is one granddaughter who lives nearby. I feel close to her and am interested in what she is doing.

You may think I'm doing a lot, but there's a woman in town over ninety who owns a large real estate business. She has many people working for her but remains active herself. She's quite remarkable.

My major project at the moment is writing a history of how I organized the art tours. Not only does it give me personal satisfaction, but I believe it will be archival material. After all, it was an important development in the art world. I think it deserves to be recorded.

A PRACTICING CLINICAL PSYCHOLOGIST AT 92: HARRIET STRACHSTEIN, Ph.D.

*A*n interview with a nonagenarian practicing psychologist is an appropriate place to reflect on the mental health of nonagenarians. A distinction must be made between emotional health and brain health, between emotional problems and organic brain disorders.

Emotional problems.

Emotional problems stem from personality features and environmental experiences. Recently, two physicians were censured for malpractice by the medical board and had their licenses suspended for six months. Both claimed that they had been judged unfairly. One of the doctors took a six-month vacation and returned to work. The other became depressed and withdrawn. Both men experienced the same loss, but one was able to adjust smoothly while the other was devastated and developed serious emotional problems. The personality of one enabled the man to deal with stress successfully. The personality of the other was not well-adapted to stress management.

Several of the nonagenarians indicated that they had suffered mild situationally-caused emotional problems. *Harry Granick was hospitalized for a short period after the death of his wife of more than fifty years with what he identified as stress related to the loss of his spouse. Similarly, Eugene Curry suffered from anxiety over the failing health of his wife. Not able to sleep or drive, he sought help from a counselor and was able to recover. Several others revealed moderate emotional problems, such as Lilian Uviller who was depressed because she was lonely and confined to the house, and Edward Corcoran who was depressed because he could no longer drive.*

Aside from these cases, no evidence of emotional problems was detected in the nonagenarians interviewed. None revealed any history of emotional or mental problems.

Organic brain disorders

The Diagnostic and Statistical Manual of Mental Disorders, *which mental health practitioners use to classify diseases, lists more than three dozen conditions under the heading "Organic Brain Syndromes." One of them, senile dementia, refers to chronic psychotic disorders which afflict some elderly people, resulting in a progressive decline in mental functioning. The condition, associated with changes in the brain, primarily the dissolution of brain cells, is especially likely to occur after age 80 and is characterized by significant memory impairment. A high proportion of the residents of nursing homes suffer from this condition.*

The most common and best known form of organic brain syndrome is Alzheimer's disease which produces intellectual deterioration and personality disintegration. As the American population ages, the number of people suffering from Alzheimer's disease is increasing substantially. Extensive research continues to search for a more complete understanding of the disorder in the hope of eventual prevention and cure.

The nonagenarians presented in this book are clear evidence that serious emotional problems and/or brain diseases are not inevitable accompaniments of old age. Quite the contrary. Increasing numbers of extremely old people are living mentally healthy lives. The 92-year-old Harriet Strachstein is a prime example.

I was born nearly 93 years ago on the Lower East Side of New York.

My parents were Polish immigrants. My father didn't know English and for many years he delivered bread to restaurants and stores. My mother made all our clothes and did all the cooking from fresh ingredients. We didn't know what a can was. She made cheese and salted her own herring. A peddler came around with large cans of milk. Mother would lower a pail from the fourth floor and he would fill it up. She would pull up the pail and send down the money.

Despite the poverty, my father put all three children through college. Both my brothers became physicians. Abner went through Columbia University on a scholarship. At the time there was a quota on Jews, only 10% in each class. When Abner received his M.D., he became an instructor at Columbia and was one of the greatest neuropathologists in the world. He discovered the virus that causes cerebral palsy for which he received many awards and appeared on the cover of *Time* magazine. He died of cancer about three years ago.

My other brother, Alexander Wolf, also was a neurologist. During World War II, he was sent to take care of soldiers who were shell-shocked. There were so many of them that he didn't have time to work with all of them individually. So he put them in groups of ten. When he came back to New York, he became a psychiatrist and began to do group therapy. He is the father of analytic group therapy. He trained me to do group therapy. Alexander is seven years younger than I am and still working.

It cost a lot to put the boys through medical school. My father wanted me to go to college but first I had to work. For a number of years I was a model. I made $75 a week which was a huge amount of money, about three times what my father was making. On that job I ran into some sexual harassment. I was modeling French blouses and my boss wanted me not to wear a brassiere. I drew the line at that.

In college, I majored in journalism and did very well. My teacher got me a job on *The New York Globe* while I was still a student. I had the lobster shift, midnight to eight.

When I finished college, I became a free-lance literary agent and helped many writers get a start. However, overall, I didn't make a great deal of money.

Harriet Strachstein, Ph.D.

When I was 20, I married a man who was our family doctor. I had met him when I was 10 years old and hated him because I had been badly burned making cocoa, and he came and pulled the skin off my thigh. I didn't think he was gentle enough. He was 23 years older than I. Unfortunately, he developed heart problems. For the last ten years of our marriage he was sick, especially in the last three. I was in and out of the hospital with him. My life became desperate. I couldn't make a living as a literary agent, and my husband had been forced to give up his practice, and the insurance had run out. We were forced to move from Park Avenue to an $85-a-month three-room apartment.

So at age 55 I went back to school, working during the day and taking classes at night. I was worn out from caring for my husband and trying to do my best for several writers. I pushed myself. You couldn't give up or feel sorry for yourself. My husband needed nurses round the clock. The children needed money to go to school.

I had two daughters and both have had serious problems in their lives. The older girl married a wonderful man who was studying to be a doctor. They had a two-year-old daughter (now a prize-winning poet) and were coming from California to New York, when their car turned over in a storm and the husband was killed. My daughter had a concussion. She and her child moved into our small apartment. So now I had to take care of them as well as my husband. I took the little girl to school. Every time it rained, my daughter would say, "It's raining on Dick's grave." Eventually, she married again, a psychiatrist who just retired.

My other daughter was a talented writer and a professor of psychology at Penn State University. She had three children, but her marriage was unhappy. Her husband was an alcoholic. She got a divorce, had a nervous breakdown, gave up her job at Penn State, and three years ago died of cancer.

My life has been a struggle.

I was the oldest person in my graduate school class. In fact, they didn't want to admit me. I took a few courses and did so well that they let me in. I got A's all the way through the program and was given the New York University Founders Day Award for being the only student to have received all A's. Twenty-eight people took the comprehensive exam and I was one of only three who passed. When I received my Ph.D. in Psychology, I was 60 years old. Most people were retiring when I was just getting started. It was shortly after I received my doctorate that my husband died. I have been a widow for over 30 years and during all that time have worked as a psychologist.

All these years I have lived in this building on the West Side of Manhattan. A stipulation in the lease permits me to practice in my apartment. A full time housekeeper does the shopping and cooking, answers the phone, and serves as receptionist when patients come.

It was only three years ago when my daughter died that I began to feel my age. Until then I used to walk the forty blocks to Macy's. I still walk quite a lot and never get tired of New York. There's so much to do. I practically live in the theatre. I love everything about plays. Since I used to represent playwrights and film writers, they still call on me for advice. They respect my criticism. I love my friends and entertain every weekend.

In the past, I had nine groups, sixty or seventy patients. Now it's down to three groups and a total of thirty-five patients. To me, that's a small practice. Groups and couples, as well as individuals, give each day a different flavor. Every hour is different. My plan is to continue working. The word "retire" to me means "retire to the grave." I love what I'm doing and I love to live well.

Patients use me as a role model. There was one woman who was a malpractice lawyer, but she hated every minute of it. She came to me depressed. This was about ten years ago. I asked her what she would prefer to do. She said, "I've always wanted to be a doctor, but my parents wouldn't allow me to go to medical school. Now it's too late. I'm 38 years old." I convinced her to do it. Three years ago, she graduated from medical school.

I don't have any medical problems except old age. Besides eye doctors, I haven't seen a doctor in years. I watch my weight. I want to look good. Looks are important in this field. When you have to sit for forty-five minutes looking at someone, that person must look fairly attractive.

At times I hug patients. Doing groups has made me less orthodox. You have to show feelings, be responsive to people's needs. I utilize the "alternate session" technique invented by my brother. A group meets once a week with me for an hour and a half. Then it meets another day in someone's house without me. This gives them the idea that peers can be valuable, that you don't always need an authority figure. I never ask them what happened at the alternate session. I tell them that I trust them. The alternate session is important because most patients have suffered from too much control by an authority figure, at home and at work. They need to experience themselves as persons capable of acting on their own.

I think I have lived so long because I do work that I love. I don't think it has anything to do with genes, because nobody in my family lived beyond their seventies. My brother once said that if you find work that you love, that is paradise; it's the only paradise that exists.

Obviously, I have had problems, but I don't dwell on them. I always remember what my mother used to say, "That which doesn't kill you will only make you stronger."

As Dr. Strachstein reached her 95th birthday, she was still practicing her profession.

PIANIST AND POET AT 93:
LILIAN UVILLER

*N*ew York City can be a lonely place for someone of any age who lives alone. Mrs. Uviller's apartment on lower Fifth Avenue is just a stone's throw from Washington Square Park, where the diversity of the metropolis is enacted in a continuously shifting pageant of noise, movement, and color. She is not a participant in the pageant, nor a member of the audience. In fact, she seems unaware of the stream of life flowing ceaselessly past her elegant but ancient building, once a hotel but now a co-op. Although Mrs. Uviller complains of loneliness and has little contact with other people, she lives a rich and varied life.

It is important not to restrict meaningful human existence too narrowly. As Etienne Saint Exupéry says in The Little Prince, *"What is essential is invisible to the eye."* The young people who see Mrs. Uviller shuffling along the street could never imagine the flexibility and depth of her mind nor the agility in her aged hands. Each day she practices the piano for two hours, reads books in psychology, and composes poems. Paint is peeling from the walls of her living *room and the antique furniture may not have been moved in decades, but at 93, Mrs. Uviller is probably not nearly as lonely as many of the young people sitting on hard benches in the shadow of the Washington Square arch.*

I have lived all my life in New York City. In fact, I was born not far from here ninety-three years ago. The city was a very different place then!

I've had a double education. My early training was in music and for many years as a young woman I gave piano lessons. I still play a great deal. One reason I took this large apartment was so that my grand piano would fit.

Then, when my children went to college, I got very lonely and in my fifties went to Columbia University where I earned an undergraduate degree in sociology and a graduate degree in psychology. I was in my sixties when I went to work as a therapist at the health center of the garment workers union. I still see two people here but officially am retired.

However, my main occupation took place before that. For twenty years I was supervisor of one of the largest of the sixty-four day centers for senior citizens conducted by the city of New York. It was when I retired from the city that I did the supportive therapy for the garment workers. I remained with them until I was in my early seventies.

I've been married twice. My first husband was chairman of the Mediation Board for New York State. We had two children, both of them Harvard graduates. My son lives here in New York with his wife, who is a judge. He's a professor at Columbia University Law School and just last week was interviewed on TV with reference to the Rodney King case. My daughter is a clinical psychologist in Cambridge, Mass.

We were married nearly 50 years and lived in a beautiful co-op on Fifth Avenue overlooking Central Park. Then 20 years ago, my husband died of cancer. At the age of 75 I married again, a man who had been a friend of my first husband. My second husband was a published author, someone I had known for 25 years and whose wife had died. It was a marriage of companionship. My second husband died five years ago of a heart attack. Both my marriages were very happy.

How I happen to be here is that when my first husband died, I just couldn't go back into our apartment. I didn't spend one night there again. I ran away, leaving behind all my beautiful furniture and moved into a furnished room here. After about six months, I had a great longing for my piano and so moved to a larger apartment. Then, when I married my second husband, I moved to this much larger apartment in the same building. Besides what you see, there is an attached studio apartment, which I have rented to an NYU student. Actually, I am in the process of looking for a retired woman, not as old as myself, who could have that apartment and provide me with some companionship.

Seven or eight years ago I had a hip fracture and since then I don't go out alone. When my husband was alive I would go out with him. Now there's a wonderful organization called the Visiting Village Neighbors. They provide escort service. When I have to go shopping or anyplace else, I just call and a volunteer comes. Aside from such local trips, I haven't been anywhere since my son drove me to my granddaughter's wedding on Cape Cod nearly a year ago. But I don't miss it much. I had the good fortune of doing extensive traveling with my first husband. In a trip to Russia, we had a room overlooking Red Square. I could look down and see the long lines of people waiting to enter Lenin's tomb.

Also, there's an agency called Homebound Repair. A man comes in once a month. If a lamp needs repair, he fixes it. He checks the floors and windows. Another service that helps me is the Caring Community which administers Meals-on-Wheels in this neighborhood. They bring a hot meal each day, so I don't have to do much cooking. By the way, years ago I gave lectures on psychology to the Caring Community. The light housework I do myself. So far, with the help of these agencies, I've been able to manage and am not a burden to my son.

Although to all intents and purposes I am housebound, I believe that I have more resources than most people. I have never given up my playing. Not only do I play for about two hours a day but am making tapes; I have about two dozen now. However, because of cataracts in my eyes, I'm finding it difficult to read music. I spoke to my doctor about a cataract operation. He said that as long as I can see as well as I do, he didn't think I should have it.

Also, I read a great deal, mostly Freudian psychology. I suppose people in their 90's who don't have my resources spend their time watching television. It is a lifesaver for them. I watch it once a day at six o'clock.

The afternoons are very lonely. I would think that for most old people, those not suffering from a grave illness, the problem is loneliness. Almost all my friends are gone and my daughter is so far away that our contact is mainly by phone. Thank God, my son, no matter how busy he is, stops by once a week.

I have three grandchildren, all of them girls, but I seldom see them. In any case, grandchildren are really an intellectual concept. By that I mean, I love them very much, but they are on a different wavelength. And they, for their part, may love me, but I am from a different time, another age. It is not so much an emotional concept as an intellectual concept—your genes are being continued.

My children never invited me to come to stay with them and I don't think I would want to. They have a right to their own private lives and I would be a burden. It used to be the custom that when a mother was left alone she would go to live with her children, but that's not very common nowadays. In earlier days, there were economic reasons for mothers living with their children. A woman didn't have a career of her own or financial resources. So they were dependent on their children. Nowadays with Social Security and pensions, you can live independently. That's what most people want.

When my second husband died, I did apply to a retirement home. But when it came down to a final decision, I found it very hard to break up this home. My piano is very dear to me and I have collected many invaluable antiques. All the paintings were done by my son. Everything here reminds me of my life. So I gained something by not breaking up my home. On the other hand, I sacrificed something because I wouldn't be so lonely. You just can't have it both ways.

I am not religious but believe there is something spiritual in man, something that sets us apart from everything else in the world. One of the challenges of the very old is to free ourselves from the fear of death. Otherwise, we would live in a very tense atmosphere. Freedom from the fear of death is something young people don't have to worry about but which, for people as old as I am, is critical to peace of mind. Now I can't say that I've completely freed myself. I'm reminded of what Woody Allen said, "I'm not afraid of dying, but I don't want to be there when it happens." What I think that means is that we want to die in our sleep. That's what is meant by not being there when it happens. When my mother was on her deathbed, she said to me, "It's not so hard to die. What's hard is to leave your family."

One problem I have is insomnia. I wake up at about 2:00 A.M. Well, a couple of years ago I felt the urge to write poems. There are now over 200. They just pop into my head. I don't have to think about them. I inherited a gift for language from my father. He was born in Austria and his native tongue was German. Although he didn't have much formal education, he was always writing. I have a diary he wrote when he and my mother went abroad in 1925. Although he never went to school here, it is written in beautiful English. Also, when you're a musician, you have a feeling for rhythm that carries over into language. I don't have any difficulty with words. I don't go to them; they come to me.

Here is a poem that I wrote recently.

MY DAY

One climbs Mt. Everest each lonely day
Ever trying sadness to allay.
The hours creep slow, one by one,
Until the day is almost done.
The evening news comes on at last,
A signal that the day is past.
A sense of repose with the nighttime meal
A time to relax, a time to heal.

MEMORY GYMNASTICS AT 91:
ISADORE WARSHAW

*O*ne of the greatest concerns of older people is the prospect of losing mental capacity, in particular, the ability to remember things. Certainly, some memory loss is a common experience. However, the extraordinary memory of Isadore Warshaw stands witness to the possibility for vigorous mental functioning into the tenth decade of life.

Warshaw invented what he calls "Geographic Gymnastics." He has compiled lists of the fifty states of the union, their capitals, and their major cities. There are a total of ten lists arranged in various orders. For example, one list of state capitals is in alphabetical order, while another has them arranged according to the alphabetical order of the states. What he has done is memorize all these lists forwards and backwards! To prove that he had done so, he insisted on reciting for me the names of the states in alphabetical order forwards and backwards and then proceeded to do the same thing for the state capitals. He has worked out an ingenious set of memory aids, such as imagining himself flying back and *forth across the country, visiting the states in alphabetical order.*

Each day Warshaw takes a mile and a half walk around the mobile home park in Sarasota, Florida, where he lives with his 79-year-old wife, Bertha. While walking, he recites the lists to himself, claiming that it makes the walk more enjoyable. He says that, since he has no one to talk to, he talks to himself!

Memorizing lists of states and cities may seem like a useless activity, but Warshaw believes that it helps keep his mind fine tuned. Also, he has "performed" his memory feat at meetings of various groups and so has received positive reinforcement for his effort.

My first wife died of tuberculosis at age 39, leaving me with two small children. At the time, I was not in very good financial shape and was emotionally drained. Well, I met Bertha who was 32 and had never been married. The kids fell in love with her. My son, who was five at the time said, "Daddy, why don't you marry Bertha so that I can have a house again." We were living in a rented apartment. My daughter was 10 and also was attracted to Bertha's warmth and cheerfulness. She turned out to be a better mother to them than are many natural mothers. The children called her Mom, and now almost fifty years later, they still relate to her as their mother.

The experience of marrying again and the good fortune of having a loving mother for the children rejuvenated me. I got a job that developed into a very satisfying long-term career. In a sense, my life began again in my forties.

I was born in Albany, New York, 91 years ago and lived there until my first wife died. Then I relocated to Bridgeport, Connecticut, where I worked for a lumber company until I retired at age 70, at which time we moved here to Florida.

I'm not rich but live on a level equivalent to when I had a job. Before coming here I had never been in a mobile home and thought they were all flimsy and cheap. Well, my sister-in-law lived in one and said that you could pay $30,000 or $40,000 for one. I thought she was crazy. She and her husband brought me to see this one. I couldn't believe how large and attractive it was. It has 1440 square feet and is

60 by 24. The cabinets are better than you would find in a $100,000 conventional home. There are two bathrooms and all the best appliances. I bought it and we've been here now for 21 years and are very happy. The mobile home park has over 900 homes, most of them double size and on large lots. We have an owners' association and work hard to keep the neighborhood looking nice. People going by don't realize the homes are mobile.

Two years ago my doctor told me that I had type two diabetes which is non-insulin dependent. Well, he didn't educate me as to what to do about it. So I went to the library to look it up and attended a lecture at the local hospital. I learned a lot. All the doctor did was keep score. So I took charge of it myself. I contacted experts in diabetes and educated myself. The hospital here has a special dining room for diabetics, offering a complete meal for $5. There's a special cook, a nurse trained in diabetes, and a dietitian who understands the needs of diabetics. My wife and I went there nearly every day for a year and a half. Well, I was overweight and lost a pound a month. Now I weigh 145 pounds. The results of my recent blood tests show that my cholesterol, triglicerides, etc. are normal. The improvement is due to diet and exercise.

Let me tell you about my experience with exercise and my doctor. I was walking a mile a day at the rate of three and a half to four miles per hour. Then I began to feel pain in my calf and consulted the doctor I have gone to for twenty-one years. Right away he wanted to send me to a surgeon. I told him that I had read in a newspaper article by a doctor that the best way to deal with pain like that is to take a rest and then keep on going. So I decided to try it. In fact, I increased my walk from one mile to a mile and a half. Each day I felt the pain later and later in the walk. Now I do the entire walk and have no pain. If I had listened to my doctor, I would have been operated on—unnecessarily.

On another occasion, I told my doctor that I experienced pain in my knees. He felt them and said that I had arthritis. It was safe to say that to a 90-year-old guy! Well, I decided that I would check it out, so I went to an orthopedic specialist. He took x-rays: front, side, and back and said, "Mr. Warshaw, you don't have arthritis. Those pictures are the best set of knees I've ever seen." And he was a specialist who used to replace knee joints. The point is that you have to take command of your own health.

Along the same line, when I moved here I weighed 205 pounds and on three occasions was hospitalized with angina attacks. But by lowering my weight and being careful with my diet, I cured all that and have not had an attack in fifteen years.

The Florida room, which was added to the house, serves as my den. I have about 600 books on business and American history. I was appointed to the Sarasota County Bicentennial Commission and worked as education director giving speeches at different clubs. I must have twenty or thirty speeches on different subjects and hundreds of slides, which I made from pictures in books. I would give a slide lecture tailored to the interests of the organization. One of my presentations on Lincoln ends with Walt Whitman's poem "O Captain! My Captain!" When I gave the talk last year, tears came to my eyes as I read the poem. When I finished, the audience was quiet for a time and then broke out in loud applause. Many asked for a copy of the speech so I had it printed up.

Now I'm working on a paper on the evolution of the Constitution. It opens with Ralph Waldo Emerson's "Concord Hymn," which contains the famous line, "And fired the shot heard round the world" referring to the start of the Revolutionary War. I go on to make the point that an even more powerful "shot" was fired twelve years later when the Constitution was framed.

I never smoked cigarettes but did chew on cigars for a number of years. It was good for relieving tension while I worked. You had to keep pulling on it to keep it lit. A philosopher once said that a cigar is like a woman: if you don't give it a lot of attention the fire will go out.

When we moved down here, I wanted to get a job but my wife wouldn't let me. So, I joined the Service Corps of Retired Executives or SCORE. It's a project of the Small Business Administration in which people with experience give free counseling to help small businesses with their problems. I worked at that for 12 or 13 years. They still call on me when they need someone to cover the office.

Then I took over the editorship of the newsletter of the local B'nai B'rith lodge. It was just a mimeographed publication which I built up to a printed 40-page monthly. I did everything. I got the ads and wrote the articles and improved it up to the point where it won awards as the best B'nai B'rith bulletin in the United States. I had been in the printing and newspaper business as a young man and so knew how to do it right. I gave up the editorship about two years ago but still help with it. This year, I'm program chairman. It's the 150th anniversary of B'nai B'rith and we're planning a major celebration. I'm going to invite the President of the United States to attend. You can never tell. If we hold it in some big hotel here and invite him long enough in advance, he might come. I never find pennies on the street because I look up and not down.

We have friends in Venice with whom we get together once a week. We drove down there yesterday. After dinner in a restaurant, we go back to the house and play cards. That gives us mental exercise.

Speaking of mental exercise, people say that when you get old you lose your memory. But I believe in the principle "use it or lose it." When I go for my walk, I recite things that I have memorized. I know by heart the 23rd Psalm, the Preamble to the Constitution, the Declaration of Independence. I can name the presidents from Washington to Clinton, forwards and backwards, and tell you the years they served. I've learned the states from Alabama to Wyoming backwards and forwards and their capitals and principal cities. I started doing this about ten years ago. I call it Geographic Gymnastics. I've done it a few times at dinner clubs. They thought it was remarkable. It shows the memory capacity of someone in his nineties. This is not to say that I don't forget things. I might go to the next room for something and forget what it was. But I go back and reconstitute it.

For my 90th birthday, my son, who is a Ph.D. chemist in Chicago, made the arrangements at a restaurant here. There were thirty people present. To me, the years are only numbers, yet I'm proud of the numbers. My wife and I both say that we are not growing old but only older.

My main concern in life is living with as little friction as possible, smoothing the way so that I can live past 100. I don't think it will be difficult. I've taken good care of myself, have a happy environment, and am not acquisitive. I'm satisfied with what I have.

PRESERVING FAMILY HISTORY AT 90:
ALICE L. WHEELER

*F*airhaven, located in Sykesville, Maryland, is a luxury "continuing-care community," where residents enjoy a secure, elegant, and enriched life. The beautiful and well-equipped complex contains 277 cottages and apartments and a 103-room health center or nursing home. An all-inclusive contract covers all health needs for life. Although related to the Episcopal Diocese of Maryland, Fairhaven is open to all who can afford to pay.

Fees vary with the accommodation. Although Mrs. Wheeler paid somewhat less five years ago when she moved in, today her one-bedroom apartment with den would cost an entrance fee of $99,000 plus a monthly charge of $1,775. Her apartment is large, airy, and fully equipped. Weekly maid service includes a change of towels and linens. The recreational facilities include a three-hole golf course, an indoor swimming pool, a library, lounge, music and game rooms, and a woodworking shop. A post office, bank, beauty parlor, and barber shop are available in a centrally located building which has the feel of the lower floors of a fine hotel.

It is important to look into total care communities while still in good health, since prospective residents must be examined by a retirement community doctor to determine that no mental or physical problem exists. Once accepted, a complete medical exam is provided once a year plus less comprehensive checkups quarterly.

Residents are required to eat one meal a day in the comfortable dining room, which has full waitress service, or to notify the office if they are to be away. The meal can be breakfast, lunch, or dinner. This requirement helps to insure that residents eat properly, encourages social interaction, and most of all, is a check on the condition of residents. Mrs. Wheeler said that on one occasion her presence in the dining room wasn't noted by the hostess and that within an hour someone called to inquire after her.

Yes, I carry myself very erect. When I was a girl my mother used to say, "Stand up straight, as if you were hung from the ceiling." A number of people here walk bent over. Not me, and that despite the fact that shortly after moving here, while on a visit back to upstate New York where I used to live, I fell and broke my back. I returned here in an ambulance and spent three months in the health center, where they took very good care of me until I was able to return to my own apartment.

I was born in a small town near Rochester, New York. Well, two months ago when I was 90, my daughter and granddaughter gave me a surprise party. They said they were taking me out for dinner, but we went to the lounge here which is used for special events. Was I ever surprised to find twenty-five of my friends from back home gathered there! I'm still getting over the shock. Never do that to someone. It was nice, but too upsetting. Here's an album of pictures. You can see how stunned I look.

My father owned a livery business. Salesmen and others would rent a horse and carriage with a driver to go off to rural areas. It was the horse and buggy age. I was the last of six children, although two had died before I came along. My mother and father were 45 when I was born. Neither of them had a college education but were very well read. I can still picture the shelf where the classics were kept, like

Scott's Waverly novels. And they knew how to use the English language. I never felt that I had uneducated parents.

I am descended from an early governor of Connecticut and am listed in the book, *The Descendants of William Lette, One of the Founders of Guilford, Ct. & the Governor of the Ct. Colony.* The first edition was complied in 1884 and the second in 1934. My marriage to Milton Wheeler and the birth of our daughter, Anne, are listed, but it's time for someone to add the next generation. Some people tell me that I shouldn't write in the book, but I've been adding information in the margins, such as my grandchildren. I don't think it desecrates the book.

Since I was very young, I saved money for a college education picking berries and other odd jobs. I attended Mechanics Institute, now known as Rochester Institute of Technology, where I lived in the girls' dormitory. In the summers, another girl and I would go across to Canada to work in a hotel. There were girls there from all over waiting on tables and cleaning the rooms. It was like a vacation, but mainly it was to make money for school.

With my B.S., I began teaching in the cooperative extension program which is directed by Cornell University. I was a home demonstration agent, which means that I went around teaching women what today is called home economics. My salary was $1,500—that's a year, not a month! But I was able to pay off school loans.

I met my future husband while we were in high school. However, his father was a physician and had delivered me. He delivered his own son in September and I came along two months later. We didn't marry until we were 26 because we wanted to pay off our college debts first. And although it was the Depression, both of us were fortunate enough to be working. Milton got a bank job and I was able to transfer to the town where he worked. I coordinated the extension program, training the leaders as well as doing much of the teaching myself. Community groups would select people to come to town for a course in food preparation, clothing construction, home furnishing, chair caning, any of a number of areas. I loved the work.

Even when my daughter was born I continued working. My father had died and my mother lived with us. She was with us until she died at the age of 88 and helped take care of Anne. So it wasn't like leaving my daughter with strangers. Also, my schedule allowed me to go home from the office every three hours to feed her.

My husband and I took early retirement at 55. We felt that life was more important than work and wanted to travel. Each winter we just closed up our house and headed off for Florida. We were very compatible and able to entertain ourselves. People wanted us to play bridge, but my husband said that there were more interesting things to do. I still don't play cards. I'm one of the few here who doesn't. I'd rather get out and do some walking. Before breakfast each morning, I walk a mile and a half, weather permitting.

My husband died at the age of 62. He smoked too much. We didn't have many years together in retirement, but it was a very precious time.

After Milton died, I lived alone in our house for twenty-five years, not realizing that as time went by my daughter and granddaughter were growing concerned. They were so subtle. I'd come down from New York on holidays to visit them in Baltimore. On one occasion my granddaughter, a lawyer, said she wanted to take me for a ride. We drove through a couple of retirement communities. When we got here, she pointed out how happy the people looked and said that she was coming back here the following week to give a talk about wills. I was unaware that she was indoctrinating me. At the time, moving to a retirement community was the furthest thing from my mind. But three years later, at the age of 85, I was ready. They didn't pressure me. They knew I would make up my own mind.

I sold my house and my car and came down here. The transition was easy because it was deliberate. I never regret what I did nor would I want to live with the children. It's not fair to them, although my mother lived with me. I feel very connected to family. My granddaughter, who's in her thirties, takes care of all my affairs. She calls me every day from work just to see how I am. My daughter calls regularly also.

This is one of the larger apartments, but some of the newer cottages are very large, even equipped with fireplaces. They're on what we call Millionaires Row. We jokingly say that the people who live there must be millionaires, but we all eat in the same dining room and don't know who's who. Everyone is friendly. I think nearly everyone is college-educated. Others wouldn't be able to afford it.

There's a nature trail and gardens and a greenhouse. I love to be outdoors and around living things, but I want to do it alone. Sometimes someone says that they'd like to walk with me, but I never say that I'd like to do so. When you're a walker, you want to go at your own pace.

When I arrived here, another woman had dinner with me and we had a good time. She suggested that we eat together regularly. I said no, that I didn't want to tie myself down like that. But I'm not a complete loner. A neighbor enjoys Scrabble. At the drop of a hat we play right here in my den. If we use that dictionary to look up a word, there's a penalty. We make up our own rules.

As far as religion is concerned, I consider myself a "floating Protestant." I can worship anywhere. While in college several other girls and I would go to a different church each Sunday. We even went to a Spiritualist church one night but were not comfortable there. When I married we joined the Congregational Church. Fairhaven has a lovely Episcopal chapel, but I don't really care for all the ritual. On Sundays there is a nondenominational service in the auditorium. Wheelchair people come over from the health center and the others walk in. As I've gotten older, my ideas on religion have not changed.

I don't read as much as I used to. My neighbor and I subscribe together to the newspaper. She reads it and then passes it on to me. It economizes on paper, but there's less and less in the paper that I want to read.

My annual physical examination has been scheduled. I feel fine and don't believe I need any medication. Sometimes I think of myself as 80 and not 90, but that's the only thing I think of as far as age is concerned. What difference does it make?

LIBRARY PAGE AT 93:
RUSSELL G. WILSON

*F*or many older people, paid
employment is a financial
necessity. Social Security has annual
cost of living increases, but most
private pensions do not. As the
years and decades pass, inflation
has eroded the value of the income
of many nonagenarians. This has
been true of Russell Wilson, but for
him as for others, psychological
and social reasons for working
outweigh the financial. Work is
closely associated with self worth
and dignity. It also provides a
setting for interacting with people,
for averting isolation and
loneliness.

Mr. Russell's work history
reveals a pattern which might be
appropriate for men and women
who wish to remain in the work force but do not have the energy or
desire to work full time. At age 65, he retired after twenty-two years of
full-time employment testing refrigerators and transformers with the
General Electric Company in Pittsfield, Massachusetts. Not happy in
retirement, he went to work as a handy man at a downtown Pittsfield
department store. His status was "part time-full time," which he

explained meant that he worked five hours a day, five days a week. Despite his part-time hours, he received full-time employee benefits. After working in the store for twenty-two years, the store went out of business, the victim of competition from suburban shopping malls. Since he had been involuntarily terminated, the now 89-year-old man was eligible for unemployment insurance.

After collecting unemployment benefits for a time, he once again decided that he preferred work to retirement and found employment with the Pittsfield Public Library as a part-time page. He works there three days a week from 9 a.m. to 12:00 p.m. Now 93 years old, Mr. Wilson has completed four years with the library and has no intention of retiring.

Since he reached age 90, Mr. Wilson has had his picture in the local newspaper on several occasions. This has made him a celebrity, and it is at the library that his "fans" can offer homage to their hero. Library patrons ask him when his picture will be in the paper again, in jest request his autograph, and insist that they can't believe that he's 93. Never in his life has he received so much attention, and the cornerstone of his status in the community is the fact that he continues to work.

I live in rent subsidized housing. It's not just for older people, but for anyone of modest means. When my wife was alive, we had a two-bedroom apartment, but when she died the regulations required that I move to a one-bedroom unit. It's adequate for my needs.

We had been married for 52 years and were watching *All in the Family* on television one evening when my wife said that she didn't feel well. She had a heart attack and died within a few hours. That was fifteen years ago.

One of my two sons lives in Pittsfield, Mass, also. He retired recently at age 65. He drops by to see me once a week, but I take care of everything for myself. I drive, shop, cook, clean. It's not a problem. When my wife was alive, we used to drive the 300 miles to visit our other son on Long Island. But my son doesn't want me to drive that distance by myself anymore and so once a year, for Fathers' Day, he picks me up and brings me to his house for the weekend. At

Christmas, I take the bus to New York but don't stay away from home for long because I have to be at work.

After the department store where I had been working closed, I was in the library one day and said to myself that I would like to work there. The library hires a number of senior citizens as pages on a part-time basis. Well, I kept pestering and pestering them until they finally hired me. I check in books that are returned, sensitize them, and put them back on the shelves. I think that it keeps my mind limber, because I have to put all the books on the right shelves.

A year ago, when I was 92, *The Pittsfield Gazette*, the weekly paper, sent a reporter to interview me and take a picture of me shelving books. The headline on the article was "The Spry Keeper of the Books." The paper has a weekly feature called "MVP," which means "Most Valuable Pittsfielder." So that week I was the MVP.

A number of people come into the library every morning and sit there for hours reading the papers. They are always asking me when I am going to retire. I couldn't do what they do. I have to be a little bit more active.

Every year the city has a Senior Ball for all the elderly people. Here's a picture which appeared in *The Gazette*. It shows me dancing with my partner at last year's ball. At 92 I was the second oldest person there, but the man who was 94 was in a wheelchair whereas I was dancing. The picture appeared in the paper a second time in their photo review of the year. I've gotten a lot of attention.

I like women and there are several whom I call upon for dancing, but I have never gotten seriously involved. At times I ask myself whether or not I should have someone, but I prefer the independence and don't think I could live with anyone else again.

Recently, our church sponsored a dinner and show in order to raise money. The organizer asked me to read a poem titled, "Observations of an Octogenarian." I told her that I was not an octogenarian but a nonagenarian. So, I doctored up the poem, read it, and acted it out as "Observations of a Nonagenarian." I wore a Boston Red Sox uniform and sneakers. It was great fun. After my act, I asked for someone to come up on stage and dance with me. I had arranged with the musicians to play "Red Sails in the Sunset." So there I was dancing. The place was packed and the local TV station was taping it. They showed it three times on Channel 5.

My father worked in the woolen mill in Pittsfield and we were quite poor. After the ninth grade, I left school and went to work and have been working ever since. My parents died fairly young and so did two of my sisters. My other sister is 91 but not doing so well; she's confined to a wheelchair. I drive up to see her once a week.

My health has been very good. I see the doctor every three months, but he says I'm OK. When I saw him the other day and told him I was going to see you, he said, "Be sure to tell him you dance a lot!" Well, there is one problem. I have an S-shaped throat. It gets constricted and I have trouble swallowing. If I don't chew my food thoroughly, I choke. Twice I've undergone a treatment in which something is put down my throat to stretch my esophagus. I could see what they were doing on a screen.

In my whole life, I had not been in a hospital until a couple of months ago when I had to have a hernia operation. My son came up from New York to be with me. Well, this nurse came and prepared me for the operation, washing me and putting iodine on me. I was flabbergasted. When I told the doctor about it, he said, "You wouldn't want a male nurse to do it because they're all gay!"

My memory is good. At the library, I write down the names of the other people working there. Writing them down seems to help me to remember them.

I don't have any special diet but do have a coffee brandy once or twice a day. Half coffee and half brandy. I have one when I get home from work. It picks me up. Other than that, I don't drink.

At our Baptist church, we have a Sixty Plus group which has a monthly dinner after the service. Older people don't like to go out at night, so we decided to have it at noon. About sixty or seventy people attend. Well, I'm the reservations officer. Since we have to know how many to prepare for, I put a sign-up list in the lobby of the church. However, many people don't sign, so I have to call them. We know who usually comes. It involves about thirty calls a month. I think some of them don't sign up just so they'll get a call from me. They want to have a long conversation, but I have to keep it short since there are so many that I have to contact.

As far as religion is concerned, I love working for the church and taking part in the activities they sponsor, but the Bible and what they teach just doesn't interest me. It's the way I've always been. Because of my job at the public library, they recently put me on the church library committee, but I'm not interested in religious books.

My alone time I spend reading, mostly mysteries, and watching sports on television. I'm a real sports enthusiast, especially for the Red Sox and Celtics. There's a minor league team in Pittsfield and I used to go to all the home games. But the last couple of years it has been too cold for me to attend at night.

My days are busy. Sometimes they call me in to work extra hours or I go and do the same work as a volunteer. I'm most happy when I'm working.

Mr. Wilson wrote that his 95th birthday had been celebrated at the Masonic Lodge to which he belongs. "I had to cut a birthday cake with a hundred men singing 'Happy Birthday.' It was thrilling."

AUDITING COLLEGE COURSES AT 90:
CATHARINE WRIGHT

"*O*ld age is ten years beyond your own chronological age."
Kay Seidell

Many active nonagenarians do not perceive themselves as old. While acknowledging the objective fact, they insist that they "don't feel old," echoing the cliche that "You're only as old as you feel." People in good health, even when in their nineties, tend to reject the label "old," thereby refusing to be negatively stereotyped. Part of their "secret" of longevity may be this tendency to avoid a socially debilitating self-image.

Of course, it might be argued that what is taking place is a refusal to accept the inevitability of decline and death. But it seems closer to the mark to suggest that active nonagenarians define age in terms of competence and well-being. The old are those no longer able to take care of themselves, to negotiate the affairs of the day with relative independence. Also, it must be remembered that for men and women who are free from disease, the deterioration of age is gradual, almost imperceptible, like the moving hands of a clock.

Catharine Wright

Perhaps the most vivid image of the "youthfulness" of some nonage-narians is to picture them as students. Reta Lasky attends courses that are designed specifically for seniors at Florida Atlantic University and Catharine Wright, the subject of this interview, audits regular classes at Swarthmore College in Pennsylvania. She's in the classroom with 20-year-olds and enjoying every moment!

Many colleges permit senior citizens to audit classes either free or for a minimal charge. School districts have inexpensive adult education pro-grams. Libraries and churches sponsor courses and book discussion groups. Elderhostel and Chautauqua offer educational programs for older people. For the more hardy and venturesome, there are educational tours to all parts of the world. Education for the elderly is a growth industry, and increasingly people in their eighties and nineties are participating.

Several years ago, Swarthmore College announced that upon reaching the fiftieth anniversary of graduation, an alumnus could audit one course per semester free of charge. Well, since I am an alum-na and live right here in town, I immediately took advantage of the opportunity. It has been marvelous! I've taken courses in literature, economics, and political science. One course was on the implications of democracy for the individual. The point was made that in the American political environment we are granted freedom and then required to establish our own personal morality. This social milieu has generated extraordinary human progress along with continuous con-flict. The stimulation and energy provided by so many people wrestling within their own minds and hearts for an authentic way of living has been the blessing and the bane of our national experience.

This semester the course I'm taking is Women's Sexuality in Literature and Film. The first third of the course is on heterosexuality, the second third on lesbianism, and the final third on pornography. Here are all these healthy young students talking and talking and making it all so academic. I'm just part of the furniture, sitting in the back and pretending I'm not there. I'm sure the students don't know how old I am. I'd like to tell them because I feel so good about it. Perhaps at the end of the course. Right now, it might scare them off.

Besides the college course, I belong to a Great Books group. Each spring we select ten books for the year and take turns leading the discussion. It's my turn next month and I'm doing *Things Fall Apart* by the Nigerian writer, Chinua Achebe. It's about the colonization of a country and the consequent disruption of the native culture.

It was only two weeks ago that I turned 90 and I had been looking forward to it for months. I feel so absolutely good! My daughter who lives with me was away in Indonesia on a trip, and so I had to send out the invitations to the party and make the arrangements myself. When some friends celebrated their father's 90th birthday, the party was held in a church hall because he kept asking more and more people. When the number reached 185, they said, "Now, daddy, that's enough!" I was so jealous of him! I had only fifty-five people. It was a crowd but not nearly everyone I would have liked to have invited.

It was a great occasion. All twenty-two members of my immediate family were here. They enjoy getting together. As you can see, the house is still full of flowers and balloons and congratulatory cards.

There's a sense of triumph to have arrived at this age. Once you're 80, people start to pay attention to you, to say how wonderful you look, to offer to help you. It reaches a new level when you turn 90. It would be easy to develop the expectation that people defer to you. But it would be a mistake.

After church each Sunday we have coffee. Well, the Sunday before my birthday, I brought a cake so that everyone could help me celebrate. But now people are treating me as if I am 90 and I don't want that.

Is there a down side to being 90, some dark clouds behind the silvery balloons? Well, I have always been an optimistic person, someone who sees the glass half full rather than half empty. It gets on my daughter's nerves sometimes. She says that I can see optimism in anything. I think I have become more like this as I got older. It's a funny thing, really. I've nothing to look forward to, yet I feel so very much at peace. I live right here in the present, not worrying about the future at all. It's a nice time. It may be that having such an attitude helps me to remain healthy. Norman Cousins said that your juices flow better when you are happy. Well, don't they?

If you want to look for a dark side of being 90, it's easy to find. Most of your friends have died or are in nursing homes. There is very little companionship with people your own age.

Of course, I'm very fortunate having my daughter here. Although I still drive and shop and get about by myself, she's a big help as well as good companionship, although I would wish that she might have married and had a home of her own.

I was born in Lansdowne, Pennsylvania. My father built houses. His father had come over from Ireland and started the business, and my father took it over. My mother was from Ireland. I was the youngest of five children. The next oldest was a brother who was six years older than me. Then, when I was 17, both my parents died. My father died of cancer in January and my mother fell down a flight of stairs and broke her neck in August. I know it was tragic, but I was getting ready to go to college and selfishly asked how their deaths would affect my plans. Well, they did. I was registered at a women's Presbyterian college at the other end of the state, but it was decided that it was too far away, and so at the last minute I went to Swarthmore. It was not for financial reasons. In my whole life there have never been financial problems.

Let me tell you about my oldest sister. She was 17 years older than I and became a second mother to me and a powerful role model. She was a real feminist. First, she went to college, to Bryn Mawr, at a time when women rarely went to college. For a time she worked as a secretary but at age 30 decided that she wanted to go to medical school. The family thought she was crazy, that she wouldn't stick it out. Well she did. For a while she practiced in Philadelphia but then went to Cambridge, England, and studied with a famous biochemist. When she returned, she taught at Penn Medical School. She didn't marry but lived with another professional woman. I became the child that she would attempt to shape. I had her to fight with in place of my parents!

After college, I was floundering. I had an interest in music but wasn't accepted in a music program. My sister suggested social work, so I went to school in Philadelphia, became a social worker, and got a position with the Children's Aid Society. I really loved it.

At 25 I married a man from Minnesota. He was an electrical engineer, who worked in the power company which his father had founded. We lived in a small town out there for 22 years and I did a lot of volunteer work, including organizing the family welfare association. In a small town there are many things which a person with some training can do.

We had five children. My oldest soon will be 65. Two are divorced, two married, and Grace, who lives here with me, has never been married. I have very successful grandchildren. Two granddaughters are engineers. Another has a doctorate in robotics.

Next we lived for 14 years in Minneapolis. During that time, we hosted Fulbright students from other countries, two from India, one from Japan, and one from Chile. They were like foster daughters and we kept up with them over the years, going to their weddings and their children's weddings.

We were in our sixties when my husband retired. The first thing we did was take a nine-month trip around the world. A year after we returned, he died. Then I applied for the Peace Corps but was turned down, because I had to put drops in my eyes and they were afraid the prescription would not be available in another country. Anyway, I was accepted by VISTA and worked near Pittsburgh for a year. It was the time of the War on Poverty and I was returning to my calling as a social worker. I remember a white woman saying, "We don't have any trouble with our blacks. They know their place." I was helping blacks in a depressed neighborhood.

How I came back to Swarthmore was somewhat accidental. I had a friend here, visited her, liked it, and decided to settle here when my year with VISTA was over. It was sort of a hub, with my children living within a couple of hours drive in several directions. After renting for a few years, I bought this house and just love it.

About five years ago I really felt weak, with all sorts of aches and pains, arthritis, and no energy. Tests were performed, but the doctor's attitude was that I was old and that nothing could be done. Finally I went to the Geriatric Center of the University of Pennsylvania. A doctor there who really knew older people gave me exercises and encouragement. My arthritis is gone—in remission, I guess. Since then I have felt very energetic. I exercise faithfully. It takes about seven minutes and keeps me limber. Earlier in life, I had never exercised.

I'm active in the Unitarian Church. The community there means very much to me. However, I'm an atheist. I don't believe in any supernatural power. Once you get rid of the idea of the supernatural, you can concentrate on the here and now, on what we owe to one another. Phillip Mayer's *The Mature Spirit: Religion without Supernatural Hope* says that as you try to become an ethical person, your spirit matures. More than needing God or not needing God, the individual needs the search, the pursuit of fuller understanding, of wisdom.

I know it seems strange for an atheist to be so attached to a church, but the Unitarian Church is open to all sorts of people who see life in different ways. Last year we had a discussion of a book titled *Can There Be Good Without God?* Of course there can. Think it out. Teilhard de Chardin wrote of mental and social evolution. Man created God in his own image. We can move beyond that, stand on our own feet: face the world, embrace it, strive to make it better.

At 90, one is somewhat detached from everything. Anything can happen and it wouldn't affect you as much as it might a younger person. It may be a sort of preparation for death. You know you are not going to be around that much longer and that you are not going to influence anything. It frees you to be somewhat distanced from the anxieties and concerns of the world.

Anyone can face death. It's dying that is the worry. To become disabled might give me a very different perspective on life. People who are in pain, who can't care for themselves, who are bedridden certainly have a greater challenge than I do to make sense out of things. Life is so wonderful when you are well. You appreciate it in particular when you have been disabled and have come out of it. There was a year there when I was ten years older than I am now. As long as I can go to school, read, drive, and take care of my affairs, it doesn't seem to matter what my chronological age might be.

After a short illness, Catharine Wright died at the age of 91 from pancreatic cancer.

PEACE AND JUSTICE ACTIVIST AT 96:
LENA WULF

A *photo in the* Hartford
Courant *shows Lena Wulf
conducting an exercise class for
residents of the nursing home in
the Connecticut retirement
community where she lives. The
picture accompanies an article
titled "Seniors Muscling In," which
features nonagenarians who engage
in vigorous exercise regularly. At
the time, Lena Wulf was 91. Now
she is 96 and still working out
regularly. On the day of our
interview, she apologized for
wearing a warm-up suit, explaining
that she had just returned from her
morning exercise class.*

*The only other time that a
picture of Miss Wulf has appeared
in a newspaper was forty years
ago. It shows her as a physical therapist working with a patient. The petite
Miss Wulf is easily recognizable, both in terms of her appearance and her
personality. The article describes her as "a real dynamo," "like a high-
geared colt," and "a wisp of a woman with brushed-back gray-streaked
hair and snapping gray eyes." At the time Miss Wulf was working for the
Hartford Rehabilitation Center. She remained a full time physical therapist*

---

until her retirement at age 73 when she began to channel her energies and apply her skills to volunteer work both within the retirement community and in the broader Hartford area.

Twice in recent years, Miss Wulf has been interviewed on area television programs. The videotapes of the programs show a woman with extraordinary poise, smoothly addressing the questions posed. Her mind is nimble and she speaks without hesitation in perfectly formed sentences and with impressive insight.

In one interview when asked what she thought of old age, she replied:

> Aging has its good side and its bad side. There are things you can't do anymore, like jump into a car and drive to the mountains. But you can move inside and discover inner resources. Since I got out of the rat race of work I find that I'm more compassionate.

In the other interview, when asked about her adjustment to retirement she responded:

> It was only when I retired that I had time to sit back and ask myself what I really wanted from life. What is really important? I decided that _doing_ isn't everything. Most people don't find the time to sit back and waste a half hour just looking at a flower. We don't live with nature anymore.

This stress on the centrality of reflection and passive pursuits did not produce an individual who distanced herself from the issues of the world and the needs of others. Quite the contrary. In one of the television interviews, she explained the origin of a peace group within the retirement community.

> We were going to view "The Day After," a film about the aftermath of a nuclear war. Advised not to watch it alone, we got together and when the film ended held a discussion. We decided that we had an obligation to hold one another up, to give each other courage. We resolved to get together regularly in order to talk about things that matter. For years we met every Saturday night, discussing the news of the world and asking ourselves, "What can we do?" Out of that group came a number of actions. We wrote to our congressman regularly so that

he would be aware of our views. We participated in nuclear freeze rallies. We formed a volunteer tutoring program and began teaching English to foreign-born people.

I guess my good health and long life are due primarily to an ancestry of strong-bodied and strong-minded women. I was born in Cologne, Germany, but raised in Frankfurt. From earliest years, I was taken on hikes in the mountains every Sunday, an event which I didn't cherish unless I could take along a friend.

My mother was very sports-minded. We skied, skated, and played tennis. As an only child, I received her undivided attention. Sadly, when I was three years old, my father died of blood poisoning. He owned a chemical factory. To this day, no one knows what happened. Mother and I went to live with grandmother and an aunt. These three vital women saw to it that I received an excellent education.

Life in Germany was wonderful for a time, or so it seemed to me. Then Hitler came and our world changed, especially for those of us who were Jewish. I might say that religion has never been part of my life. I have studied the various religions but just can't believe. I can't cope with a vengeful God or a religion for which Law is the most important thing. I could cope with a religion where love is the most important thing, like Christianity. The Christ-figure to me is very important, not as the Son of God but as a great prophet. There are many great prophets, and I am grateful to all of them. All feed my heart and my mind.

Many people can believe. I envy them. They have that wonderful child-like faith that whatever happens is God's will. They are the lucky ones. But for me, if there is a God, He must have larger dimensions than what these people see. I just can't imagine a lovely old man with a white beard, who spends his time listening to our complaints. For those who can believe, religion is a warm nest. But I just can't get into that nest, as comforting as it might be. I have a great yearning for whatever you call God. It would be wonderful if I could put my head in somebody's hand and say, "You take over; I don't have to do it any more."

Recently, I was sick, some sort of virus. I felt very weak and got depressed. My best friend is in the nursing home with Alzheimer's disease. I look into her eyes and remember the good times we had together. I'm well again and my spirits have returned, but a cloud of uncertainty hangs over me. Perhaps the kindnesses that come to us are the loving hands of God.

Since I underwent Jungian analysis years ago I have been interested in myths. Jung bases so much of his collective unconscious on myths. Joseph Campbell also helps us to connect with deep recesses of the human experience through stories which represent the fears and dreams and hopes of human nature as it gropes for an understanding of itself.

I'm 96 years old. I should understand more by now, but I feel that I know less now than I did ten years ago. It isn't just that the deeper one goes the darker it gets; it's also that things are not black and white. I suffer over the state of the world, but I can't say this is right and that is wrong. I can see the other guy's side too. Bosnia is a terrible situation. We should send in food but not troops or planes. That would just sharpen their hatreds and resolve nothing.

Another support which other people have which I lack is family. Other than a niece in England whom I hear from once a year and another in Switzerland, I have no one. We have a mind line but not a heart line. As a young woman, I was engaged but had to flee the Nazis leaving my fiancé behind. He didn't follow me. So I don't have religion and I don't have family.

The family of one of the women here has sort of adopted me and invites me to their home for holidays, but it doesn't feel the same. I have friends, but really, I'm very much alone.

Every day there are reminders that I am getting old, something that I can't do that I used to be able to do. It may be fingertips that have no feeling so that I can't pick things up, or it takes me half an hour to button my blouse. It may be that I can't thread a needle because my eyesight is weak. Piddling little things. Nevertheless, although my vision is not as good as before, I can still see. I can still smell a rose and touch things. Life has narrowed but not ended. What I can do, I try to do well.

So that I not lose perspective, I write down the good things that happen to me each day. Then, when I feel depressed, I look at the list. Perhaps someone unexpectedly called me on the phone or invited me to go someplace with them. There are many rainbows, but we tend to see only dark clouds.

My experience as a therapist has enabled me to help many people in the nursing home here. I start at a level where I know they can respond. Perhaps it's only hand movement or neck movement. Everyone can do something. I have people sit in a circle in their wheelchairs and throw them a beach ball. Everyone reaches out to catch it. It must be an instinct. They look at it and throw it back. If someone says, "I'm too old; I can't do anything," I tell them that I'm older than they are.

It was about thirty years ago, while I was still employed, that another woman and I moved here to Avery House, which was built by the Congregational churches of Hartford. It was designed in what is called a village concept from complete independence to complete dependence. So far I have been able to live with complete independence. Since my friend moved out some years ago, I have lived alone, moving to this smaller house. It is just one large room but I love it. I do my own shopping and cooking and housekeeping.

What would I do if I could not continue to live independently? That's my nightmare. But I've come to terms with it since it is beyond my control. The first level of help would be provided by the home health agency, which supplies aides who would help me in whatever way necessary. They might shop or prepare meals or help me get dressed. As long as it was not something insurmountable. This service is very popular.

The next step would be to enter the intermediate care facility where I would be provided with needed medication, meals, and other support. Finally, if it came to that, there is the nursing home which provides total care. All these various stages are reversible. Someone who regained her health could return to a more independent status.

Several years ago some local school teachers came here and provided training in the teaching of English. Eight of us are tutors. Here's a picture of the Polish woman with whom I have been working. She comes here each week and is making great progress.

There is a new building here with younger people. They are more active than those of us who arrived years ago. As our group gets older, there are fewer and fewer people to participate in things, such as the college courses and Great Decisions groups. I do read a lot, although not as much as before. I get tired more quickly. Recently I read *Upon This Rock*, the story of a black church in Brooklyn. I was fascinated with the bold vision of the Reverend Johnnie Youngblood and the way he brought self respect into the black community and, particularly, to the men who had been completely demoralized. That's the kind of thing I like to read. It gives me some glimpse of the meaning of life.

I have had to discontinue conducting exercise classes in our senior day care center, not because I couldn't do it, but because there was concern about insurance. What if someone got hurt? Legal considerations impede the human dimension and limit what can be done. But there is a wonderful exercise teacher who comes twice a week for the residents in general. I never miss that class. From my training in physical therapy I know how important it is to keep active.

In my seventies, I discovered yoga and with it, meditation. On my 75th birthday I could stand on my head. But that's not what's important. It's not standing on your head but what's *in* your head and in your heart that counts. For me, to be alive is to be open to the world, interested in people and events, to love nature, and to seek to develop an inner center.

More than a year after the interview, Miss Wulf wrote to say that she had arrived at age 97 and commented, "This fall was worth being alive for." She added that she had "attended an exhibition of portraits of old people done by stitching cloth." She concluded by saying, "They were incredibly expressive. I guess life does the 'stitching'."

THE WISDOM OF THE NONAGENARIANS

"When we are really honest with ourselves,
we must admit that our lives are all that really
belong to us. So it is how we use our lives that
determines what kind of people we are."

Cesar Chavez

Talking with dozens of nonagenarians over the course of a year has made me keenly aware of the precious gift of life, a gift at once fragile and durable. The hands that shook mine in friendly greeting were nearly a century old, yet warm, strong, and trusting. The eyes that looked at me glistened with curiosity and interest, windows to minds that had not tired of processing new information. Questions evoked memories of childhood lived at the beginning of the twentieth century but also prompted opinions and hopes for the soon-to-begin twenty-first century.

Life for each human being is a succession of days, a calendar of pages each with its hastily written notations. No time to tarry. Soon it will be tomorrow. For the nonagenarian, there have been more than 32,000 days—and still counting. What impressed me about these wonderful people was that they were mature adults continuing to live their lives, not worrying about things beyond their control. There is today and hopefully tomorrow and the day after. The sun came up today; no need to fret about whether or not it will rise tomorrow.

What sparked my curiosity about nonagenarians was a Census Bureau report that people over ninety are the fastest growing segment of the American population. In fact, it is projected that about one quarter of today's 65-year-olds will live to be 90 and that, contrary to popular belief, elderly Americans are physically and financially healthy.

Not knowing anyone who was ninety, I asked my 85-year-old mother if she did. Well, she did and introduced me to several. They were women who attended her church and were active in her senior citizens group. When I saw these women, my initial reaction was disbelief. They couldn't be that old; they looked much younger! I came to learn that quite a few of the people I would see shopping or in a restaurant or at church or driving their cars were indeed nonagenarians. They don't wear a label identifying themselves as 90 years old and are virtually indistinguishable from their more numerous octogenarian friends.

There remains the question: How might I live to be 90? Do today's active nonagenarians offer any insight as to how others might join their ranks? While there is no magic formula for successful aging, lessons are indeed there to be learned. Most of them are so obvious that the tendency may be to slough them off as too trivial to merit much attention. But beware! Life is the accumulation of many small steps, not a few giant leaps.

In the Fourth Book of Kings, the story is told of a Syrian general, Naaman, who contracted leprosy and was advised by his Jewish maid to go to Israel where the prophet Eliseus had the power to cure him. Loaded with treasure, Naaman journeyed to Israel where the prophet told him to wash in the River Jordan and he would be healed. Naaman was indignant at the instructions, which he considered too jejune to merit compliance. As he prepared to return home, his servants said to him that if the prophet had asked of him "some great thing" he would have done it; why not do the very simple thing that was asked. Naaman took the advice, washed in the Jordan, and was healed.

The active nonagenarians do not ask "some great thing" either. They are ordinary people who have done ordinary things. Nor did they deliberately try to live to ninety. What they did was live each day just as all of us must, one at a time, only perhaps with some special wisdom to protect them. The challenge is to uncover the messages for long life revealed by the stories they tell, to move beyond the details of individual lives in order to discover that which has universal application.

I have attempted to do that by organizing *the wisdom of the nonage-*

narians under ten headings. Each can stand alone as a facet of the "secret" of health, happiness, and longevity. Taken together, they offer the distillation of hundreds of hours of interviews, reading, and reflection. Nevertheless, when all is said and done, there remain other factors that cannot be identified, measured, or controlled. Human life remains a candle on a mountain top, whose flame can be extinguished by a tiny breeze that comes from some Power beyond our understanding.

1. Develop a positive attitude toward life.

When he was 87 years old, George Burns wrote *How to Live to Be 100*. A decade later, the venerable entertainer was still going strong, well-positioned to be a living illustration of the book's title. In 1993, on the occasion of receiving an honorary doctorate from Brandeis University, he quipped, "I can hardly wait to go home and tell my mother and father that they finally have a son, a doctor."

To a large extent Burns' book is a collection of what he calls "age jokes," such as that Dean Martin is likely to live to 100 because he's already 80-proof. Or, that Phyllis Diller will make it because her face-lifts alone will hold her up until she's past 100. However, tucked away among the pictures of Burns with his cigar and beautiful young women are some valuable suggestions. Perhaps the most important lesson which Burns communicates is the health-conferring power of humor. We enjoy being in the electronic presence of this active nonagenarian, not because he's so old, but because he makes us laugh. Laughter is a potent prescription for a long life.

When George Burns tries to identify the key to longevity, what he comes up with is the apparently simplistic answer, "think positively." This phrase echoes Norman Vincent Peale's extraordinarily influential 1952 book, *The Power of Positive Thinking*. Peale himself has outlived many of those who derided him for superficiality. When he became a nonagenarian himself in 1988, one headline read, "Norman Vincent Peale: Positively 90." An article two years later was titled "High Priest of Optimism Still Positive." Long before the healing power of positive attitudes had been studied scientifically and before Bernie Siegel in *Love, Medicine and Miracles* invested positive thinking with medical respectability, Peale had put his finger on something powerful: that patterns of thought can nourish or poison both spirit and body.

What came across in the interviews with nonagenarians was the striking unanimity with which they manifest a positive attitude toward life. There were few complaints about aches and pains, few criticisms of relatives or friends, and a view of the future that was, in general, strongly optimistic. When asked about problems or worries which they might have, more than one replied, "I don't think that way." Others fumbled around, searching for something negative to say, but typically came up with superficial complaints.

Without realizing it, they were following George Burns' advice, "I look to the future, because that's where I'm going to spend the rest of my life."

2. Discover your personal activity signature.

When describing his approach to music students, the nonagenarian concert violinist, Joseph Fuchs, said that each student had a distinctive "musical signature" and that the responsibility of the teacher was to discover, respect, and develop that unique "signature." While listening to Mr. Fuchs explain this concept, it dawned on me that each of the nonagenarians, as well as each of us, has an "activity signature," a characteristic approach to life. Some people engage in vigorous activities, while others are more sedentary. Some are more socially active, while others expend their energies on intellectual or artistic pursuits. The nonagenarian artist, Arthur Cohn, spends hours each day alone in his studio painting, while Anna Cassidy is out showing houses to her real estate clients. Harriet Strachstein's sense of self-worth is linked to her practice as a clinical psychologist and Isadore Warshaw's to his daily memory-developing exercises. Joe Mishkin has to get in that round of golf, and Kathryn Donovan needs to start each day by attending Mass in her neighborhood church. Each is at peace when engaged in his or her distinctive form of activity.

We are not only creatures of habit but are created by habits. The personal life structure shapes and guides individual consciousness and provides continuous feedback. A sense of well being and pleasure flows from the capacity to maintain accustomed routines. Russell Wilson goes to his job as a library page, Edward Corcoran to his law office, Al Ross to his desk at the Palm Beach newspaper. Ann Jordan coordinates the senior citizen club; Reta Lasky attends her exercise class and college course; Anne and Grayson Holt engage in their church renewal projects.

The "signature" of other nonagenarians is less social but equally clear cut and distinctive, like a fingerprint. In the privacy of her apartment, Dorothy Redfield works on projects for promoting her father-in-law's paintings; Peter Comerford says his prayers, reads the newspapers, and writes letters to the editor; Lilian Uviller plays the piano.

A crisis can occur when someone is not able to maintain an accustomed and valued pattern. For example, Edward Corcoran has not fully adjusted to the loss of his driver's license, and Lilian Uviller is frustrated because she can no longer leave her home unaccompanied. However, these were exceptions. The vast majority of the subjects were happy and fulfilled in the day-by-day enactment of their "signature" routines which they subtly modify as circumstances change.

What is my activity signature? Do I enjoy doing something that I might continue to do when I am in my nineties? Or do I need to work on a new signature, perhaps replacing work with volunteer service or some leisure activity such as gardening, golfing, or writing? The challenge is to find a truly satisfying project. It need not take many hours each day, although it might. What is essential is that it provide what might be called "status conferring value." When Harry Granick is asked what he does, who he is, he can answer, "I write one act plays." Leroy Campbell can point to the beautiful garden which he has created. Nida Neel can speak of her role as informal counselor for the women who come for afternoon tea.

3. Take time for reflection.

The actress Helen Hayes died in 1993 at the age of 92. The seeds of her long life were planted decades before and beautifully revealed in her 1965 bestseller *A Gift of Joy*. The book is not so much an autobiography as a set of meditations on life, similar to Dag Hammarskjoold's *Markings* and Anne Morrow Lindbergh's *Gifts from the Sea*.

In the chapter titled "Solitude," Miss Hayes relates how she bought a home in Mexico where she would spend long periods of time away from the distractions of fame. Her friends did not understand why she would leave the glamour and celebrity of New York and Hollywood for what they imagined to be the loneliness of Cuernavaca. Miss Hayes makes a distinction between loneliness and solitude and argues that it is in solitude that truly marvelous and life-conferring work is done. Among other things, she says, it is in solitude that she is "able to make some infinitesimally small progress toward acquaintance with myself, something you cannot do unless you can be alone and, therefore, free."

To be 65 years old must have seemed old to a woman who had been an actress since childhood. Although she could not have dreamed that she would live to be 92, Miss Hayes' reflections in the chapter titled "Age," reveal a philosophy which certainly helped her to live with dignity and charm for another twenty-seven years. For example, in commenting on the desperate effort of most people to disguise old age, she says, "I know there is nothing more beautiful than an unadorned old face with lines that tell a story, a story of a life that has been lived with some fullness." In her quiet time away from the spotlights, Helen Hayes learned how to play the most important role of her career—herself.

Few of the active nonagenarians complained of loneliness, even those who spend a considerable amount of time alone. Like Helen Hayes, they have discovered the richness of solitude. Tonio Selwart, who had performed on the stage and the radio with Miss Hayes, is especially remarkable. It is impossible for me to forget the peaceful smile which suffused his face while we were together, the positive tone of his words, and the pleasant letters which he has written to me. And Selwart is blind. In the solitude of endless darkness he has somehow found enlightenment.

Not all the people interviewed were especially articulate or introspective. But most had spent time in reflection and had fashioned an approach to life which obviously has been very effective. Orville Davis does his thinking at his word processor, Sheila McGuth with her cat on her lap, and Morris Rubin while he does his morning yoga exercises.

Perhaps the most thoughtful nonagenarian of all is Lena Wulf from whose lips wisdom flows in every sentence. Paradoxically, whereas Helen Hayes, like Sister John Baptist and the Holts, achieved a high level of contemplation in the context of religious faith, Lena Wulf has plumbed the depths of meaning in the lonely world of agnosticism. Catharine Wright has done the same as an avowed atheist, demonstrating that there are many channels to inner vision.

4. Eat normal, nutritious meals.

There are countless books on nutrition and magazines are awash with articles on the importance of limiting the intake of fat, salt, and sugar. But the active nonagenarians have not read these books and articles. With virtual unanimity, they insist that they eat moderately but without counting calories. Since it is assumed that diet is an important element in long life, the nonagenarians were asked about their eating habits. They shrugged their shoulders and said that they have no food restrictions. Many prefer fish and chicken to beef but none are vegetarians. Most are thin; none are overweight.

These findings correspond to those of a survey of active nonagenarians reported in 1992 by the Humana Seniors Association affiliated with the Humana hospital chain. In that study, 58% of the hundreds of respondents said that they eat whatever they want, and 53% reported that they eat balanced meals. Only 28% limit their salt intake, and 24% try to eat a low-fat diet.

While some nonagenarians have an alcoholic drink or two each day, others are teetotalers. Some have a sweet tooth, but others eschew desserts. Ruth Bennett offered me a high-fat ice cream from her freezer, while Lena Wulf gave me strawberries and tea. Several take vitamins with religious fidelity, but most do not. A few eat in communal settings, but most prepare their own meals. None smokes, although a few had smoked when younger.

With reference to food, I think especially of Magnus Lundstrom who rents a room in a private house and has his meals with the family which includes school-age children. While I was interviewing Magnus, a young girl bounded in from school, came over, and gave him a hug. She offered us a cold drink and went to prepare dinner. It was clear that this robust Swedish immigrant looked forward to his evening dinner with his adoptive family.

I think of Dr. Giuseppe Maltese, who smacked his lips when he told me how much he enjoyed going out for dinner each evening with his lady friend, and of Isadore Warshaw, who has a loving wife to cook his meals and who insisted I take some grapefruits from his Florida tree.

Dorothy Redfield invited my wife and myself to dine with her in the elegant dining room of the total-care retirement community where she lives. The choice and quality of food was excellent and the service, friendly and attentive. The residents dress each evening and make dinner hour a highlight of the day.

What is the lesson with reference to diet? It is to be conscious of proper nutrition but not to become obsessed with food. Eat what you enjoy, what your body tells you is right for you. We who are not yet nonagenarians know more about food groups and fiber and polyunsaturated fats than they do. So, if we have the discipline to follow the advice so widely disseminated, we should be in excellent shape nutritionally to live a long life.

5. Exercise regularly.

Frank Regan takes a long walk each day or works out on the exercise machines in his basement. Chapman O'Connor rides his bicycle and square dances. Evelyn Golbe swims laps in her community pool. Lena Wulf and Reta Lasky participate in physical fitness classes. Ruth Bennett and Grayson Holt have medals which attest to their participation in Senior Olympics events. Joe Mishkin's ruddy complexion and strong hands attest to his daily round of golf. Even after a minor injury, Ann Jordan continues to bowl. Leroy Campbell bends and lifts and digs each day in his prize-winning garden.

Although such physical activities are impressive, many of the nonagenarians interviewed have no exercise routine other than walking. As with diet, physical fitness is not something to which much attention was paid in the past, and many older people did not develop the habit of regular exercise. For women, in particular, sports and exercise were not encouraged, with participation in rigorous pursuits considered unladylike. In light of this cultural reality, it is perhaps significant that Margery Curry played baseball in college and that Ruth Bennett also was involved in athletics as a student.

Numerous studies support the value of physical exercise for older people, including the very old. Physiologist William Evans of the Tufts University Center on Aging says, "There is no group in our population that can benefit more from exercise than senior citizens. For a young person, exercise can increase physical functioning by perhaps 10%. But in an old person, you can increase it by 50%." What is recommended is at least three half-hour periods a week of vigorous exercise such as jogging, swimming, fast walking, biking, dancing, or indoor exercise programs.

One of the often overlooked benefits of retirement communities is the availability of fitness programs and facilities. All the nonagenarians living in any type of housing for the elderly mentioned this aspect of life in their community. Lena Wulf, whose career as a physical therapist had sensitized her to the importance of exercise, spoke not only of her own exercise routines but of how she did volunteer work as a recreation therapist with nursing home patients.

Physical activity not only substantially reduces the risk of hip fractures and heart disease, but has impressive psychological advantages as well. Studies have found that anxiety declines with exercise and that 15 minutes of walking at a heart rate of 100 beats/minute induces substantial muscular relaxation. In fact, it has been established that exercise has a greater calming effect than a popular tranquilizer.

Furthermore, exercise can have a valuable social dimension. Both Russell Wilson and Chapman O'Connor look forward to dancing, not primarily because it is good exercise but because it gets them out with other people. Also, although some people are disciplined enough to maintain an exercise schedule alone, the thousands of stationary bicycles and rowing machines gathering dust in American homes are witness to how difficult this can be. The best way to insure faithfulness to an exercise plan is to work out with others on a set schedule.

6. Have a plan for each day.

The nonagenarians who are still working have appointment books which they had to consult when I called to arrange a meeting. Several others said things such as, "I can't see you on Tuesdays, because that's when I bowl," or "Eleven o'clock will be OK. My exercise class is over by then." Most of the men and women interviewed could describe a clear, full, and satisfying schedule for their days. They know how essential it is to keep busy and how depressing it is to be idle. Periods of quiet reflection are valued only when integrated into a well-rounded set of activities.

Lilian Uviller is one of the few nonagenarians who complained about too much empty time. She has a schedule for her mornings, including two hours practicing the piano, but loneliness characterizes her afternoons. She is particularly vulnerable because she lives alone in the anonymity of a New York City apartment, cannot go out by herself, and has few friends capable of visiting her. Although she reads psychological literature and writes poems, the long hours alone are oppressive.

Mrs. Uviller knows that in retirement housing she would have companionship, a range of activities, and assistance were an emergency to arise. On the other hand, except in a prohibitively expensive facility, she could not have her piano or the paintings by her son which cover the walls of her apartment. Perhaps the sign of Mrs. Uviller's strength and spirit of independence is that she realizes that trade-offs have to be made in life and she has adjusted as best she can to a less-than-ideal situation.

Many people dread the prospect of going to a nursing home and equate all forms of housing for older people with the images they have seen of incontinent, zombie-like men and women tied to their chairs. It cannot be stressed strongly enough that there are many adult homes and communities which are characterized by health, happiness, and security. The range of programs available in such places make it virtually impossible for anyone to be isolated. Great sophistication has emerged to provide a framework for living capable of satisfying the needs and tastes of nearly everyone.

Men and women in their 60's and 70's could find it enlightening to visit several types of retirement housing. Financial considerations as well as life style factors must be taken into account, of course, but early assessment of the options available can not only correct inaccurate stereotypes but some day might avoid the necessity of making an uninformed decision under crisis conditions.

This suggestion should not obscure the fact that the majority of active nonagenarians live in their own homes and have no intention of moving to any form of retirement world. They enjoy good health, both physical and mental, have arranged for adequate social support, and plan their days so as to enable them to continue to live satisfying lives.

7. Remain connected to the world.

In their 1961 book, *Growing Old*, Elaine Cumming and William B. Henry developed the first sociological theory of aging as they attempted to answer the question, "What happens as people age?" Their conclusion was that *disengagement* occurs. The world of aging people shrinks as they move into a smaller and smaller range of relationships, activities, and interests. For Cumming and Henry, such *disengagement* is normal and valuable. It frees people from the distractions of adult life and provides them with the tranquillity to attend to the task of preparing for death.

In a similar vein, other gerontologists speak of *a life review*, the idea that looking back over the road that has been traveled is a desirable characteristic in elderly people. Erik Erikson in his theory of development postulates that the final human challenge is to assess one's life and to find that it was worthwhile, that it made sense. Erikson called this task *integrity*.

What about the active nonagenarians? Are they disengaging, undertaking a life review, wrestling with the issue of integrity? In general, they are not—at least they do not spend most of their time in such a process.

Rather, they exemplify an approach to aging which emerged in reaction to Disengagement Theory. It is called *Activity Theory.*

Activity theory holds that later adulthood is best lived as is young adulthood and middle age, that is, with full engagement in life. Retirement from work may be appropriate but *not* retirement from participation in the world. As long as the human mind functions, it craves stimulation, challenge, and novelty. Although educational and occupational differences influence life at 90 as much as they do life at 40 or 60, almost all the nonagenarians read the newspaper, watch world events on television, vote in elections, discuss contemporary issues with zest, and derive satisfaction from forming and sharing opinions about current events. If they are at all representative of what healthy people do in the final stage of life, then remaining connected to the world is the norm.

Some of the fastest growing occupations are those for men and women trained in keeping older people active, either in institutional settings or in community-based programs. With the number of older people rising rapidly, the demand for innovative programs is sure to rise and with it opportunities for entrepreneurs. For example, on Long Island, New York, Community Care Companions (CCC) provides "companions" who assist elderly people with such chores as shopping and going to the doctor. One octogenarian uses a young companion to accompany him when he plays golf. The client pays $11 an hour of which the companion receives $7. Within a few years, CCC had more than 800 clients, including several nonagenarians, providing part time employment to several hundred people.

Products designed to enhance mobility for older people and for those with handicaps have created a new specialized market. Catalogs with hundreds of devices provide occupational therapists with creative ways to "get them moving." A video called "Armchair Fitness" offers stretching and strengthening low-impact aerobic workouts, which can be performed sitting in a chair. A 12-part series, *Exercise with Billie*, which has been broadcast on hundreds of television stations, contains progressively more challenging exercises beginning with many that can be done while seated.

The rapid proliferation of services and products for the very old will enable ever greater numbers of people to remain active and to maintain substantial independence.

8. Cherish family relationships.

Older people tend to have vivid memories of their childhood, as if by recalling the freshness of their youth they could neutralize the lengthening shadows of age. Almost all the nonagenarians told stories of their mothers and fathers, always happy or heroic tales of people who had acquired near mythical proportions with the passage of time. Religious nonagenarians, like Sister John Baptist, spoke of their parents with such pleasure that it was as if they were about to see them again soon. And that, of course, is precisely what their faith tells them is the truth.

Most nonagenarians, however, do not have to romanticize long departed family members. They have living children, grandchildren, and great-grandchildren about whom they speak with pride and whose pictures and gifts surround them like a warm sweater to ward off the chill of winter.

Those nonagenarians who are still working or actively engaged in current projects tend not to refer to family as much as do those for whom memories of the past occupy more and more of their present. Nevertheless, everyone interviewed who is a parent shared with pride the educational and occupational achievements of their children, many of whom are quite successful indeed, evidence of the upward social mobility which has made America such a land of opportunity for immigrants and the poor.

The four married couples in the sample of nonagenarians are perhaps the most fortunate of all. As if by some miracle, in defiance of the laws of probability, they maintain what for many humans is the most precious relationship of life, the marital bond. They continue to live in their own homes and to care for their own needs just as they have done for upwards of sixty years. All have children with whom they maintain regular contact, but none of the sons and daughters live nearby.

Four other nonagenarians, all of them men, live in marriage relationships with spouses who are not nonagenarians. Their wives, happy to have husbands who still are healthy, certainly have contributed substantially to that health by their supportive companionship. Peter Comerford's wife, Ethyl, insisted that I come for lunch, providing me with a close-up view of the give-and-take of their relationship. Joseph Fuchs' wife, Doris, is a self-effacing companion to a strong man consumed with his career as a musician. Al Ross's wife, Etta, a gracious lady at 88, is having trouble keeping up with her energetic husband. Similarly, Isadore Warshaw's wife, Bertha, keeps a lovely home for her dynamic husband.

For six other nonagenarians, all of them widowed, family life includes living with one of their children in apparent harmony. In all cases, the children are well into middle age. Frank Regan lives in the comfortable suburban home of his son and daughter-in-law, both of whom work, providing everyone with privacy and independence. About two years ago when Leroy Campbell was widowed, his son and daughter-in-law moved into his large Cape Cod house. Although all are retired, each has independent interests which keep them busy and out of one another's way. Edward Corcoran lives with an unmarried son who, like his 99-year-old father, works. Nida Neel's daughter lives with her, and within the past two years both women were widowed. Eloise Spaeth owns a house which she shares with her unmarried daughter, as does Catharine Wright.

The diversity of housing arrangement includes several nonagenarians who live with people to whom they are not related, but in family-like settings. Sister John Baptist continues to live with women who in a spiritual sense are her sisters. Ruth Bennett and Dorothy Redfield reside in retirement communities, which might be considered families in which one pays for membership. Magnus Lundstrom rents a room in a private house and is treated like a beloved grandfather by his host family. The remaining nonagenarians live in their own homes or apartments, most of them maintaining regular contact with family.

Nonagenarians may outlive their friends but most do not outlive sons and daughters, who cannot avoid being concerned about their healthy yet vulnerable ancient progenitors. In the relay race of the species, the baton of duty is passed backwards as well as forwards. There is no resting on the course. Just when one's children have run off on their own for a season of independence, the needs of parents assert themselves.

Some dimensions of the demographic and sociological revolution that is occurring in the American family were noted in a 1991 article by Marjorie H. Cantor:

* By the year 2020, the typical family will consist of at least four generations.

* Middle generation women in the future will spend, on average, more years with parents over 65 than with children under 18.

* The caregivers of the future will be the "young-old" (people over 60), instead of the 45 to 59-year-olds currently making up the largest group of caregivers.

* For the first time in history, the average married couple will have more parents than children, leading to a heavier burden for the middle generation as their parents age.

A federal study of middle-aged Americans reported in 1993 that despite myths about the disintegration of the family, the predominant pattern is that family relationships remain close and intergenerational assistance, high. Forty-four percent of Americans aged 58-66 have one or both parents surviving. Eighty-five percent of people over 80 report that they see or speak to their children two to seven times a week. One researcher summarized the findings by saying: "Family members are the most important source of help for older people." The active nonagenarians pride themselves on their independence but know they can count on their children should the need arise.

9. Trust in the goodness of others & don't be a complainer.

Before undertaking the interviews I had two concerns. One was that the nonagenarians would be suspicious of a stranger who wanted to ask them a lot of questions. The other was that I would be subjected to a rambling catalog of complaints. To my surprise and delight, neither misgiving materialized. I was welcomed with great trust and heard few complaints.

Although the media presents a picture of America as a violent, exploitative society, none of the interviewees expressed any fear of people or had installed security devices. Most saw me alone in their homes, were comfortable with the tape recorder, and spoke not only with clarity and insightfulness, but did so with the relaxed demeanor one might experience with an old and trusted friend. They seem to take for granted that people are good.

Despite tales of elderly people being swindled and mugged, few nonagenarians had encountered any such problems. They may lead charmed lives in this regard, or perhaps are naive, but there's no avoiding the fact that their trusting approach to dealing with others has not hurt their exceptional longevity. There's a saying that people who fear diseases are the ones who get them. It may also be true that those who fear other people are the very ones who are given reason to be fearful.

In her 1991 book, *Remarkable Survivors*, a study of successful aging among women, Alice Taylor Day constructed what she called "markers" of successful aging. The markers were grouped under three headings:

1) *Capacity for Independent Activity*, which includes such markers as being able to do one's own shopping, meal preparation, and house-work.

2) *Private Safety Net*, marked by social supports, such as living with one's spouse, knowing friends who would help for a short time if one were ill, and ownership of one's own home.

3) *Personal Well-being*, which includes a global sense of happiness, a feeling that one is useful and well occupied, and a sense that life does not get worse as one gets older.

All of these markers have been applied in some respect in the assessment of the active nonagenarians. Of particular interest here is the final marker, the attitude that life does not get worse as one gets older. Considering the inevitable losses that nonagenarians have experienced, it is remarkable how little complaining they did about their health, their children, their living conditions, or society in general.

Kathryn Donovan was mugged on a New York City street but not deterred from continuing to go out alone. Harriet Strachstein expressed no fear of the Manhattan city streets. Harry Granick shops without anxiety in Harlem.

10. Be flexible, because everything changes.

It is said that love must be handled like a flower—gently, in an open hand, not a closed fist. If grasped too tightly, it dies. So also with life itself and all its relationships and activities. There comes a time to say goodbye, to close the desk, to put down the tools, to pack the suitcase. When asked if it was difficult giving up the beautiful house, which had been her home for more than fifty years, Dorothy Redfield said no, that she knew it was time to move on and that sometimes now she passes it without even giving it a look.

Prompted by a question to recall his wife who had died some years ago, tears welled up in the eyes of Orville Davis as the pain of memory overwhelmed his cheerful spirit. But he quickly recovered his composure, wiped away the tears, and pulled himself back into the present, a present filled with activities which he had added in adjusting to the realities of life.

In *A Fresh Map of Life* (1989), Peter Laslett argues that for more and more people a "third age" in life is emerging. Young adulthood is filled with enthusiasm, energy, and hope. Middle adulthood is characterized by productivity and child rearing. The third age, beginning in the 60's and continuing into the 90's, is an increasingly long and fruitful stage of life, not at all a "rocking chair" existence or a morbid waiting for the end, but a time of health, affluence, and opportunity with ever expanding vistas and promise.

With a flair for alliteration, Gail Sheehy, in *New Passages* (1995), speaks of the Serene Sixties, the Sage Seventies, the Uninhibited Eighties, and the Nobility of the Nineties. For Sheehy, nonagenarians are "the new aristocracy of successful aging."

Although demographic changes portend a dramatic increase in the number of active nonagenarians, it nonetheless remains true that the likelihood of physical and mental problems increases with age, making the final years of life a time of considerable pain and expense for many older persons and their loved ones. To avoid despair and anger, deep reflection on the mystery of suffering is essential, such as the biblical Job undertook when he lost health, possessions, family, and friends.

Although losses are unavoidable and death the great equalizer, it appears inevitable that hundreds of thousands, even millions, of today's younger adults will join the ranks of the active nonagenarians and experience life and happiness beyond the biblical four score and ten years. The nonagenarians in this book are trailblazers, scouts. They have entered the new frontier and are staking out claims for those who will come after them.

Some younger people have said to me that they wouldn't want to live to be 90. They imagine such an age as burdened with helplessness and pain. Even those younger people, who know active nonagenarians, continue to be influenced by the anachronistic stereotype that "old age" inevitably means dependence and loneliness, a nursing home, or a sick bed. What must be emphasized one last time is that none of the men and women interviewed was unhappy with life. No one wanted to die. No one felt that there was no reason to continue living.

Some years ago, Don Gold interviewed twenty older Americans to explore their range of concerns and to uncover clues for others to use in their quest of a longer and fuller life. His book has a title which would be a fitting slogan for the active nonagenarians, *Until the Singing Stops: A Celebration of Life and Old Age in America*. The active nonagenarians whose stories have been told here insist that for them the music has not stopped, and until it does, they are going to keep on singing.